Displaced Donkeys

A Guernsey Family's War

Displaced Donkeys

A Guernsey Family's War

Suzanne Lang

Pinknote Press

First published 2009

ISBN 978-0-473-15352-6
Published by Pinknote Press
40 Rangimoana Avenue
Turangi 3382, New Zealand

Copies of *Displaced Donkeys* are available by post from:
Susan Knott
Je Reviens
Grande Cloture
Portinfer Vale
Guernsey GY6 8LJ
tel: 0481 259170
email: gateandgaragedoorco@cwgsy.net

Cover picture by Suzanne Lang

Composed by
Rawhiti Editorial Services
Christchurch, New Zealand

Printed in Great Britain

For my dear late mother

Dorothy May Knott née Ogier

Preface

The protagonist in this book is my mother Dorothy, who was the grandchild of Charlie Duncombe, a locally well-known black immigrant to Guernsey. Dorothy, her siblings and her mother Dolly were conspicuous by their skin colour. They were among the poorer town families that relied on handouts from charitable organizations. But this status became irrelevant when the people of Guernsey were faced with the imminent arrival of German troops at the beginning of WW2. Some of the islanders who chose to be evacuated to Britain had to leave their worldly goods behind and, being limited as to the amount of cash they could take with them, they were literally all in the same boat as they were ferried to safety. Others who remained saw their homes and possessions taken from them by the Germans.

This book is the result of interviews and correspondence with my mother over the last few years. During our conversations I learned much about her thoughts and memories of her family life and relationships up to and during the war years 1940–1945. Hers is a candid account of her wartime experiences and those of her family of displaced Guernsey donkeys.

Thanks to the *Guernsey Press* and the Stockport Public Library, and to Aunty Edna (Nunoos) for helping me to tell her story. And I thank my wonderful late husband David, who encouraged and supported me throughout my writing efforts, and my mum who sadly did not live to see her story in print.

Some of the characters in this book have been given fictitious names to protect their identity.

Suzanne Lang

Contents

Stockport, 1945

It was a Monday in late September 1945 and an unusually warm day with hazy sunshine. My brothers and sisters were playing out in the street in their best charity-donated clothes, with their faces scrubbed clean, the girls' hair neatly brushed and the boys' curly hair clipped short at the back and sides with the kitchen scissors. They stood out alongside the other kids because we were the only coloured family in the street.

We'd been told that our Dad could come home from the war any day soon, so that morning we were up early just in case he turned up. Most of my friends' dads had been back for ages. One of them, Vera's dad, had an arm missing; it had been blown off by a grenade and he had to wear his sleeve folded up and held with a safety pin. A couple of the dads in our street acted really strange and their wives told our mum that they had bad nightmares and woke up screaming and sweating. Mrs. Ashworth, who lived three doors up from us, told Aunty Elise that since Mr Ashworth had returned from the war he just sat in an armchair rocking back and forwards and crying a lot but he refused to tell her why. There were hardly any men wearing uniforms in the streets any more. On Sundays they wore new suits that all looked the same; they called them "demob suits". I expected my dad would get one of those too when he came back. Nearly all the dads in our street had been back for a while since "Victory in Europe"… except the ones who had got killed. Our dad had been fighting in Burma and even though those "Bastard Japs" as Mum called them had surrendered too in August, our Dad still hadn't come home yet. His last letter to Mum had arrived months ago but she didn't let us read it as she usually did. She had warned me not to tell my brothers and sisters, but said that he was angry in his letter and had made threats. Then out of the blue the telegram arrived and she was a bag of nerves.

'I knew I shouldn't have told him in a letter. I should have waited until he came home,' she said when she told me about his reply.

'Did you tell him everything?' I asked.

'Yes, well… no, not all of it – you know what your father is like,' she replied. She was perched on the edge of a chair at the table in our living room and I watched her press the crumpled telegram onto the table and smooth out the creases. As she leaned forward onto her elbows to re-read it she pushed the fingers of both hands into her thick frizzy hair and dragged them down her face until they covered her full painted mouth. She was wearing her best loose-fitting cotton summer dress – it was a faded blue – and her smooth coffee-coloured skin was dusted to a paler shade with face powder. She must have been crying all night because her eyelids were puffy and red. She didn't cry very often but she had cried, I remember, when she'd danced with us and we'd sung *Rule Britannia* with the neighbours at our street party to celebrate victory in Japan and the end of the war. However, those were tears of happiness and relief, not of the dread she was feeling now.

2

Guernsey, 1940

It was during the Easter school holidays in 1940 that I first learned more about my mum Dolly's life as a child. The weather was getting warmer so she had packed some sandwiches and lemonade and walked us a half-mile to what we called "the first beach" but was really called Havelet Bay. We liked the sandy part of the beach best but when we got there it was high tide – the choppy sea covered the sand and big rolling waves crashed against the high granite wall built to protect the road above. We had to walk along the road past the beach to the far end where a granite slipway sloped down to a pebbled beach that remained dry at high tide. Aunty Elise was already sitting on a blanket spread over the pebbles and her kids were playing further down the beach. A friend who was visiting her from St Sampson's in the north of the island was sitting beside her and she introduced her to Mum as June. Mum had jammed the old black pram against the thick bumpy grey granite wall that curved around and down the slipway so as to keep baby Leonard in the shade and then she put the brake on leaving my brother Little Cliffy, who was named after our dad, at the front in a pram seat. Aunty Elise stood up to take Mum's bags as she lowered herself onto the slipway and slid down the waist-high drop to place her feet on the pebbles. I handed her Little Cliffy after I'd lifted him from the front of the pram and she swung him down to sit at her feet. My younger sisters Pamela and Nunoos had already stripped off and were pulling the straps of their woollen bathers over their shoulders. I hurriedly copied them and we ran down the slipway and over the smoothed worn rocks that separated the pebbled beach from the rolling waves that roared towards the wall with frothing crests, smashed into it, and then were sent flying back in a silvery foaming waterfall.

'You stay this side of those rocks until the tide goes down, you kids – d'you 'ear Dorothy!' Mum shouted, as we squealed under the cold drifting spray of the waterfall. I waved to her and we searched out the deepest puddles in the rocks that had been warmed by the sun and sat in them splashing with our feet. It wasn't as much fun as running through the waves on the sand so after a little while I decided to go back to our mum's spot up the beach until the tide had gone down a bit and I could walk on the sand. I wobbled and tipped from side to side with my arms outspread as I carefully stepped on the knobbly stones that jabbed into the soles of my feet. My wet woollen bathers had stretched, and the crutch was hanging down nearly to my knees. When I reached Mum she shouted at me for dripping all over the blanket and threw a towel at me. I wrapped it around my shoulders and clutched it under my chin with both hands.

'Can I have a drink please Mum?' I asked and she reached into one of the paper carrier bags and passed me a bottle filled with a sherbet lemonade drink. I could tell she had already got to know the lady called June because she had her laughing and pressing her hand on her chest as I approached them. I swigged from the bottle and handed it back to Mum.

'Move out of the way Dorothy, so I can see the other kids,' Mum said pushing against my leg. I stepped aside then climbed up onto the slipway above them. I spread out the towel and lay down on my front resting the side of my head on my forearms. My belly and thighs soaked up the heat from the granite through the towel; I closed my eyes and the hot sun made the skin on my back tingle as I listened to the women talking.

'So, Dolly, your father is Charlie Duncombe, that black man who used to tap dance and sing in the pubs and who worked on the docks unloading the coal boats. Didn't they say he jumped ship from a merchant navy vessel and stayed here... is that true? And your mum, wasn't she that local girl Susan Inder who married him and then died young, poor woman, with that terrible consumption, when you were still a child?' June quizzed Mum.

Mum shrugged. 'I don't know how my dad got to be in Guernsey, but you're right about my poor mum – she was sick for years, but she was a good mother to me, not like my stepmother Grace.'

'Were you an only child then? Who looked after you when your mum died? I heard Charlie went to live in Jersey?' June was firing questions at Mum and had to lean back so she could see Mum past Aunty Elise who already knew the answers and had her elbows on her knees and her face cupped in her hands watching the kids playing on the rocks.

'He put me in the children's home – I was about nine then – but after he'd met Grace he sent for me to go to live with them in Jersey. I'd have been about ten then I s'pose. I remember getting off the boat at Jersey me, and walking the gangplank that was lowered onto the jetty at a level under the road because of the half-tide. I didn't know where to go so I just walked along that level but it was covered in green mossy seaweed and really slippery and I nearly went arse over a couple of times,' she laughed. 'Anyway,' she continued, 'I headed towards the shore then I climbed down a rusty old ladder fixed against the harbour wall to the sand with my bundle of clothes from the children's home stuffed into a pillowcase under my arm. I walked all the way up between the beached boats until I came to the road, but there was nobody there to meet me so I just sat there feeling lost and started crying.'

'You mean nobody came to meet you?' June asked.

'Oh yes they was there in the end. I heard my dad shouting and when I looked for him I saw him and Grace standing at road level above the boat – he was waving at me. He told me later that one of the crew had seen me walking off and guessed I must be his daughter so pointed me out to him. My dad laughed about it later and so did I, but Grace called me stupid. I wasn't happy living there – bad things happened to me but I was warned to keep it a secret or else I'd be sent back to the children's home.'

Aunty Elise's head turned quickly round towards Mum and she sat bolt upright. 'What kind of bad things?' she asked. Mum covered her mouth as though she hadn't meant to say what she'd said. June's mouth was hanging open and she was leaning forward because Aunty Elise had blocked her view of my mum. I'd also lifted my head to look at Mum and she'd caught my movement out of the corner of her eye and looked straight at me. Quickly she turned back to the women and said, 'Never mind that, I've put it all behind me, you can't change the past, you've got to get on with life.' The two women saw me watching them and smiled at me before raising their eyebrows at each other and turning their attention back to Mum.

5

Displaced Donkeys

'Where is your Cliff from, is he country?' June asked, quickly changing the subject. I thought this lady was a really nosy person but Mum still answered her.

'He's from Grande Rocques on the west coast. He grew up there and lived in a little cottage with his brothers and sister. His parents are Alfred and Sarah Ogier and they call themselves real "Guernsey donkeys" born and bred because their families go back generations. What about you, are you married, June?' Mum asked.

'I was engaged once but the swine broke it off and started courting my best friend. I was livid when I found out that they had been going up the Cow's Horn to do their courting behind my back. It took me ages to get over him, Dolly, I can tell you. I thought he was bloody handsome, my Henry.' Her turned-down mouth changed to a hint of a smile as she said his name.

Aunty Elise had stopped watching her kids and joined in the conversation. 'Oh we've all done a bit of courting up the Cows Horn,' she chipped in and laughed, 'in the ruins of the old Clarence Battery where we couldn't be seen, eh Dolly?

Mum slapped her on the arm and said, 'Yes, and you always got the handsome ones, you lucky mare.'

'What about your Cliff, Dolly, he's bloody handsome. How did you catch him – you never did tell me?' She laughed, rubbing her slapped arm. Leonard started to grizzle in his pram and Mum shouted to me without turning her head, 'Go and see to your brother, Dorothy, and bring him here, he probably needs changing.' I put my hands under his arms and lifted him out of the pram – his full nappy sagged in his rubber pants and I kept my arms held out straight as I carried him across to Mum so he didn't lean on me.

Nunoos and Pamela came running up the slipway – their bathers had stretched too, so their tiny nipples poked out above the drooped neckline and the crutch flapped between their knees as they ran towards us. Pamela leaned down and picked up the towel to dry her face then she wrapped it around her shoulders. Nunoos asked Mum if she had a towel so she could dry herself.

'You'll have to share that one,' she snapped as she peeled off Leonard's soaked nappy.

'I'm hungwy Mummy,' Nunoos said rubbing her belly, 'and thuwsty.' Mum sighed. She rooted through the carrier bag again and held up a packet of sandwiches and bottle of lemonade and Nunoos leaned down to take them. They sat down on the wet patch where I had been earlier and while Pamela drank Nunoos unwrapped the jam sandwiches. She handed me one off the top and then gave Pamela another before taking one herself and placing the packet beside her.

'The tide is going out: look, you can see the sand,' Pamela said pointing at the beach.

'You comin' with us after to go wunnin' in the waves Dowothy?' Nunoos asked. I wanted to stay there and hear about how Mum and Dad met but not as much as I wanted to run through the waves on the beach, so after we'd finished eating, the three of us ran down to the sand. We followed the shallow rippling waves as they seeped away from the beach dragging at our legs and leaving our footprints in the soft sand, and then we turned to run squealing with laughter as they rushed back at us swirling around our ankles and licking at the back of our knees.

Sometime later, as the sun sank lower down towards the top of Le Val des Terres – the winding hill that climbs high above the beach – I noticed that a dark cool shadow was cast down over our mum and the others. They had already started to pack up their blankets and Mum was waving to us to go to her, so we left the waves, which were now well down the beach. The damp towel barely dried our skin and we struggled to push our arms through the vests that stuck to our backs and shoulders as we shivered in the cool shade.

'Make haste you kids!' Mum shouted 'I've got to get home for your father's tea.' The boys were loaded into the pram and it bounced and juddered as Mum pushed it over the cobbled slipway. When we got on the flat road above the beach Mum told me to push the pram and Pamela and Nunoos skipped ahead with Aunty Elise's kids. The women walked shoulder to shoulder behind me and June asked Mum if it was true that Charlie, her father, really did used to dance and jig along the narrow bending plank between the dock and the coal boats with a coal sack on each shoulder. Mum laughed and said it was true and that she remembered how he used to teach her to dance and sing when she was a little girl.

Displaced Donkeys

Aunty Elise started laughing and said to Mum, 'I bet he didn't teach you to go down the tram sheds and lift up your smock to show the drivers your drawers, did he?'

'Oh shut your mouth, you cheeky mare! I only did it because they promised to give me a penny and they always did. Then I spent it on sweets.' Mum laughed.

Aunty Elise turned to June and said, 'Do you know what, June? Dolly told me that when her mother Susan took her to register her birth those old town gossips Flossie and Margot were waiting outside the Greffe Registry Office because they'd heard she was going to be there. Nobody had seen Dolly since she'd been born, you see, so they went to find out if the rumour was true that she looked like a little nigger-doll. What do you think of that?' June's mouth dropped open and she shook her head and turned to look at Mum.

'It's true, June,' Mum said. 'My mum told me that when I was a little girl all the townspeople's tongues were wagging because she'd had a baby and married this foreign black man.' Aunty Elise changed the subject and started talking about the war and June told them that her brother had volunteered and gone to England to sign up. By the time we'd walked past the Esplanade in front of the harbour and reached the bottom of Cornet Street opposite the Town Church, June had headed off to catch her bus home. Aunty Elise and her kids had left us earlier and taken the short cut behind the Yacht Hotel and up Cliff Street steps to get to their house.

Mum took the pram from me to push it up the Cornet Street hill and Nunoos and Pamela held hands and skipped ahead chanting loudly 'Give him Bovril, give him Bovril!' – the slogan that was written on the large tin advert fixed to the wall above our heads. It was cool in the shade and I shivered as we reached our house and went inside. We lived in a small terraced house in the corner near the bottom of Cornet Street. The front door opened into the street and at the back a lean-to scullery opened out to a back yard. We could see the Town Church from our house: it was across the road from where the hill wound around a bend then went out of sight down towards the harbour.

The house was empty. Dad wasn't home from work yet. Our dad had a good job as a glazier and there was plenty of work for him from the tomato growers, glazing or repairing their greenhouses, but he drank most of his wages away every weekend and this left Mum without money for rent or food for her family. She often sent us to the Notre Dame du Rosaire Church's soup kitchen to be fed by the nuns who fed the hungry children from the poorer families in the town – but she usually did without herself. Sometimes when the rent man called she would pretend we weren't at home. If we were in the front room when he knocked she'd make us sit with her in silence, huddled under the window where we couldn't be seen if he cupped his face in his hands and peered inside. With five kids under eight years, our mum struggled and when she wasn't fighting with our dad she was screaming at us or giving us hidings in her frustration. She pleaded and humbled herself to whoever she had to in order feed and clothe her ragged brood. When she took us into town with her to go shopping she would shout greetings across the street to the people she knew. I often saw people turn and look away from her but some people who were just as poor and in the same boat found her a bit comic and would shout back. It seemed that just like Charlie, our grandpa, she was becoming a well-known character amongst locals and the poorer townsfolk, as well as the authorities of Guernsey.

3
The reality of the war hits home

Our island was bathed in lovely spring sunshine and while we kids played in the streets the grown-ups listened to Churchill's speeches about the German advance across Europe on the wireless and they read about it in our local paper alongside big adverts urging British tourists to "Come to visit sunny Guernsey!" Meanwhile gas masks and blackout curtain material had arrived on the island and sirens were tested – all in accordance with rules issued in Britain. Many islanders thought that the Germans would have no interest in invading our tiny island and thought the precautions unnecessary. But others had already left for Britain or were preparing to. The grown-ups were all talking about how, across the Channel in France, the Germans had forced the French and British troops down to the beaches at Dunkirk, where they had been rescued by ships and hundreds of smaller vessels and evacuated to the safety of Britain. I was a seven year-old girl and my young life seemed unaffected by the war in Europe – but that was soon to change.

A few weeks after the Dunkirk evacuation, Lollie – who I called my cousin – and I were sitting on the low granite wall on Le Mignot Plateau near St Barnabas Church above Cornet Street, each quietly absorbed in our own thoughts. The sun had warmed the rough grey granite and we dangled our legs over the edge, our feet bare and browned from daily sunburn. The drop on the other side of the wall to the sloping grass below was so steep I was afraid to fall and I gripped onto the edge. The sky was cloudless, and there was no wind. I could see the tall steeple of the Town Church below. On the harbour jetties the cranes poked their noses upwards and their big hooks hung very still. The tide was out and the pungent smell of the seaweed drying under the sun on the harbour bed filled my nose. Idle wooden fishing boats were heeled over, their bow ropes drooping then climbing upward to the metal mooring rings fixed high on the stone-built harbour wall. Their stern ropes were draped in strands of slimy weed and snaked in and out of the clumps of bubbly dark brown vraic where heavy chains attached them to the harbour bed.

Down on the quayside an old fisherman was sitting repairing a wicker crab pot that he'd rested on coiled nets, another was squatting inspecting his own nets and others were standing around clad in knitted Guernsey sweaters, with baggy trousers tucked into rubber boots, nodding at each other and puffing thoughtfully on their pipes. I looked out beyond the harbour mouth towards the offshore islands in the distance. The sea was a turquoise blue and its surface sparkled in the sunlight. The islands of Herm and Jethou appeared to be floating on the shimmering cushion of a heat haze that surrounded them. They seemed to be close enough to swim across to, even though it actually took nearly an hour to reach them from Guernsey on one of the little wooden ferry boats painted white with gleaming varnish on their slatted wooden bench seats. My thoughts drifted back to the time we all went to Herm Island for the day, Dad, Mum, me, my sisters Nunoos and Pamela, and our brother Little Cliffy, and Lollie came with us too. The tide was high, I remember, and the boat named *Lady Dorothy* was tied up alongside the harbour slipway in front of the Town Church. Dad knew the man who owned the boat. He was an old grey-whiskered man with glinting eyes and brown wrinkly skin wearing a traditional Guernsey sweater and a navy blue captain's cap. He was squeezed into a little wooden kiosk at the top of the slipway where he sold tickets through an open window.

'OK Cliff,' he smiled as Dad approached, then he waved us on and we didn't have to pay. Another man stood further down on the slipway alongside the boat helping people to step aboard. He nodded at our dad then picked us younger kids up and lowered us onto the deck, and we ran between the lines of seats toward the long seat at the stern. Our family took up the whole seat and Mum soon struck up a noisy conversation with the other passengers and made them laugh. The diesel engines fired up and smoke belched out at the stern above the waterline. After we had left the harbour Dad pointed out the porpoises to us. Black, sleek and shiny, they moved faster than the boat, swimming close alongside then diving under, in and out of the white frothy wake that churned behind the boat. I stared into the rolling waves and tried to guess where they would pop up next from their deep dives as they played hide and seek with us. When the crew had tied up in the tiny harbour of Herm Island we got off the boat carrying our bathers rolled up in frayed towels under our arms and ran along barefoot to the sandy harbour beach. Dad followed slowly, loaded with bags of sandwiches and bottles of sherbet lemonade, puffing on a thin fag pressed between his lips, and Mum with Leonard in her arms shouted at me to watch out for one of the younger kids.

'Wake up you!' Lollie called out to me and my thoughts were jerked back.. 'Do you want to walk all around the top of these walls with me?' she asked, standing up and holding out her arms like a tightrope walker to balance herself.

'No thanks, I'm scared I might fall off. Hey Lollie, do you remember when we went to Herm on the ferry that time and we saw the porpoises?' I asked.

'Oh yeh, I remember me, we nearly missed the last ferry back to Guernsey 'cos the tide was going out and we had to run to Rosaire Steps further along the island where there was enough water for the boat to pull alongside for us to get on it and I remember your mum was puffing and swearing. You know you won't fall, Dorothy, if you just hold out your arms for balance, like this.' She demonstrated, taking a few steps away from me hardly wobbling at all, her curled toes gripping the top edge of the narrow wall. Through her legs I could see the ridge of the orange pantiled roofs of the terrace of town houses and shops below in Fountain Street. It sagged and rose in a higgledy-piggledy line with crooked chimneystacks marking the end of each property along the terrace. Above, the granite weather-beaten houses, each built to get the best view over the islands, clung to the hillside. Below us, near the bottom of Cornet Street in a small graveyard stood a tall white Celtic cross. The sunlight danced over its surface challenging the dappled shade cast onto it by the overhanging branches of a nearby tree. The fishermen on the Albert Pier were calling out to each other; I could hear their excited voices but not their words and a dozen seagulls that circled high above them began screeching.

The reality of the war hits home

Lollie walked towards me concentrating on keeping her balance and as I looked up at her the sunlight shone through her ball of frizzy hair like a golden halo. Her full fat lips were clenched and a dusting of pale freckles spread into a patch across her nose and cheeks. Lollie was like her dad Charlie, my Grandpa Duncombe, in her features but her skin was quite pale, more like her mother Grace's. She was comic. She was fearless. The week before, a boy called Bobby Green, who lived in Union Street, had been behind us as we walked home from Vauvert School and he'd shouted after us 'Nigger, nigger, pull the trigger, bang, bang, bang!' He had pointed his fingers like a gun. Lollie chased him and smacked him across his head, before he ran off up Allez Street swearing back at her. She skipped back brushing her palms and grinning at me. 'That'll teach the cheeky bugger not to call us niggers, eh?

Back on the Plateau wall I stiffened as Lollie flapped her arms and pretended to lose her balance. 'Scared you!' she jeered. She straightened up and pointed toward Castle Cornet at the edge of the harbour and beyond to the coast of France. 'Look out there at the black smoke, Dorothy. Quickly, stand up so you can see!' Her voice was high-pitched and excited. There was a distant rumbling sound followed by some muffled bangs and more black clouds of smoke. I jumped down from the wall. The fishermen below fell quiet, their faces turned toward the noise. Even the seagulls seemed to be silent. 'That'll be the Germans, they're bombing the French and then they're going to kill them. Did you know they put you in Concentrater Camps where they starve you first, and then they kill you? My brothers Ronald and Ernest told me.' Suddenly, a loud roaring sound overhead startled us. We shaded our eyes from the piercing sun and looked up towards the noise. 'That's a German plane, quickly hide!' Lollie shrieked. She leapt off the wall and we crouched down, hands clasping the back of our heads. My eyes tightly shut, I held my breath until my chest hurt and waited for a bomb to drop on us. The noise faded away and we slowly lifted our heads to see the plane flying south towards Jersey or France. The fishermen below were sprawled around lying flat amongst their nets. They stared up at the disappearing plane then picked themselves up and began shouting, and pointing towards the sky, and the gulls circled and screeched again in concert with them.

'Quick, let's go home in case he comes back to bomb us,' Lollie said, pulling my arm.

'How do you know it was a German plane, Lollie, it might have been a British one?' We were running, feet pounding on the cobbled stones in the shaded alleyway between the high granite walls that wound down between the Plateau and Cornet Street.

'I could see a black cross under its wings. I just quickly saw it,' she called back as I struggled to keep up with her. 'It might have been a Mrs Smith – that's what my brother called it when he did drawings of enemy planes for us. Did you know the Germans have got square heads? It's true, my brothers told me.' We stopped to catch our breath at the top of the steps down to the road.

'How do they know?' I asked panting.

'Because they wears square helmets I s'pose,' she replied. We jumped down the steps two at a time into Cornet Street and headed for home.

4
A shock for Uncle Beano

Near the big gates in the tall granite wall near the bottom corner of the street we saw my sister Nunoos. She had her hand pushed into a hole in the wall. Lollie hushed me with her finger and we crept up behind her. She was singing

Colimachaöns, colimachaöns, show me your horns,
If you don't I will kill you!

'Here's my horns!' shouted Lollie, her two fingers pointed upwards on each side of her head as she sprang up behind her.

Nunoos screamed, pulled out her hand, and jumped backwards: 'Lollie, you fwightened me!'

'That'll teach you to kill snails,' Lollie wagged a finger at her.

'I never kill them, honest, they always show me their horns and I just sing that to make sure they do – tell her Dowothy.' She shifted close to me, clutched my arm and pushed me between her and Lollie.

'Leave her alone Lollie! Did you see the German plane?' I asked Nunoos.

'No, I didn't see a plane, I just wanted the colimachaön to show me his horns.' She looked at me through big brown doe eyes. She was wearing a shabby old cotton dress of mine from the Red Cross. It was too long, her bare ankles and little brown feet just visible below the hemline. Her hair was just like Lollie's, a big round frizzy ball but darker, her olive skin was smooth and her little nose flared slightly at the nostrils above pouting lips that hid the gap of her missing front teeth. She was small for a six-year-old and everyone loved her sweet nature and what Dad called her wide-eyed innocence, He never explained why he called her Nunoos, but the name stuck.

'Anyway,' Nunoos said as she pushed out her chin, 'Mummy was looking for you Dowothy, and Gwanny wanted you Lollie. I was coming to get you but I couldn't find you and then I saw the colimachaön. Gwanny's at home with aunty Elise, they're saying

Jewwy's on our doorstep but when I went outside to look he wasn't there. Who's Jewwy, Dowothy?'

'Don't tell her, Lollie,' I shook my head frowning.

Lollie shrugged and yelled as she ran past us, 'Last one there's a sissy!'

I chased her up Cornet Street but stopped when I heard Nunoos' loud wail from behind me. She had tripped over her long dress. Tears were running down her crumpled face as she pulled up the dress to peer at the blood seeping through the graze on her knee. I gave up the chase and went back to her.

'You started wunnin' up the woad and I was wunnin' after you and I twipped,' she sobbed.

'It's only a graze.' I said and took her hand. She looked up at me with sad watery eyes and wiped away the tears smearing her cheeks with the backs of grubby wet hands. We walked slowly hand-in-hand and by the time we reached our house she'd stopped limping. Lollie was sitting on the doorstep waiting for us.

'You were slow!' she sneered.

'She fell over – anyway it wasn't a fair start,' I snapped back at her.

'Is Uncle Jewwy inside our house… can I see him?' Nunoos asked.

Granny Duncombe shouted to us from inside. She always shouted. 'Lollie! You there you?'

'I'm here, me Mum, just waiting for Dorothy and Nunoos.'

'Get in yer all of you!' We pushed Nunoos ahead as we entered the living room because nobody ever shouted at her. Granny, Mum, and Aunty Elise Churchill – not our real aunty although we'd been told to call her Aunty – were all perched stiffly on their chairs. They turned towards us but said nothing, not smiling or frowning, I'd never seen that look before, it was as if they were sharing a secret from us and they looked guilty.

After the bright sunshine the cramped little room was dark. A shaft of sunlight sneaked through a tear in the ragged curtains at the open window above the big kitchen sink in the scullery. It crept along the blackened floorboards and climbed up the side of a metal bucket full of soaking nappies in the corner and reflected off the yellowy water's surface. The familiar smell of Rinso soap hovered over the bucket. Granny was sitting on a wooden chair next to the coal range although you couldn't see the chair beneath her full skirt. Although she was only in her early thirties she seemed much older. She peered at us from behind her thick round glasses that had circles spiralling into the centre and made her eyes looked really small. She would often just go to sleep, anywhere, at any time – Mum told us it was a sickness but we didn't always know she was asleep because we couldn't see her eyes very well through her glasses. She wore her straight dark hair pulled back tight into a roll. Her knees were wide apart under her long black dress and the toes of her scuffed wooden clogs were peeping out at the front. Our mum was sitting at the solid wooden kitchen table – made by Grandpa Ogier from greenhouse timbers – with our baby brother Leonard draped over her shoulder and she was rubbing his back. She looked tired and anxious; her breasts were heavy with milk and a wet patch had seeped through her cotton smock where it was mixed with streaks of dried dribble. Small and wiry, with large brown eyes like Nunoos', full lips and skin silky smooth the colour of coffee, our mum's dark hair also stood out stiff and frizzy from her head – but it didn't shine for it wasn't healthy.

Leonard burped and spurted out thick curdled milk onto her shoulder.

'Good boy!' the women said together, breaking the silence. Aunty Elise gripped her rolled cigarette between tightened red lips and closed one eye to keep out the smoke that coiled upwards like a snake charmed from a basket. She reached her long thin hand across the table, handed Mum a cloth, and then took Leonard from her. I'd heard Dad tell Mum that Aunty Elise reminded him of a gypsy with her long black hair, toothy smile and big loop earrings, and I'd wondered what a gypsy was.

'Guess what, Mum?' I said, 'Lollie saw a German plane up the Plateau when she was on the wall and she nearly fell off when it came down low and flew right over us!'

I thought they would be shocked. Mum's face stiffened and she reached past Nunoos and clipped Lollie around the ear.

'What have I told you about playing on that wall up there – by Christ you'll fall and break your neck one day, you keep off that wall d'you 'ear? Anyway there's no German planes, yer – they're over in France – it was most likely a British one, so just mind you keep off that bloody wall,' she shouted.

'It *was* a German plane because I saw...' Lollie was rubbing her ear and starting to back me up before Granny's palm slapped against the back of her head cutting her short. 'Don't answer back,' she warned her.

I lowered my head so as not to provoke a slap too or meet with Granny's angry eyes and I noticed on the table a large yellow enamelled bowl with a green lip painted around the top edge, full of cooling red jelly – it smelled of raspberries. Aunty Elise must have made it for us. I was just wondering if there would be some custard to go with it for tea, when my sister Pamela came running in from outside and weaved her way through the room crammed full of bodies. She pulled a chair up to the table and stood on it.

'Cor jelly!' she cried, as she reached over to the jelly and poked her finger into the centre then licked it clean. Granny slapped her hard across the legs. At first she just looked shocked then in an instant she gave a yell, tears flowed and Granny pulled her roughly off the chair and sent her to play outside. Nunoos gently put her arm around her and told her not to cry – that she'd go out to play with her and they could look for colimachaöns.

Pamela was nearly four, with slim features, and was small and wiry like our mother. Her hair was curly and short – she'd had it cut because she caught nits from the kids up the road. Little Cliffy, nearly two, was asleep on a blanket on the floor under the table – he often crawled there to curl up and sleep with Tibby the cat.

'Yer, take Leonard out in his pram for some fresh air Dorothy,' Mum said, nodding towards Aunty Elise who passed me the baby. I cradled him in my arms: he smelled of spewed milk and his nappy was wet. I took him out to the old black pram in the narrow passage, put him in and wheeled him outside, nearly tipping him out as I struggled down the doorstep before Lollie came out to help. Nunoos was asking Pamela if she'd seen Jewwy yet and if he was our uncle.

'Not everyone we're told to call Uncle or Aunty is really a true uncle or aunty,' I explained to Nunoos. 'It's because they're Mum and Dad's grown-up friends. But you know that Lollie really is our aunty because Mummy is her step-sister, but we don't call her aunty: we call her our cousin 'cos she's only seven and not old yet.'

'Aunty Lollie!' Nunoos gave a toothless sneer and laughed and Pamela laughed too, pointing at Lollie and screwing up her face.

Our mum appeared at the door with Little Cliffy in her arms. He was wearing only his vest so he could let the air get to his bum, raw from nappy rash. She lowered him into the pram in front of Leonard. 'Keep these kids outside until I calls you in for tea Dorothy – us grown-ups wants to talk.'

Granny's loud voice drifted down the passage 'They're saying in the Press that Guernsey men might get "called up" now, but they can't call them up according to the Guernsey law.' I watched Mum go back into the passage then turned to my sisters. Pamela was sitting on the kerbside and Nunoos was kneeling behind her peering into her hair looking for nits as she had seen Mum doing, with her fingers poised to strike.

'Look, I can see one. I want to make it click,' she cried. We gathered around bending over close to Pamela's head as Nunoos squeezed her little thumbnails hard together crushing the tiny creature. 'I can't make it click like Mummy does,' she whined.

'Let me see,' I said, leaning over the top of Nunoos' head and concentrating hard on Pamela's in case another one appeared. I thought I saw one but Pamela moved her head.

'Keep still,' I shouted.

'There, it just jumped on you, Nunoos!' Lollie pointed at Nunoos and laughed.

'Where?' Nunoos screamed and jumped up banging me under the chin with her head. I felt a sharp pain as I bit into my tongue and tears filled my eyes.

'Thuddup Lollie!' I shouted. 'Thee what you made her do.' I pointed to my tongue hanging out over my bottom lip. 'I bet ith bleeding now.'

'Nah it's not,' she said with hardly a glance at it. 'Now show me where that bloney nit is – I'll get the little bugger,' and she pushed me aside.

'There's one, look,' she pretended, 'ooh and another one there – bugger, I missed it!'

Pamela had had enough. She stood up. 'Leave my head alone: Mum will do it later,' she said, frowning and scratching her head. Nunoos was rubbing her banged head and I still had my tongue hanging out. We stood and watched Pamela scratching her scalp; then soon we were all scratching imaginary itches on our heads.

Displaced Donkeys

'C'mon let's go and play up the Plateau,' I nodded towards the top of the street.

It was hard to push the pram up the street and I could barely see over the handle so Lollie pushed it with me. Pamela and Nunoos took hold of the sides and we straightened our arms and leaned forwards, putting our weight behind it. We reached the top, turned to go up past St Barnabas Church and then arrived on the Plateau. As I pulled the pram brake onto the wheel I saw that Leonard was sound asleep and Little Cliffy was rubbing his eyes with chubby fists. His shock of fair curly hair was matted at the back where he had slept and crusty lines of dried snot joined his nostrils to his upper lip. His skin was quite pale compared to ours. He filled his little mouth with his thumb and lazily watched me draw a grid pattern in the dry cracked ground with a stick and number each square from one to ten for a game of hopscotch. Nunoos looked for some stones to throw, one each for her, Pamela, Lollie and me. I played first. Pamela complained that she wouldn't be able to jump the squares because I had made them too big. Nunoos agreed with her but while we argued Lollie took her turn, hopped all the squares and declared herself the winner.

Later I began to feel cold for the sun had gone down. It was well past teatime and I wondered if it would be okay to go home now as I was hungry and we'd seen Aunty Elise leave our house a long time earlier. Leonard was grizzling and Little Cliffy was shivering in the pram as we leaned on the wall to look down at our house. Suddenly the door opened and Mum cupped her hands to her mouth and called 'Dorotheeee!' in a high-pitched yell. I waved to her and we hurried down for tea. We sat at the table – Nunoos and Pamela with grubby tear-stained faces and Lollie and me with dirty hands from playing hopscotch – our eyes fixed on the plate piled with doorstep-thick sandwiches and the bowl of jelly. Mum fed and changed Leonard and put him down for a sleep. She dropped Little Cliffy, still with a dried snotty nose, into a grimy wooden high chair that Grandpa Ogier had made for me as a toddler, and handed him a sandwich without a crust. Granny poured us each a cup of sweet tea. Lollie grabbed at a sandwich first, quickly followed by the rest of us. Little Cliffy spat his half-chewed bread out, scrunched it up and smeared it over his tray.

A shock for Uncle Beano

'Look at the bloody time,' Mum shouted, waking up Granny who had put the teapot back on the range hotplate and sat down again, chin on chest, eyes closed, elbows out, and hands on her knees. 'The drunken bastard will drink every penny he's earned if we don't get him home.' Granny opened her eyes, sat bolt upright and nodded at Mum.

'Send Dorothy to bring him home: she's daddy's girl that one,' Granny sneered and poked me. 'You get down the pub and tell your father to come home right now for his tea.' I sat open-mouthed, my sandwich held suspended in the air. I looked desperately at the jelly thinking they'll have eaten it all before I get back. No jelly for me and no custard, I thought as I gave a pleading look at Lollie.

'Can't Lollie go?' A slap from Granny stung my leg.

'Don't you answer back, now get! You can go too Lollie and fetch your father. Now get going before it gets dark.'

On the doorstep outside I groaned to Lollie, 'There'll be no jelly left for us if we don't hurry up.' The pub was down by Woolworth's facing the Victoria harbour. Grandpa and Dad always used to drink there every Friday night. We ran down Cornet Street hand-in-hand as fast as we could and stood outside the door waiting for a man to come out so that we could send him back in to call our dads outside. The black paint on the heavy door was peeling and cracked and below the dull brass doorknob someone had scratched *Jack loves Mary* and surrounded it with a heart with an arrow through it. The door was wide open and an old man wearing a collarless shirt and braces covered by a long, shaggy, greying, full beard staggered out and stood for a moment looking down at us through screwed up eyes. He rocked gently back and forth, the rolled fag in his mouth had burned down and was close to catching his nicotine-stained moustache alight.

'Hello little ladies. I know you, let me think… you're Charlie's girl, eh? And you pretty little thing look like Cliff's eldest.' The fag moved up and down as he slurred through his hidden mouth.

'Can you call them outside for us please, mister?' I asked.

He turned and leaned against the open door and caught the attention of the barman. 'These little ladies would like to speak to Charlie and Cliff, Jack. Can you give them a shout?' As he said 'shout' he lost his balance and his hand slid down the door until he ended up with both hands on the doorstep, the patched seat of his trousers raised in front of our faces. He let out a loud fart. I cupped my hands to my mouth to smother a burst of giggles but Lollie just roared with laughter. I peered over his back to try to see my dad. The old man struggled to stand up and we each took an arm to help. Once he was upright he dug into his pocket and handed us a penny each. He leaned down towards us and we stepped back to get clear of his teetering body and drunken breath as he patted our heads and told us that we were good girls, and then he staggered away – two steps forward, one to the side, then one back, two steps forward, one to the side....

'Thanks mister!' Lollie shouted after him then gave me a grin. Dad came to the doorway, stepped outside, picked me up and sat me on his forearm. Leaning his head back to look into my face he stroked my hair allowing his hand to follow the long dark loose flowing waves until they curled under his forearm. He gave me a wet kiss on the cheek. His breath smelled just like the drunkard's.

'Mum says your tea is ready and you're to come home now before you spend all of your wages, and Granny said so is Grandpa.' A lock of his sun-bleached fair hair fell onto his tanned forehead as he lowered me to the ground and his soft blue eyes hardened for a moment. He patted my head as he stood up.

'You go home now both of you, before it gets too dark. Tell that mother of yours Grandpa and me will come when we're ready and not before – off you go.' Then he stepped back in through the open door. We walked home in silence, knowing what to expect, and I didn't want to go in the house.

'You go in first and tell her, Lollie. I'll come in behind you,' and we went inside.

'When he's ready! I'll swing for that bastard, mark my words.' Mum shoved us onto our chairs at the table. 'Finish your tea, both of you,' she snapped. The other kids were still seated around the table in front of empty plates waiting for the jelly but there was no custard to be seen. The pile of sandwiches had gone but there was one each on my plate and on Lollie's.

'They won't be home now until closing time and once he's spent his wages he'll help your father to empty his wallet,' Granny said.

She was slurping tea out of a cup without a handle and cupping her other hand underneath it.

'Bastard! Bastard! I'm like Mother bastard Hubbard,' Mum screamed. She snatched at our chipped enamel plates and threw them into the sink in the scullery. I grabbed my half-eaten sandwich just in time as my plate disappeared. Mum was like a whirlwind. She grabbed the chewed scrunched bread from between Little Cliffy's fingers and threw it on the floor for Tibby, the skinny tortoiseshell family cat with sagging teats from the last litter that Dad had drowned. Tibby survived on mice and scraps and was skulking in the corner, sniffing the nappy bucket. Little Cliffy's eyes followed his food and he clapped his hands as Tibby pounced on it.

'Tibby's tea!' he squealed happily, but the rest of us kept quiet.

'I'll give the bastard "when he's ready"!' She emptied the teapot into the sink and shiny brown tea leaves splattered the curtain as she thrust the pot up and down. Her face was twisted, her lips drawn in so tightly they looked like Tibby's bum when her tail was up. Little Cliffy hung over the arm of his highchair watching Tibby under the table where she was choking on the bread. We all sat in silence, heads bowed, trying to disappear and not attract an angry slap around the head. Then suddenly Mum stood still and quiet as the creaking sound of the front door opening drifted up the passage.

'Right: that's him!' She scooped the jelly up from the table and rushed out into the darkened passage. 'Here's your bloody tea you useless drunken bastard!' she screamed.

'Jeeezus Christ, Dolly! What the hell?' We jumped from our chairs and ran to the door peeping down into the passage but afraid to step out. As our eyes grew used to the dark we could see our mum with her hand over her mouth staring wide-eyed at Uncle Beano, Dad's drinking friend, with the upturned bowl on his head. Jelly was oozing down his face and neck. He was looking down at his white shirt and when he saw the thick dark red globules dropping down onto his chest his face filled with horror and he screamed, 'Oh Jesus, oh shit, I'm bleeding!' He grabbed the bowl from his head and, flinging it to the floor, ran like a madman down the street clutching his head.

Mum ran out and shouted after him as he reached the corner, 'It's only jelly, Beano! I thought you was Cliff you!' Then she started to laugh, clutching her stomach. We danced around her, laughing because she was laughing and pointing at Beano as he disappeared around the corner.

'It's only jelly, Uncle Beano!' we called after him. Eventually Mum ushered us back inside. I rescued the bowl from the floor and wiped my fingers around the inside edge and put them into my mouth before she took it away. Her rage was over for the moment and she packed us off to bed unwashed and still a little hungry. We shared a double bed, girls at the top and boys at the bottom. Leonard usually slept in our parent's room but that night I brought him into our bed in case there was another fight.

The next morning Granny had gone home and Dad had gone out when Mum got us all up. Leonard had disappeared from our bed during the night but Lollie, who had stayed the night, was complaining because Little Cliffy had wet the bed and her knickers were soaked. She took them off for Mum to wash them and she went without until they had dried. I noticed that the glass in the mirror over the mantelpiece was cracked – seven years bad luck, Mum said that meant – and there were bits of broken cups in the hearth. There was a cut on Mum's cheek and on her lip.

'I want you to look after the girls and Little Cliffy today, Dorothy, just keep them out from under my feet d'you 'ear?' I nodded, my mouth full of bread. We played all day in the lanes around our street and on the steep flights of steps behind the Yacht Inn, and banged on the big wooden cellar doors of the terraced house near the top of the steps under the gas lamp. Lollie had told us a bogeyman lived there who jumped out and grabbed kids and took them into the cellar to eat them. Lollie did the banging and we all ran screeching and terrified, pushing the pram along the Strand Road, which was lined with houses overlooking the beach, searching desperately for somewhere to hide. Later we had races up Tower Hill Steps where Dad once told us a mother and her two grown-up daughters had been burned for being witches in 1556. He said one of the daughters gave birth to her baby and when it rolled clear of the flames it was still alive. Nunoos asked him if they took care of the baby for her, but Dad shook his head and told her that the men just threw it back into the fire to burn with its mother. When she heard this Nunoos' jaw dropped and she got very upset.

After a while we lay exhausted on the top step next to the pram. We'd stayed out until our bellies hurt with hunger and Little Cliffy's nappy was full and smelly. Finally we drifted home and made Nunoos tap on our door while we all waited to see if we we would be allowed in. The following week when Nunoos and I came home from school Dad was at home early sitting at the table with Mum. They hadn't been talking to each other properly since the fight and I'd warned the kids to be well behaved so as not to get them shouting at us and then at each other. Pamela was sitting on his lap with her head against his chest and he smiled at us. Nunoos ran to him with a drawing she had done at school and he swept her up beside Pamela. I hesitated: I wanted to be on his lap and to be hugged too, so I moved over and leaned against his shoulder. He stroked and kissed my hair. He told Nunoos it was the best picture he'd ever seen and she was his clever girl, then he showed Mum the picture of a house and our matchstick-drawn family standing in front of the door with a cat. Mum told Nunoos it was lovely but there would be someone missing from the picture soon, and she glared at Dad.

'Well, you'd better tell them,' she sighed, then got up and filled the kettle.

'Daddy's going away to join the army and fight the wicked Germans soon and when I'm gone I want you all to be good kids and do what Mummy says.'

'Will you drive an aeroplane and fly home to see us playing up the Plateau sometimes?' Nunoos asked.

'No. Daddy will be a soldier like he was here in the Guernsey Militia.' He answered that 'yes' he'd have a gun and 'no' he wouldn't come home for his tea, and more daft questions from Nunoos, then told us he'd bring us a present when he came back and sent us outside to play until teatime. We talked about what we hoped our present might be but not at all about his leaving us.

There were no more drunken fights before he left. We all went down the harbour to see him off. Nunoos and Pamela were crying, I was crying, Little Cliffy was crying because we were crying, and even

Displaced Donkeys

Mum was crying. My arm ached as we stood waving until the boat sailed around the White Rock pier heads and disappeared out of sight. I was thinking I wish I could have gone with him. Nunoos just came right out and said it. After we left our tearful grandparents, aunties, uncles and cousins who had also been there to see him off we walked home. Nunoos kept asking when he was coming back and Mum told her to shut up or she'd get a clout, so we all walked in a silence broken only by the squeak, squeak of a pram wheel until we reached the house.

5

The move

Soon after Dad had gone Mum announced that we were moving to Brazil House in Pedvin Street to live in rooms above Granny and Grandpa Duncombe. I thought this was a great idea because I could spend more time with Lollie. Everyone in the family carried something and helped with the move including Granny's kids – Ronald, Ernest, Lollie and her five-year old sister Barbara and our little Pamela. We marched up the road in a long line with our arms full of bundles of bedding or clothes, dropping the odd sock as we followed our Grandpa as though he was the Pied Piper. He had loaded a wooden handcart with furniture and every now and then he would do a little jig with his feet.

'Show us a dance Grandpa,' Nunoos shouted. He put down the cart and took an old broad-rimmed hat of our mum's off the top of Ronald's bundle of clothes and placed it on his head then he tilted it jauntily to one side and pulled a broom from his cartload. A wide grin spread across his black face and his big lips peeled back to show huge dark gums above his straight white teeth – like a chimpanzee. With his feet spread apart, he threw the broom across his chest from one outstretched hand to the other and did some nifty footwork tapping his toes and heels to a rhythm in his head as he twirled round and spun the broom in his hand. Although he was a big man in his late fifties he was really light on his feet. The neighbours came out and stood on their front steps and we all clapped in time and cheered him on as he twirled and tapped until, finally breathless, he lifted his hat and, still grinning broadly, took a bow.

The move took all day. We stacked old stained mattresses high on the pram, struggled with boxes and put upturned saucepans on our heads pretending we were soldiers, until the house was finally empty and we were all dead on our feet. As Mum locked the door to the empty house the next door neighbours waved and called, 'Cheerie Dolly, see you around. It'll be quiet around here without you.'

'Cheeky mares,' she shouted back and they all laughed.

Over the next couple of weeks the sun shone daily and we kids played outside without a care for the war or fear of attack from the Germans. Lollie and I took turns pumping water with the iron handle over the granite horse trough on Trinity Square into each other's cupped hands so that we could drink it. Across the road – where the bottom of Pedvin Street meets the top of Le Bordage Road – we saw a lady dressed in a smart skirt and a white blouse talking to Nunoos who had her hand in a hole in a wall again looking for colimachaöns, so we ran over to them.

'Is Edna your sister?' the lady asked Lollie.

'No she's hers,' Lollie pointed at me.

'My hand is stuck Dowothy,' Nunoos whined. It was. I pulled and she yelled and it came out dirty and grazed.

'Can I speak to your mother about Edna?' the lady asked and I told her our mum was at home. We walked up Pedvin Street wondering what Nunoos had done wrong. Lollie ran inside to tell Mum about the lady and she came to the door wiping her hands on a towel.

'What have I told you about sticking your hand in holes? I'll give you such a clout my girl.' Mum raised a warning hand at Nunoos.

'I hope you don't mind,' the lady interrupted her, 'but I was listening to Edna sing and watching her dance as I followed her up the road. She has real talent and I was wondering if you would mind if I gave her lessons in song and dance?'

'We've got no money for stuff like that, missus,' Mum huffed.

'Oh there wouldn't be a charge, it would be free to Edna.'

'Do you want to do that, Nunoos?' Mum asked. Nunoos raised her doe-like eyes to the lady and nodded, flashing a toothless smile. The following Saturday afternoon the lady called for her and Nunoos went to start her lessons. Once Mum learned that the lady lived in Upper Hauteville just up the road from Pedvin Street, I had to take Nunoos there and go to fetch her back.

'What did you do today?' I would ask her on our way home.

'The lady played the piano and I sang this song. Listen – I'll sing it for you Dowothy:

If I had one wish to make,
A wish that could come twue,
I would like and old stwaw hat…'

The move

All the way home she would sing happily at the top of her voice and tap and twirl showing me what she had learned. She tried to teach me but I had no rhythm and anyway I didn't know the words. From then on Nunoos danced or skipped everywhere, she never just walked. She would sometimes sing to her rag doll Missy and teach her the steps as she bounced her up and down and after a while the lady even taught her to pronounce her R's properly and not like a W.

6

Crabbing with the boys

It was a Sunday and we were going crabbing with Ronald and Ernest off the rocks at Havelet Bay. Lollie had asked her brothers if we could go, just her and me, but they didn't want girls hanging around them. Granny overheard and shouted, 'Let them go with you or you stay at home!'

It was decided. We took a short cut down the steps behind the Yacht Inn and past the Slaughter House, a long tall granite building with curved corners a bit like the main market building in Fountain Street. All around the slaughterhouse just below the roof were slatted windows through which you could sometimes hear squealing sounds. The boys told us they were the sounds of little girls being killed by the monsters that lived there. Ernest was twelve and big for his age, and Ronald was eleven. They both looked like paler versions of our grandpa. They climbed high up onto the wide Havelet Bay breakwater wall and walked along the top with their crab-catcher bicycle wheels and string slung over their shoulders, but they wouldn't help us up so we had to walk alongside down on the road. We headed towards La Vallette bathing pools where we clambered over the rocks next to the gents' pool so as to get close to the sea. At the water's edge, where the waves lapped amongst the dark silky swirling tendrils of seaweed that clung to the rocks beneath us, we sat down and waited while the boys prepared their crab catchers. They undid the coil of string wrapped around the bicycle wheels and laid the wheels on the rocks. Each wheel had no spokes but instead string threaded across the wheel and through the spoke holes around the edge then back again criss-crossing like a net. Four pieces of shorter lengths of string were tied at equal spaces around the edge of the wheel and knotted together above the centre where they were attached to the long length they had uncoiled. For bait they used some smelly fish heads, scrounged from the fish market the day before, which they tied into the centre of each wheel. From the rocks they lowered the baited wheels carefully into the sea right down to the seabed and we waited.

'Lollie, you and Dorothy go and find some limpets and winkles," Ernest said. We found a sharp stone to knock off the limpets and climbed barefoot over the warm brown craggy rocks plucking off curly grey winkle shells and dropping them into our scooped-up skirts. The limpets were trickier because if you didn't knock them off the rock with the first blow they held on so tight that when you tried again you just ended up smashing their shell, and we gave up on the ones that did that.

'Oi!' Ronald shouted, 'we've got one.' We scrambled across the rocks clutching our skirt pouches of limpets and winkles. There in the middle of Ronald's wheel was a big orangey-brown spider crab with lots of knobbly spikes all over its back and down its legs that dangled and danced through the string. There was a little brown crab too but it was under the net and fell back into the sea.

'I nearly lost mine, look,' Ernest said, gently lifting his wheel clear of the drop to the sea. His crab was a lady spider crab – you could tell by the skinny claws and the dish-shaped flap under her belly that was full of tiny round brown eggs. She had caught her claw and legs in the string at the rim of the wheel and was hanging over the side. They carefully put the crabs into a cloth sack. I sat down beside the sack to watch as they dropped their wheels again but I screamed and jumped clear as the sack seemed to come to life and jerked towards me. They caught three more crabs before we packed up and headed home.

'Crabs for tea tonight, Mum.' Ronald grinned, holding up his catch to Granny who was sunning herself as she sat on her front doorstep.

'Who's that?' she growled opening her eyes.

'And winkles and limpets, Mum,' Lollie added ignoring the question.

An hour later we were seated around the still warm, bright red cooked crabs and shellfish piled onto newspaper spread out on the table. We poked into the winkle shells with a sewing needle to prise out what Mum called "the eye" – a hard dark brown disc with lots of rings on it like Granny's glasses. We weren't to eat that, Dad had told us. Once it was out we pushed the needle in again and wiggled it around until we could stab the soft flesh of the winkle inside and drag it out, stretching its coiled body and letting it spring back into a coil before popping it into our mouths. Grandpa cracked the crab claws with a hammer to get to the white meaty flesh which was shared among the grownups. The boys sucked on the legs after they had pulled them off and snapped them at the knuckles before passing them to Grandpa to crack open. Granny picked at each crab's body and scooped the brown slimy stuff from inside their spiky shells into a bowl and mixed it with the tiny eggs to spread onto our bread.

'There's only one thing better than spider crab, Dad,' said Ernest through lips full of crab legs, 'and that's ormers.' Grandpa nodded and grinned.

After she'd picked the crabs clean Granny began to wrap the empty shells and legs in the newspaper when she suddenly stopped to read something.

'Look, Dolly, here's your Cliff's name in the *Press*.' She smoothed out the crumpled page on the table and showed Mum.

'What does it say about him?' Ernest asked. We eagerly waited for her to read it.

'Wait a minute. How old is this paper?' Granny said searching for the front-page headline, her nose almost touching the page. 'Yer 'tis Saturday the eighth of June 1940.' She read the headline aloud to us: '"British Tanks help France on the Aisne" and yer at the bottom of the page it says that four Channel Islands men have joined the Royal Artillery.' We huddled around her and she continued… "Clifford Ogier, son of Mr and Mrs A. Ogier of Grandes Rocques, Castel, who has served three years in the Royal Guernsey Militia, is now in the army on the mainland. Gunner Ogier, 33, was employed as a glazier. His wife and family are living at 36 Pedvin Street." She passed the paper to our mum and we strained to see the writing on the paper.

'I can't see him, Mummy,' Nunoos said peering at the paper through a gap in our bodies.

'There's no picture – just writing, stupid,' snapped Ernest. Mum stood up, pushed us aside, folded the paper and silently left the room.

After we moved to Pedvin Street Nunoos spent more time with Lollie's sister Barbara, who was small for her age with a big gummy grin like her father and a mop of black curls. Pamela tagged along with them too so I didn't have to look after them. We were all playing together out in the street sticking our heads through the iron railings on the small wall in Pedvin Street above the gents' urinals that were built into the wall behind a carved iron screen below in the Le Bordage Street. The boys spat down onto the caps of the men coming out then quickly pulled their heads back out of sight. We girls didn't spit but we shouted 'Hello mister!' as they came out onto the pavement buttoning their flies, then pulled our heads back so they couldn't see us when they looked up. Lollie shouted to an old man 'Your flies are undone mister!' but got her ears stuck and couldn't pull her head back in time. He looked up, wagged his finger and shouted at her, 'I'll tell your mother, Lollie Duncombe!' Everyone knew Charlie Duncombe's kids. Granny didn't hear him. She and Mum were standing on the doorstep shouting across the road to our neighbours. They all leaned against the walls in their doorways and had their arms folded underneath their bosoms. It seemed they all either nodded in agreement, or else shook their heads, at the same time.

'The picture houses are closing down so we can't go to see *The Flying Deuces* with Laurel and Hardy at The Regal this week,' Mrs Leggett across the road complained. Her snotty-onosed toddler was sitting on the kerbside peeling off a trodden-in sweet and putting it into his mouth.

'Seems to me, with these practice air raid warnings and all, we might as well be in the bloody war,' Granny said, 'and did you read about all those French people turning up in Guernsey on those fishing boats – whole families with kids and babies? They said those bastard Germans had burned down their houses and everyone had fled their town. They'll be yer in Guernsey next, mark my words.' They all slowly nodded. Mum seemed to be less angry with us now that there were no more fights and rows with Dad. She was kept busy though, doing the housework for Granny, who had just had another baby girl called Delia.

7
The note from school

On Wednesday 19 June 1940 we were crammed around Granny's table with the younger ones sitting two to a chair, all scoffing down bread and jam with tea as quickly as we could. We were still eating as Granny hurried us out to school shouting, 'Now get a bloody move on or you'll be late for school.' Ernest and Ronald pushed past us and ran ahead. I held Nunoos' hand and pulled her along faster than her legs could carry her.

'Stop running so fast, Dorothy, my legs can't catch up with my feet,' she moaned. Lollie held Barbara's hand as we hurried up Vauvert past the Cats Ladder and into the school gates. The playground was empty. We took the younger girls to their classrooms then went to our own. My teacher looked down at me over her glasses.

'Why are you late, Dorothy Ogier?' her face looked stern.

'We all overslept, miss,' I answered staring at the floor, twisting my finger.

'Poor punctuality is the height of bad manners, my girl. Now go to your desk.'

The sun was shining at playtime as we ran out into the playground for break. Excited girls shrieked and ran into their own special groups and unrolled their skipping ropes. I could never do skipping so I always ended up turning the rope. In a separate playground the boys chased or hid from each other pretending to be Germans and British, firing fingers shaped into guns and pretending to fall down dead clutching their chests. In next to no time it seemed, the bell rang high on the roof and we walked quietly back inside in single file, girls in one door and boys in another.

When the bell rang again at half-past three for home time the teacher gave us each a letter from a pile on her desk as we filed out of the classroom. 'Make sure you give this letter straight to your mother, Dorothy, do you understand?' I nodded. Outside the gates Lollie, Nunoos, and Barbara were waiting for me. Lollie had opened her letter.

'That's for Granny, not you,' I said.

'She won't care if I've read it. Shall I tell you what it says? It says there's going to be an *evac… evacu…*oh, some big word, on a boat to the mainland and our mums and dads have to go to school tonight at seven o'clock.' All the way home she tried to pronounce the big word on the letter for us and only when Ronald and Ernest came running and caught us up at Trinity Square did we hear the words *evacuation* and *evacuated* read out properly.

'The Germans are coming from France to kill us – that's why we have to escape before they get here and some of the older boys at school told us that Britain said Guernsey is demilitarised and that means there won't be any soldiers here to fight to save us from the Germans,' gasped Ronald.

'It's true what he says,' Ernest called over his shoulder as the boys ran on ahead to our house.

When we reached home later Nunoos rushed inside waving her letter.

'Mummy, we're being *evacutated* because the Germans are coming to kill us,' she yelled running up the passage.

'I know all about it. I read Ernest's letter when he came in, Nunoos. Don't you worry, Mummy won't let any Germans kill you. Now leave those letters and go outside all of you and play until your tea is ready.' Granny sent Ernest and Ronald to the Red Cross to see if they had any small suitcases but they had run out and only had some brown carrier bags with string handles. While we played outside Granny and Mum were busy gathering together the things we were to take from the list sent with the letter from school. They found what they could: vests, knickers, socks, cardigan, pullover, blouse, shirt and shoes. Some things we did without: handkerchief, toothbrush (we never used one), nightclothes (we slept in our vest and drawers), comb, flannel, soap and towel (the whole family shared these so there was none spare to take). The list suggested rations for the journey: sandwiches (egg or cheese), packets of nuts and seedless raisins, dry biscuits with cheese, barley sugar and an apple or orange. But we got only a bottle of sherbet lemonade and two slices of bread and butter each – that's all there was in the cupboard.

'Inside now for your tea,' Mum shouted from the doorstep and we had fish and chips that Ronald had been sent for earlier. Granny shouted at Grandpa for starting to eat our packs of bread and butter and he hung his head like a naughty little boy.

Granny and Mum had got all dressed up in their best dresses. Mum was wearing red lipstick, her hair was flattened down under a scarf and she had patted her face a creamy-white colour with face powder though her neck was still brown. Granny's face was powdered a brownish shade but her neck was white. I wondered why they didn't swap face powder so it would match their necks.

'While we go to your school Grandpa is going to get you all scrubbed in the big tin bath – the young ones first – then all of you straight to bed,' Mum said. There was a knock at the door and we ran to the window to see who it was. A group of women and some men were standing outside – our neighbours calling Mum and Granny. We watched them walking down the road huddled together, heads bobbing and gabbling like a gaggle of geese, all heading for the school meeting at seven o'clock.

We squeezed into the bath, girls or boys in twos, and every time we climbed out the next pair in got another bucket of warm water, so that by the time Ernest and Ronald got in it was quite deep but the soapy scum floated on the surface and stuck on their bodies. In our double bed at Granny's, Pamela and Barbara and Nunoos slept at the bottom and Lollie and I slept at the top. We talked about going to the mainland on a big boat together and maybe seeing Dad when we got there – we were excited and couldn't sleep. Grandpa came into our room and told us all about ships and being at sea and made it sound like a great adventure that we'd be going on.

'Will we go on the boat Daddy went on, eh?' asked Nunoos.

'Maybe so, maybe so,' said Grandpa in his slow melodic drawl.

'Has Mummy been on a big boat?' Pamela asked.

'Well yes, she came on the boat to live with me and Granny in Jersey when she was a young girl.' He told us the story the way I'd heard Mum tell it, but he missed out the bit where she had cried. Then he laughed out loud so we all laughed too but I hoped I wouldn't get lost in the big harbour in England.

When we awoke the next morning there were three neat piles of clean clothes on top of the chest of drawers in our bedroom. We each recognised our own clothes and dressed. Downstairs the table was laid. Our sugary tea had been poured into jam jars because there weren't enough cups, and we had boiled eggs with toast soldiers as a special treat from Aunty Elise. Mum had put fresh bread and butter into our carrier bags and toasted the rest. Pamela and Barbara asked if they could go on the big boat with us but were told it was only we three older girls going with our school and Ernest and Ronald were going with the big school. We finished breakfast and left the table. Nunoos ran towards Mum, who was sitting feeding Leonard, and started to cry, 'Why can't you come with us, Mummy? I want you to come.' Mum put her arm around her shoulders, pulled her close and pressed her mouth into Nunoos' hair.

'Mummy has to look after the babies. Your teacher is going with you and she'll look after you for me and you'll have to look after Missy. We'll put her in your bag so you don't lose her,' she said, picking up the rag doll and handing her to Nunoos. She stood up and put Leonard into his pram. 'And anyway the letter from your school says we're not allowed to come to the boat because there will be too many people, so we have to say goodbye here.'

'Come on now, get your coats on – hurry up,' Granny ordered. I tried to tell Mum it was too warm for a coat but she ignored me. She pulled me towards her and brushed my hair roughly before yanking it up into a pony-tail and tying it with a piece of red wool.

'There, you're done and don't let anyone up there on the mainland cut this lot off or your father will go mad – he loves your hair.' Then she gave me a quick kiss on the cheek and turned me away to fetch my coat. Nunoos' hair looked the same brushed or not so she was ready and Mum hugged her close to her. I wanted a hug like that but knew I was the eldest and was lucky to get a kiss on the cheek. We stood there in our coats by the door looking back at those who weren't coming with us and it was as if already we didn't belong in this ragged lumped-together family. The pieces of cotton material hurriedly sewn onto our coat lapels – which would set us apart from our school friends because we never had or would ever buy parcel labels in our house – had our names written on them in ink. Our mum's best writing in capital letters spelled "Dorothy May Ogier, Vauvert School" and "Edna May Ogier, Vauvert School" as instructed in the school's letter.

Displaced Donkeys

'Don't forget these,' Mum said as she hung our gas mask boxes around our necks. Granny hung Lollie's around her neck and gave her a kiss on the cheek. Lollie reached towards our Grandpa, who came over to her and swept her up into a big long hug. His eyes were watery and he didn't seem able to speak as she buried her face into his neck. He put her down and came towards us with open arms and gave Nunoos and me a big hug, then he hugged Ernest and Ronald, who tried not to cry in front of us but when they let Granny hug them she wiped their tears. We were all tearful as we spilled into the street, and as they watched us walk down Pedvin Street in the morning sunshine in our thick coats carrying our little carrier bags the grown-ups dabbed away their tears. Ernest and Ronnie acted all brave: slinging their bags of belongings over their shoulders they strode on ahead.

We sat and waited all day at school. We asked the teachers when we were going, but they didn't know and we got so hungry by the afternoon that we ate our bread and butter and drank our drinks. Later the teachers sent us all home telling us there was no boat so to come back tomorrow and a boat would come for sure. We all carried our overcoats as it was hot and sunny and I had to carry Nunoos' bag because she complained it was too heavy. All the way home she skipped around me and asked why the boat didn't come and were we staying in Guernsey now and would there be a boat tomorrow and could we go to the beach for a swim before tea because she was hot? Aunty Elise was there when we got home. The front door was open and inside we could hear her squeaky voice telling Granny and Mum that her kids weren't going anywhere without her as she couldn't be sure where they might end up over there on the mainland. We stepped into the passage and I held my finger to my lips as we stood still and listened.

'They'll probably drop bombs on the places where our kids are being sent, and there's no bombs dropping here nor is there likely to be if we don't put up a fight,' she yelled angrily.

'They'll be all right with the school teachers looking after them,' Granny snapped. 'Anyway haven't you heard what they're saying, that the Germans will be here in Guernsey in a day or so and you know what those bastards do to their prisoners...they murder kids and rape women and put the men in slave labour or prison camps. Would you prefer that?'

Mum tried to calm them down. 'Look, they're saying that women with younger children and babies can leave here straight after the schoolchildren have all gone. There's going to be more boats coming for us and we can meet up with them again when we get there.'

'So what's to say those German bastards won't drop bombs on the ships as they go across the sea to the mainland? No, I think we should stay here where we'll all be safer. They won't come here, they'll go straight to Britain and that's where we'll be sending our poor kids,' Aunty Elise replied.

'She could be right, Grace,' our mum said to Granny. 'What if they drop their bombs on the boats and sink them all on the way across the Channel? The kids might be safer here in Guernsey: we all might be. I'm not sure now that I should let them go. I'd never forgive myself if they got killed – maybe we should all stay here?'

'No they'll be safer away from Guernsey and we can go too so we'll all be bloody safe,' Granny shouted. I'd heard enough and turned to Lollie and Nunoos who looked as scared as I was at what we were hearing. I beckoned them to follow me into the living room.

'The boat didn't come, so they sent us home,' I announced as I came into the room, interrupting their conversation. 'We'll be going tomorrow instead.'

'We know, a neighbour called in to tell us,' Mum replied. We were sent out to play but not to the beach. We went down to Trinity Square, stripped to our knickers and jumped in and out of the horse trough. Carved in the iron water tank above the granite trough was a fierce lion's face with a big curly mane around his head but he didn't frighten us because he had no teeth – just a thick pipe sticking out of his mouth for a waterspout. Lollie reached up and pumped the big handle on the back of the tank and the lion face gushed water into the trough. We splashed it over each other and squealed with laughter until we heard Mum shout and wave to us from the doorstep. We all ran across the road with our dry clothes bundled under our arms, leaving little wet footprints behind us.

After our tea we were all sent to bed early again. There was an uncomfortable silence in the bedroom. I was thinking about the German plane that flew over the plateau and imagined it dropping bombs on our boat and all the kids jumping into the sea and drowning because of the heavy coats their mothers had made them wear.

Lollie whispered to me, 'Are you awake, Dorothy?' I didn't answer because I was quietly crying. Eventually I fell asleep like the others.

I awoke to a firm hand shaking my shoulder and I heard my mum whisper in the dark.

'Wake up Dorothy, and you Lollie, and wake Nunoos but try not to wake the others. You can get dressed downstairs then I'm taking you up to the school.'

'What's the time?' I asked

'Shush, it's very early in the morning – now make haste downstairs.' Ernest and Ronald were already up, rushing their breakfasts and once we were dressed and fed Granny handed us crumpled brown paper bags containing some dry bread – there was no butter left – and another sherbet lemonade drink to put in our carrier bags. The sun wasn't up yet as we walked to our school and there was silence in the streets except for Granny's wheezing as we climbed Vauvert hill. It got noisier though with loud voices as we approached the school carrying our gas masks, bags, and wearing our coats with the sewn-on labels to join other bleary-eyed children who stood around tearful and bewildered with their mums and dads. Granny hugged Lollie and then the boys, who ran off afterwards up the hill to St Joseph's, their school. Mum sent us off with a tearful kiss and a stern warning to me to look after Nunoos. Then she waved as the teacher led us inside the school. I took one last look back at her and Granny standing at the gates with the other weeping mothers and comforting fathers – then the teacher pulled the door closed.

8
The evacuation

The pupils of our school were walked down The Grange past Elizabeth College in long lines of three abreast, all the way down St Julian's Avenue underneath the shelter of the tall elm trees that grew out from the pavement, each class headed by a teacher, until we reached the harbour. There were buses loaded with children lined up along the road to the docks. There were more people crowded around the docks than I'd ever seen in my life. Hundreds of men, women, young children and young babies in prams were all looking at the big boat in the dock. The noise of the crowd was frightening – some women were crying and hugging their children and others were waving to children as they boarded. It seems that most parents came to the dock despite the letter from the school. As we got near the boat I peered among the tearful, unhappy faces searching for our mum. I saw Grandpa, his face easily recognizable, and with him Granny Duncombe and Mum and our Granny and Grandpa Ogier too. They saw us and waved like mad. Mum shouted out to me, 'Mind you look after your sister, Dorothy.'

'I will Mum,' I shouted back and waved. We all waved. The dockworkers helped us up the gangplank and we followed our teacher to some deck space on the seaward side. Later as the boat moved away from the docks, Lollie found me and then we found Nunoos and pushed our way through the crowded deck toward the dockside to catch one last sight of our parents and grandparents. It was hopeless – we couldn't see them in the crowd amongst all those waving arms – so, feeling disappointed, we returned to our separate school classes.

The boat was called *Antonia*. It was black and grey with two big funnels and rusting railings around the decks. High above the rails were small boats hanging on big hooks. It had recently been used to carry troops and was smelly and dirty. There was no room to run around and play. After it had steamed out of the harbour mouth into the Russell Channel heading north, some of the younger children started feeling sick and were crying for their mothers. A teacher was sick over the side and the wind blew it back over her coat sleeve. I went down below and tried to get comfortable but began to feel unwell as the boat leaned and rolled. Down in the hold where my class had been sent it was crammed with children. Many of the younger children were now curled up on the floor sleeping or sobbing. I wondered where Lollie and Nunoos were. I'm supposed to look after Nunoos, I thought. I should go and find her but the teacher had warned us not to leave our class. I was worried but eventually, exhausted, I fell asleep.

I had been asleep for what seemed a long time when I was awakened by a man who brought us mugs of tea – it was very strong and sweet. We also got tomatoes and cheese triangles. I took out my dry bread, spread the cheese on it with my fingers and rolled it in half. I dipped the end of my bread and cheese into the dark brown liquid just long enough for it not to fall off when I pulled it out and shoved it into my mouth. After the sandwich I ate the tomato. The juice and pips spurted out as I bit into it and ran down my chin but it was sweet like the best Guernsey toms. When I finished eating I asked the teacher if I could go and find my sister. She was busy wiping the tomato spew off the coat of a boy in our class and she waved me away, so I went looking for Nunoos and Lollie. I couldn't see them among the children in the hold and decided to search upstairs. Up on the deck the sea-air blew through my hair and I could taste the salt on my lips. There were loads of tomatoes bobbing on the sea among the waves – I thought that maybe they had fallen off a cargo boat that was shipping them to England. But then suddenly I shuddered and I thought perhaps a German bomber had sunk that boat, as Aunty Elise had said, and would get us next. I looked up and searched among streaks of purple and red clouds but saw no German plane. In the distance on the horizon the sky was bright orange and a big red sun was sinking towards the sea. I was surrounded by groups of strange young faces from various Island schools. Some young ones were sleeping on blankets and others who were older were wide-awake and talkative, but there was no sign of Nunoos or Lollie. I went back to my class down below just in time for the lesson on how to use our gas masks. My class was standing in a circle around our teacher and she was showing them how to put their chins in first then pull the straps at the back of the mask over their heads. I quickly joined in. The mask smelled of rubber and made me feel sick as I breathed in and out, and some of the boys found it made a noise like a fart and started laughing. Later I curled up on the blanket and fell asleep until someone stepped on my hair and I awoke to a noisy commotion, as bodies around me were standing up and gathering up their belongings.

'We've arrived at the mainland, now stay together in your class and follow me when you are told,' our teacher announced. I remembered Nunoos and pretended to my teacher that I needed the lavatory so I could find her. It was darker up on the deck now. I could just make out in the fading light what turned out to be the port of Weymouth in the distance. I found Nunoos sitting on her coat that was spread out on the deck playing cat's cradle with her friend while the rest of her class were putting on their coats and getting ready to follow their teacher.

'Where were you earlier when I came looking for you? Have you seen Lollie?' I asked crouching beside her.

'No I haven't seen Lollie, I've been here all the time me. I want to go to the lavatory: will you show me where to go?' I asked her teacher where it was and I took her in the direction pointed out by the teacher.

'You're not wearing your coat. Where is it, Nunoos?' I asked her.

'On the floor back there – I was sitting on it.' She looked back pointing to where she had been sitting but now it was just crammed with kids standing and waiting. We turned and spotted Lollie hanging over the deck rails being sick – her face looked green in the dim yellow glow of the boat's deck lights.

'Watch it doesn't blow back at you in the wind, Lollie,' I warned.

'Oh Dorothy, will you stay with me? I feel really sick,' she pleaded.

'No, Dorothy, you need to take me to the lavatory – I need to go now!' Nunoos was tugging my arm with one hand and the other was between her crossed legs. I could see a queue of children and a couple of teachers standing outside a door so I sent her to join the end of the line and took care of Lollie. After a short while Nunoos came back towards us – she was crying and walking oddly.

'I had an accident,' she sobbed, hanging her head. Lollie moved closer to her.

'What kind of accident?' I asked

'Pooh: she's shit her pants!' Lollie was holding her nose and pulling away from her. Nunoos frowned at me and said, 'It's your fault, Dorothy, you sent me there and when I reached the front of that queue the teacher told me it was giving out medicine for the children who'd been sea sick, so she sent me to another queue and I went there but then it was too late: it just came and I couldn't stop it. And you can shuddup Lollie, tell her, Dorothy.' Her bottom lip was pouted and she was snivelling as I took her to join the lavatory queue. We stood at the end and waited. Lollie had followed us. She held her nose and announced loudly to the others in the queue that her cousin had shit her pants. Suddenly a big space opened up around us as the other children all stepped away imitating Lollie – which made Nunoos cry even more. Soon we found ourselves in the front of the queue at the lavatory door and then inside standing at the basin. Nunoos took off her pants and I emptied them into the lavatory before rinsing them in the basin under the tap and then I used them to wash her dirty bum down before rinsing them out again.

'Stop crying now, Nunoos,' I said, as I tried to wring out the rinsing water. 'You'll have to wear these damp but they'll soon dry, don't worry.' We came out to Lollie who had been outside barring anyone except maybe a teacher from entering the lavatory. The boat had stopped. It was waiting for the boats in front of us to unload and clear the pier. When it started to move again we were all hurried back to our classes by the teachers. We moved like a flock of sheep without any sense of direction.

'See you later,' I called to Lollie. I glanced around but couldn't see Nunoos. I thought she must be back with her class too. Everyone was pushing and shoving. Some of the girls in my class started crying for their mothers and we were all tired and hungry.

9
Arrival in Britain

The boat finally docked. We filed down the gangplank and then walked in the dark behind our teacher in a long line two-by-two until we reached a large building that looked like a cinema. I thought we were going to see a film but we were told to sit with our class in each row and wait. The Salvation Army ladies gave us sandwiches and drinks and we had our hair checked for nits. Then we were looked over by doctors in white coats; they asked us if we had any illnesses or were feeling sick. I looked around at the hundreds of faces, trying to see my sister, but I couldn't and I wondered if she was walking under the jetty here in Weymouth and up the beach as Mum had done in Jersey, with nobody to meet her and no coat with her name sewn on to tell anyone who she was.

It was still dark when we were taken to the railway station. There were loads of kids in the dimly lit station and the boys in our class were pointing excitedly at the huge trains. We had never seen a real train and I was a bit scared of the loud hissing noises and white clouds of steam coming from under the half-hidden wheels. The driver leaned out of his window, grinned at the boys and beckoned them to come closer to the engine. They moved cautiously towards him and he climbed down to meet them. He started to point to things and explain how they worked. Some other boys joined them – they were older and wore uniforms and caps and I thought they must be from Elizabeth College. Soon teachers and kids began climbing up through the open doors of the long line of carriages and our teacher called us together to climb aboard too. A man had to lift us up as we couldn't reach the step, and we squeezed together onto the seats with our feet sticking out over the edge. Our teacher took our bags and gas masks and placed them on a rack above the seats. The train whistle blew a few times and then, hissing and juddering, the train slowly moved out of the station. The kids who sat next to the open windows waved goodbye to the children and teachers on the platform who were waiting for the next train. As the train left the station our teacher pulled down the black blinds at the windows and then suddenly someone put out the lights and everything went black. A few girls screamed and at first I was a bit frightened of the jerking and rocking of the train but my heavy lids and tiredness took over and I drifted in and out of sleep.

The next morning we soon got fidgety and left our seats to press our palms and noses against the windows and take in the passing scenery.

'Look at those cows, miss, they're not brown like Guernsey cows – they're black and white. Funny, eh?' shouted Percy le Patourel whose dad was a farmer in Guernsey.

'They're called Friesians, Percy,' the teacher explained.

The patchwork of fields stretched as far as my eyes could see. I was thinking they must reach the other side of the world as the sea does at Grande Rocques near Granny and Grandpa Ogier's house. When the train came into places where there were lots of houses we stopped at the stations and kind people came out and gave us sandwiches and sweets before we moved on again. We didn't know where we were and even the teacher didn't know. She showed us that the names of the stations had been painted out.

'How will the driver know where he's going, miss?' asked Lollie, who had managed to find me by wandering through the carriages. She never was one to sit and do as she was told – not by a teacher.

'I'm sure he knows his way,' our teacher replied.

'Have you seen Nunoos?' I asked Lollie.

'No not yet. She may be in another carriage though. Hey, miss, is Dorothy's sister Edna on this train with her class and teacher?' she shouted to our teacher.

'Don't shout at me, Lollie Duncombe,' came the reply, and to me she said, 'Don't worry Dorothy, we'll all meet up again at the final destination and you'll find your sister then.' As the day went on the rhythmic clickety-click of the wheels on the track made me drowsy and I wondered if the journey would ever end. Lollie was told by my teacher to return to her classmates. My friend Jean Ogier – who was no relation – was sitting beside me asleep with her head against the teacher's shoulder and so I put my head on

Jean's shoulder and listened to the clickety-click until I was lulled into sleep.

'Wake up children. I think we're finally here.' Our teacher was standing up straightening her skirt and buttoning her cardigan as the train chuffed slowly to a halt. She grabbed her hat, placed it on her head and then began passing us our gas masks and bags. It was chaos. Bags were lost or handed to the wrong child and Mary Falla from my class wet herself and was crying because she wanted the lavatory and nobody heard her asking for it. We congregated on the platform where standing waiting for us were some smartly dressed men and women who spoke to our teachers. We followed them through the station and it was getting dark as we approached the lines of strange tall buses.

'Those are funny buses, miss, they've got an upstairs like a house,' Percy shouted.

'You'll see lots of these Percy – they're called double-deckers. Now get aboard quickly, you're holding everyone up.'

We all wanted to go upstairs but the driver told Percy it was already full up there. We drove past rows of brick houses which all looked the same, but soon it was too dark to see out of the windows so we slept. Suddenly the bus lurched to a halt. We were all thrown forward and I banged my head on the seat in front.

'Ah'm sorry aboot that, weans,' the driver called over his shoulder in a strange-sounding language.

'Hurry now, children, gather your belongings together – we're getting out here,' a matronly teacher at the front of the bus shouted back to us. We pulled our bags from under the seats and stepped out into the street. Across the road there was an old building like a church hall and we were marched inside where the lighting was dim and the windows were blocked out with heavy black curtains. There were camp beds in rows with a pillow and a blanket and beside each one a small wooden box. Class by class we were allocated beds until the hall was full. Lollie's class was in the row next to mine, so she asked a girl classmate next to my bed to swap beds with her and she wasn't taking no for an answer.

'Put your belongings into your boxes, everyone, then change into your nightdresses or pyjamas and try to get some sleep,' our headmistress Miss Naftel's voice called out. We sat on our beds and I looked around at everyone changing into nightwear and then pulled a "what should we do?" face at Lollie.

Just then Miss Naftel appeared beside our beds. 'Hurry up girls and get changed.'

'We don't have nightdresses, miss,' Lollie said, raising her palms.

'We'll see what we can do for you.' She smiled and left us. She returned with two long white cotton nightdresses. I pulled mine on and laughed at Lollie struggling to pull the partially unbuttoned neck down over her mass of bushy hair.

'Shuddup laughing, the stupid hole is too small for my head.' I undid the buttons for her and she pulled her head through the hole.

'Ta,' she said and got into her bed. It was so good to be able to stretch out and as I lay there in the quietness a whimper and sniffle at the far end of the hall faded into silence. I stared up at the chapel-style ceiling with its wooden planks and heavy beams wondering if I would ever see my sister Nunoos again. I pictured her lost and wandering amongst the beached boats in Weymouth calling out to me but I wasn't there. Soon the weight of my heavy lids forced me into sleep.

In the morning when I awoke there were ladies wandering among the beds with drinks for us.

'They're called the WVS,' Lollie, already up and dressed, told me when I asked her who they were.

'Is Nunoos' class in here with us, Lollie?' I asked, rubbing the sleep from my eyes.

'No, but don't worry. I'll ask Miss Naftel where she is,' she replied.

We were loaded unto buses again and taken to the municipal baths where we had lovely hot showers. I'd never had a shower so I had to be shown where to stand but I soon decided that I liked showers better than the tin bath.

'Don't forget to clean your teeth,' a strict teacher bellowed as we all lined up beside a long row of square white basins.

'Please miss, we haven't got a toothbrush,' Lollie called with her arm raised to get her attention. The teacher turned to a WVS lady who disappeared from sight and then came back to hand us a toothbrush and a round tin of toothpowder each. We opened the tins and carefully imitated the other children cleaning their teeth to make sure we did it right.

Over the next week or so lots of nice people came to visit the hall, some bringing jigsaw puzzles and toys and books. Others stood in front of us eyeing us up and down and asking us where we came from and our names because we didn't have our coats on with the labels so they didn't know. My friend Jean Ogier ran over to tell me she was going out for the day to the park and then she was led away by a man and woman. We had our lessons in a room next to where we slept and our meals were served on long trestle tables down the middle of the makeshift classroom. We had minced meat with mash and peas, and rice pudding for afters. It tasted great, much better than the food we had at home. Lollie stopped wearing her nightdress and went to bed in her pants, vest and socks so she could be first dressed at the door when we had a random air raid drill because the first ready always got a sweet.

One sunny morning we were walked through lanes out to the countryside for our lessons. Our teacher set up her blackboard and easel at the edge of a field where a man was driving a pair of horses while sitting on a strange-looking machine with two big wheels on each side and underneath some sort of cutting thing that could chop off the long dry grass near the roots as the horses pulled it along. We did times tables, all reading together out loud from the blackboard in a tuneless chant, and after a picnic lunch we had a nap in the sunshine before we were walked back to the hall.

I noticed that some of the children like Jean went away with grown-ups and didn't come back.

'They're being billeted,' Lollie explained when I asked why.

'What's billeted and how come you know all about it?' I asked.

'Because I asks what's happening that's why,' she retorted.

'Well why don't you know where Nunoos is then?' She replied that Miss Naftel was finding out for her and had told her not to worry.

'That's what *my* teacher told me but what will I tell my mum if she's been lost. I'll get a good hiding.' Tears welled up in my eyes and Lollie's look softened as she put her arm around my shoulders.

'She'll be yer somewhere, eh Dorothy, you'll see,' she reassured me. I wiped my tears on my cardigan sleeve and nodded silently.

That afternoon we were sitting on my bed playing snap when a lady in uniform came up to us with a Red Cross lady.

'This is Dorothy,' the Red Cross lady told her. 'She is a pleasant little girl and she's well behaved. Dorothy, this lady has come to meet you and would like to talk to you.' The lady in uniform looked down at me and I noticed her soft blue eyes were like my dad's. She was wearing a peaked cap, the top of the cap tucked all the way around into a band with a badge on the front above the peak, and her dark curly hair was pinned back at the sides. Her jacket had big breast pockets with buttons and the letters ATS were stuck on each of her shoulders. She smelled lovely, like flowers – her lips were bright red and when she spoke to me and smiled her teeth shone clean and white.

'Can I sit beside you on your bed and talk to you, Dorothy?' she asked.

'Yes miss,' I replied shyly, and grabbing at Lollie's hand I said, 'This is my cousin Lollie but really she's my aunty.' Lollie shifted away from me to make room for the lady to sit down.

Soon she noticed that the lady was showing a real interest only in me, so she stood up and said, 'I'm going outside for a bit Dorothy. I'll be back soon.' I told the lady where we had come from and about losing my sister Nunoos, whose real name was Edna, and asked if she could help me to find her. She told me she'd ask somebody about it and asked if I'd like to go and stay with her and her mother for a while.

'Can Lollie come too?' I asked. She shook her head and said she was sorry but they really only had room for one child as she was out at war-work with the ATS and her mother was getting a bit old to have too many children to look after. She told me she'd call for me the next day if I'd like her to and I agreed. She seemed kind and I liked her eyes, like my dad's. Lollie came back after she had gone.

'I'm going to live with that lady tomorrow,' I told her.

'I'll come with you,' she said with a grin.

'You can't come, the lady said she can only take one child.' I noticed a flash of disappointment in her eyes but she quickly turned away and sat on her bed.

'I'm not bothered anyway, it's okay here.' Later that night I could hear her quietly sobbing into her pillow and went and sat on the edge of her bed to comfort her. She turned her head away from me and I stroked her soft, bushy hair.

'Someone will billet you too soon, don't worry Lollie,' I whispered.

'I don't want to be left here on my own,' she sobbed into her pillow. 'Nearly everyone else has gone – it's just the ugly ones left behind and that means I must be ugly too.'

'No you're not, I don't think you're ugly. Look, if I don't go, will you stop crying?' She nodded without lifting her head. 'Anyway we should try to stay together,' I said, 'and tomorrow I'm going to tell the lady I don't want to go with her – okay?'

'Are you really going to tell her that?' she asked as she lifted her head and looked up at me. Then she sat up and wiped her wet cheeks and runny nose on her blanket.

'I promise.' I smiled at her. 'Maybe we can find someone to take both of us to live with them and even Nunoos too when we find her. Yeh, that's what we'll do – and we'll say we'll only go if we can all go together.'

'Oh thanks Dorothy,' she whispered and we hugged each other. Then I slipped back to my bed.

Early the following afternoon our teacher called Lollie over to where she was standing with a man and a lady. The lady had bushy hair just like Lollie's. I watched them from my bed and they smiled as they were talking to her and the man crouched down to her level and she was making him laugh. After they left she came running over to me with a beaming smile.

'I've got billeted, Dorothy! That lady and man wants to take me to live with them tomorrow so you can go with that lady 'cos now we'll both be all right.'

'But what about Nunoos and us all staying together?' I asked.

'I reckon she's already with billeters and that's why she didn't come here.'

'Do you think so – did Miss Naftel say that to you?'

'No, but I think that's what she thinks too. So Dorothy, we should go with these billeters and if we find out Nunoos hasn't found billeters I'll ask mine if she can come and stay with me

since your lady can only take one and I'll look after her for you
– okay?'

'Do you promise to look after her and stop teasing her?'

'I cross my heart and hope to die me.'

'All right then we'll go,' I said, and she turned and waved at the
couple still talking to the teacher near the door and gave them her
sweetest smile.

10

Life with the Thorntons

When my lady came I was packed and ready to go, but I was a bit frightened to be going somewhere alone with strangers. I gave Lollie a hug and began to cry.

'Don't be upset, girls, you're both going to be very happy in nice homes,' Miss Naftel said, smiling at my lady. 'Come on, we'll wave them off, shall we Lollie?' She took Lollie's hand and they followed us outside where a big shiny black car was waiting. The driver, who wore a dark blazer and a peaked cap, took my carrier bag from the lady and we climbed into the back onto a soft, springy brown leather seat. I stroked it with my fingers – it was warm and had a strange smell. I had never been in a car before and felt small as I stretched my neck to look out of the windows. As we drove away we all waved goodbye. I kneeled on the seat and waved out of the small back window until Lollie and Miss Naftel became tiny far away figures. My heart sank and I suddenly felt scared of what was to happen now I had lost Nunoos *and* Lollie.

'You can call me Margaret instead of Miss if you'd like, Dorothy. I'd prefer that,' she said, smiling as I looked up at her face through my tear-filled eyes. I had got used to the Scottish accent now and found her soft-spoken voice easy to understand.

'All right Mi… I mean Margaret,' I said the name, slowly, uncomfortably. We had always called grown-ups Mrs So-and-so, or Mr So-and-so, or if they were family friends Aunty or Uncle. A teardrop rolled slowly down my cheek and she took out her hanky, gently patted my cheek and reached her arm around my shoulders.

'Now now hen, don't be upset, we'll look after you and you'll be happy with us.' We drove out of the built-up town area and into country lanes with tall thick hedges covered in little white flowers. We drove for what seemed a long time. The warm sunshine shone through the window and the swaying motion of the car made me drowsy and I fell asleep. When I awoke I was cradled in the arms of the driver. He was carrying me from the car towards a white house with tall windows. We climbed up three wide stone steps to where a plump old lady with white wavy hair, a kind face and the same soft blue eyes as Margaret, stood framed in the open doorway smiling at me. She was wearing an apron covered in little red roses over a pale blue short-sleeved dress and her arms reached out to me. Sitting quietly beside her with his head cocked to one side and eyeing me curiously, was a little white whiskery dog. The sunlight glinted on the polished brass doorknocker behind the old woman. It was a roaring lion's head just like the one on the pump on Trinity Square but it was smaller, had sharp teeth and it looked angry. It didn't have the big wavy mane all around its head or the pipe shoved into its mouth for a waterspout. The driver lowered me to the doorstep and I stood with my head down, nervously twisting my finger.

'Och you're a pretty wee lass. Welcome to our home, Dorothy.' The old lady lifted my chin with her fingers. I looked up into her eyes and saw kindness in them and decided that she was a good person. I stepped into her open arms and sank into her soft body as she hugged me close to her. The little dog was jumping up at me, scratching at my coat with his little claws and wagging his tail.

'And this is wee Kenny. He's a Scottie and he's a very friendly little dog. Aren't you, Kenny?' She bent down and patted his rough bristly fur as he licked her hand. We went inside and my mouth fell open as I took in my surroundings. My feet sank into a deep red carpet with a wild flowery pattern in the entrance hall which swept up the stairs held firm to each stair by brass rods. The banisters and rails were dark polished wood, and part way up, the walls were panelled with dark wood and the biggest paintings I'd ever seen with wide carved golden frames hung high on the white walls. One that hung above the staircase was a picture of an old man sitting upright in a leather chair. He was thoughtfully smoking a pipe, a gold watch chain draped across his waistcoat, and his glistening eyes stared down at me making me feel scared.

'That's my grandfather,' Margaret said as she followed my gaze.

'Can he see me?' I asked.

'No,' she laughed, 'it's just a portrait, he's not alive anymore'.

'Well noo, I'm sure Dorothy would like to see her room, wouldn't you Dorothy?' The old lady gestured to Margaret to take me upstairs as she closed the door. Upstairs the landing was wide and I glanced back through the banister rails at the grandfather with eyes that seemed to be following me.

'Here's your room, it used to be mine when I was a wee girl,' Margaret said pushing open a heavy wooden door. Inside there was a bed with a dark carved headboard and a lovely soft-looking pink flowered eiderdown with a matching pillow. Next to the tall window that overlooked the fields and woods stretching on for miles, was a wooden washstand with a large patterned china bowl, a matching water jug, a neatly folded face flannel, soap and a towel. Sitting on a chest of drawers in the corner was a beautiful doll with rosy cheeks and painted lips and wide staring eyes. She was wearing a white frilly lace dress and soft white shoes, and her long black hair was wound into plaits. She was leaning against a teddy bear with patches of his brown fur smoothed or worn away, and a stitch or two missing from the edge of his sewn-on smile. A lace-covered doll's crib stood against a wall and a rug beside the bed covered the polished floorboards. Margaret put down my bag and picked up the teddy and gave him a quick hug. I noticed that her face looked girlish as she kissed his little black nose.

'Its been a while since Thomas has had a hug, Dorothy – he'll be glad of a new playmate.' She carefully put him back beside the doll she called Rosemary.

'Would you like a bath before tea, Dorothy?' Margaret asked.

'Is it Sunday today?' I asked her.

'No, it's Monday,' she replied.

'We only have a bath on Sunday at home, so I'd better not.'

'Well, while you're here you can have a bath more often than that, Dorothy. I think that would make my mother Mrs Thornton very happy. Will you do that for us?' I nodded and she took me to the bathroom. There was just a big bath in the room with a curled edge and claws for feet that looked like they might have been cut off the lion whose head was downstairs on the front door. Large thick white towels were draped over a freestanding wooden rail. The walls were white and the sun shining through the stained glass window cast colourful shapes and patterns right up to the high ceilings – just like the kaleidoscope the teacher had once shown us at school. Margaret turned the taps and water poured out of a wide spout to partly fill the bath. Later, after she had bathed me with creamy Lux soap and washed and towel-dried my hair she helped me into my change of clothes and brushed my hair leaving it loose to dry properly. We went downstairs and I gripped her hand firmly as we passed the grandfather picture.

When we entered the dining room Mrs Thornton was seated at the long polished table. She had taken off her apron and she greeted me with a warm smile.

'Are you hungry Dorothy?' she asked.

'Yes, I am, Mrs Thornton,' I replied, eagerly eyeing the pile of cakes and jam tarts on the table.

'Well, pull up a chair lass, and have some tea and cake.' Margaret sat down with us and poured the tea into dainty china cups with saucers ringed with roses. She passed me the plate of cakes and a small empty plate to put a cake on and I drooled over the assortment. I wanted one of everything on the plate – but I settled for the jam tart. I reached into my cup of tea with my tart and dunked it into the tea then I tilted my head back and dropped it into my open mouth.

'Ahem, we'll have to give her some lessons in table manners, hen,' Mrs Thornton whispered to Margaret.

'Noo we don't put our food into our drinks here, Dorothy: that's not good table manners, lass,' she said with a slight frown. I hung my head hoping I wouldn't get a clout and I was sorry to have already made this nice old lady upset with me. There was a white cloth rolled up inside a ring by my plate and Margaret removed the ring and spread the cloth open then tucked it inside my dress collar. I watched them use their cloths to dab the crumbs away from their lips after each bite of cake and sip of tea. I carefully imitated with exactly three dabs, one side, then the other, then the middle. They put the cloth down beside their plates but I left mine around my neck and just lifted the bottom edge to my mouth. Margaret offered me more cake after I'd finished the tart and Mrs Thornton poured more tea into my cup from the shiny silver teapot. She smiled at me and added sugar and milk from the little silver bowl and jug. We had a silver spoon on the saucer to stir our tea, so the sugar bowl wasn't full of brown lumps like ours at home from the wet spoon. During our tea Margaret told me that she was on a few days' leave and the next day I would be going to town with them to buy some clothes and a school uniform for the local girls' school. Mrs Thornton told me that if I had any worries about anything at all, I was to tell her – so I asked about my sister Nunoos and the two glanced at each other, then at me and Margaret answered.

'Don't worry Dorothy, I'm sure she's with a family and is quite happy.'

'Can I visit her or can she come here to see me?'

'We'll see what can be arranged, lass – now eat up and drink your tea,' said her mother. That night as I snuggled into the fluffy eiderdown I had never felt so special or been in such a posh clean house before. It was so quiet – no kids whispering after lights out or crying for their mum. In the stillness I whispered into the soft pillow 'It's all right, Nunoos, these nice people will find you for me,' and I soon fell asleep.

The next day after breakfast we waited for the driver. Margaret explained that Mr Jack, as I was to call him, lived nearby and was employed as the gardener, driver and handyman since Mrs Thornton's husband had died. He arrived and, opening the doors of the shiny car for us, he nodded a greeting at Margaret and her mother and touched the peak of his cap. He drove slowly towards town. Glasgow town centre was bustling with activity. It had lots of tall buildings and shops with big glass windows criss-crossed with wide strips of tape. There were trams clattering down the centre of the street, buses parked at the kerb and horses pulling overloaded carts. The streets were full of soldiers and lots of people wearing different uniforms and everybody was in a hurry.

In a big department store in Argyle Street called Lewis's I tried on my uniform: first the grey gymslip and yellow blouse, then the grey blazer with gold piping around the edges, a matching striped tie, a round broad-rimmed hat with a gold band and finally grey ankle socks and black lace-up shoes. I stood in front of the mirror, Margaret and her mother were pleased with the look, I hardly recognised myself and I wondered if Nunoos and Lollie were trying on their uniforms somewhere for their new schools. Mrs Thornton bought me a dress (but she called it a frock) – with pink roses all over it, her favourite flowers – and a cardigan, extra underwear, blouses, slips, socks and a change of nightdress. I liked Glasgow because everyone was treating me nicely: even the lady serving us smiled at me and stroked my hair. If I'd been in Guernsey with my family she would have eyed me suspiciously and told me not to touch anything, or sent my sisters and me outside to wait for our mum – mind you, we wouldn't have come into such a posh shop in the first place.

During her leave Margaret took me to the park where we fed the ducks in the pond and Kenny stood at the edge and barked at them but he wasn't sure about getting into the pond. The ducks all flapped and quacked and it sounded as though they were all laughing at him. I liked Margaret because at bedtimes she would read me stories from the books she had kept from her childhood. I liked "Snow White" and "Little Red Riding Hood" but I found "The Big Bad Wolf" a bit scary. After my story one night Margaret told me I'd be starting school on the following Monday. She said she'd take me and not to worry, but afterwards she'd have to return to her ATS duties because her leave would be over. In future she explained that I'd be spending more time with only Mrs Thornton and Kenny. She leaned over and tucked me in, wished me goodnight, kissed me on the forehead and quietly left the room. I lay awake thinking about what the new school would be like and if Nunoos or Lollie might be at the same school.

Monday came and I was up early and proudly dressed in my smart uniform. Mrs Thornton plaited my hair and tied in a yellow ribbon to match my blouse and Kenny danced around my feet aware of all of the excitement.

'Och I remember when I took you for your first day at the school, hen,' Mrs Thornton said to Margaret. 'It seems like only yesterday.' Margaret smiled at her.

'You'll like Green Lanes Girls' School, Dorothy,' Margaret said. 'I enjoyed my time there and I'm sure you will too. Now let me look at you, lass. Och you look so smart.' She kissed me on the cheek.

The house had a long winding drive bordered with trees and large black wooden gates at the entrance opening onto the narrow country lane. Just a few yards from the gate was a bus stop where

Margaret explained I was to catch the bus for school in future but on my first day I was to be taken in the car. As we drove up to the school gates I saw some girls grouped together near the entrance and they turned to look when Mr Jack opened the door for me. A teacher appeared in the doorway to the old school building. She was wearing a brown tweed two-piece suit and was clanging a hand bell. Just like our school in Guernsey, it was built of grey stone with steep roofs.

'It's time to go in now Dorothy,' Margaret urged. 'We must report to the headmistress, Miss MacDonald.'

Miss MacDonald seemed to know all about me and welcomed me to the school.

'Is that a French name, Ogier?' She asked, but I just shrugged and held on to Margaret's hand. There was a knock at the door and a tall girl came in when told to enter. She closed the door behind her and stood with her hands clasped behind her back. She had straight brown hair cut short below her ears and a fringe, and her long nose overshadowed her small mouth.

'This is Debbie McKenzie. I've asked her to look after you, Dorothy, and to help you settle in at our school. She will take you to your class now. Go with her and I will speak to Miss Thornton.' At break time in the playground Debbie stood over me as the other girls gathered around full of questions. They thought my name was funny and asked if it was really sunny where I came from because I was so brown. They thought the way I talked was strange but Debbie told them not to be unkind. Although she was only seven, she was unusually tall and looked about ten or eleven and this made the other girls a little wary of her, so they smiled at me and invited me to join in their skipping game. I chose to turn the rope so they wouldn't know I couldn't skip. I didn't sit next to Debbie in my class. I was put at the front next to Kate – a chubby girl with long fair hair in a plait with a yellow ribbon the same as Mrs Thornton had done mine. She showed me where they were up to in her subject books and I saw that they were doing the same sums as I had done at my school.

Every day Mrs Thornton and Kenny met the school bus as it dropped me at home and she asked me all about my day at school. After I'd changed out of my school clothes I played outside with

Kenny on the lawns and he chased me around the trees. Later Mrs Thornton showed me how to set the table with cutlery and plates for our meals and I watched the way she cut up her food with a knife and fork, chewed with her mouth closed, and did the dab, dab, dab with her napkin, and I carefully copied her. Beth, a cheerful plump lady who was related to Mr Jack and also lived in the nearby village, was Mrs Thornton's "daily". She would sing all the latest war songs as she dusted and cleaned the house and told me to call her Aunty Beth.

'D'ye ken this wan, Dorothy?' she would ask as I followed her around the house.

'*Run rabbit, run rabbit, run, run, run...*' she'd sing, then bend down and hold my hands in hers and swing them from side to side as I laughed and sang along with her.

Sometimes Mrs Thornton would call out, 'It's Children's Hour on the radio, Dorothy,' and I'd sit on a footstool beside her chair and we'd listen to the voice of Uncle Mac and laugh at Larry the Lamb and Dennis the Dachshund.

'Hiv ye heerd frae yer Vincent, Mrs T?' Aunty Beth asked one morning in mid-July as I was finishing my breakfast. ''Cause ma auld mum tellt me last night that they didnae ken wit wiz happenin aboot their hoose in Glasgow. An air raid in broad daylight it wiz, the hoose wiz shaken ahn the windae blew oot. It shoulda sent them tae shelter but old Da said that nae German was sending him oot a his hoose tae nae shelter. Then all of a sudden there wiz a helluva bang and the hoose shook and a wee bit o' the plaster ceiling fell oan his heed. Weel then he couldna get oot o' there quick enough.' She threw back her head and laughed with her hand on her ample chest. 'Och I shouldna laugh – I wouldna want him taken away frae us.'

'Och Beth, thank the Lord that they're safe,' said Mrs Thornton. 'I've not heard from Vincent recently. He's with the Glasgow Squadron and he's very excited that now they have new Spitfires and he's recently been posted somewhere but says he mustn't say where. Anyway, he's due some leave soon and I'm so looking forward to seeing the lad again, but you can't help but worry can you?' Aunty Beth nodded.

'We're going to have a special visitor, Dorothy', Mrs Thornton said a week later as she met me at the bus stop. 'My son Vincent, who's in the RAF, is coming home on leave tomorrow and he's looking forward to meeting you.' Her face was glowing with happiness, her eyes twinkled and she looked suddenly younger. I'd seen a photograph of a young man in uniform with dark curly hair and a handsome smiling face in a silver frame on the sideboard and guessed that was her son but nobody had actually told me who it was.

'Is he the man in the photo on the sideboard, Mrs Thornton?' I asked.

'Yes lass, that's him. Och, did I not show him to you before – he's the image of his late father, don't you know?' She glowed with pride. That night in bed I thought for the first time about my dad fighting the Germans. I pictured him in the silver photo frame looking smart in his uniform and Vincent's handsome face became my dad's.

The next day was Saturday. No school, although I really liked school and Mrs Thornton told me that the teacher said I was doing quite well. Kenny wasn't allowed upstairs and was sitting patiently at the bottom waiting for me. He leapt up and down wagging his tail when I appeared at the top and I ran down to pat him. I always ran down sideways and stayed close to the wall underneath the Grandfather picture so he couldn't follow me with his eyes and I tried to never look up at him from the hall. The noise of tyres grinding to a halt on the gravel came from outside and Mrs Thornton came running to open the front door. She flung it open and held out her arms to Vincent who was climbing the steps looking just like the photograph and wearing a broad grin. They hugged for ages until he noticed me over her shoulder and released his hold on her.

'You must be Dorothy,' he said.

'Yes I am, Mr Vincent.' I felt a bit shy and began twisting my finger.

'Och, you can call me Vincent – no Mister, lass. Hey you'll never guess what happened, Dorothy? A little bird flew alongside my plane and he told me that I had a new wee sister at home and I thought I'd better come and see for myself.' His white teeth shone as he smiled, just like Margaret's. After he had settled in and had a talk with his mother he came out to Kenny and me in the garden.

'Can you ride a bicycle, Dorothy?' he asked.

'I've never tried.'

'Well, in the shed out the back are my sister Margaret's and my bikes from when we were children about your age. Shall we see if Margaret's still works?' I nodded and he took me to the big wooden shed with padlocked double doors and unlocked them. Inside was stacked high with tea chests, an old fashioned pram, some wicker baskets, bedheads and there, hanging by their frames on hooks just near the doors, were two small bikes. Vincent lifted down the girl's bike and brushed off the dust and cobwebs with a cloth before wheeling it outside. He had to pump air into the flat tyres and he squeezed them to test their hardness.

'There we are – just the right size for you, Dorothy. Sit on it, lass, and try to put your feet on the ground and don't worry if you can't I'll adjust the seat a wee bit for you,' he said. I sat on the bike and put down my feet. It was like new, no scratches or rust, I just sat there speechless.

'It's just about right,' he said. 'Now put your feet on the pedals and I'll hold the seat to steady you and we'll see if you can ride it.' I put up my feet and felt myself fall to one side so I quickly put my foot down on that side.

'Trust me Dorothy, I won't let you fall. Have another try, go on,' he reassured me. I tried again, pushing the pedals, leaning into his steadying arm. Slowly I rode around and around trusting him with my full weight and then a bit less weight as I found my balance and then straight along the drive. He ran to keep up as I became more balanced and pedalled faster. Kenny ran alongside barking at me and Mrs Thornton stood in the doorway above the steps, clapping me. Suddenly I was on my own – he had let go. I heard his laughter and he called after me 'Well done Dorothy, you're riding it by yourself.' I wobbled but steadied myself and rode down to the gates but I didn't know how to stop. I began to wobble again and the bicycle crashed into the gate, tipping me head first over the handlebars. I looked back through tear-filled eyes, untangling myself from the bicycle and rubbing my head. I could just about see them in the distance – they were standing together on the top step where they'd been watching and clapping me. Vincent rushed down the drive to pick me up and I smiled up at him.

'I'm all right, I couldn't stop but I didn't hurt myself – honest,' I lied. I didn't want him to take the bicycle away.

'Right then, we need to learn how to use the brakes.' He grinned and showed me, then held on to the seat again until I was balanced and could apply the brakes when he told me to. I was left alone then and I rode all around the garden chased by Kenny until I was called inside to wash for dinner. That night after I'd said my prayers the way Mrs Thornton had taught me I thanked God for the lovely bicycle. I also asked him to look after my mum and dad and brothers and sisters wherever they were.

The summer holidays came around and Debbie and Kate were allowed to come to the house and play and sometimes Mrs Thornton would take us to the park or she would take me into the town with her – but not very often because petrol was rationed. Margaret came home on leave and took me to the cinema to see *Snow White and the Seven Dwarfs*. When we got home she carried a big parcel into my bedroom and said, 'I wrote to tell my pen-pal Angela in America all about you, Dorothy, and she sent this for you. Let's see what we have in here, shall we?' She undid the string and pulled it from the brown paper, then passed me the parcel. I lifted out beautiful Shirley Temple style dresses and a red woollen knee length coat with a soft black velvet collar and flap pockets and shiny red buttons. Best of all was a pair of black patent leather shoes with a t-bar strap. I kicked off my slippers and tried on the shoes,which were a little bit loose but Margaret told me not to worry, as I'd grow into them in no time.

'Thank you, Margaret, for these, thank you. All the girls at school would love to have real Shirley Temple clothes like this – wait till I show Kate and Debbie.' I put on the coat and twirled around clasping it closed with my hands. I looked down at my shoes, spread open my arms and began to dance and sing the way I'd seen my sister Nunoos doing back in Guernsey. '*On the good ship lollipop, it's a nice trip to the candy shop…*'

Mrs Thornton was standing in the doorway. She laughed out loud at me and winked at Margaret who was also laughing and they both clapped. They were clapping for me, the way we had all clapped for Nunoos but this time I was the centre of attention. I couldn't stop smiling. I hugged Margaret and she patted my head and then helped me to try on the other dresses for size.

'Och that's pretty on you, lass,' said Mrs Thornton as I stood before the mirror.

'They're just the right size for her, Mother. I love the pale blue one don't you?' After I'd tried the dresses on and Margaret had hung them up in the wardrobe we went downstairs and I helped to set the table for dinner. At bedtime Margaret read me a story about Cinderella and after she'd gone downstairs I pictured myself at the ball wearing one of my Shirley Temple dresses and dancing with the prince. Then I said my prayers before going to sleep. That night I had lots to thank God for, and as usual I asked him to look after my family.

Over the next couple of months Margaret and Vincent usually came for only a couple of days at a time. They spoke to Mrs Thornton about the war but it seemed to me the war must be somewhere else, far away from rural Glasgow where we were living. But the war did grow closer to home after a raid on Glasgow on the eighteenth of September. That night as I lay in bed I was awoken by the sound of a heavy throbbing and drone of plane engines overhead. I was frightened and I pulled the sheet up over my head and clenched my eyes shut. I guessed it was the Germans and wondered if they would soon drop bombs and kill Mrs Thornton and Kenny and me. I sensed movement in the room and opened my eyes to peep over the sheet. Mrs Thornton had opened my bedroom door. She was carrying a candle in a holder; its flickering flame lit up the room and as she came in a tall black shadow slunk into the room behind her. She sat on the edge of my bed.

'Did the noise waken you Dorothy?' I lowered the sheets from my face and nodded. She gently stroked my hair.

'Let's see what all the noise is aboot shall we?' She walked to the window, blew out the candle and opened the heavy drapes. The moon was nearly full and we could see lots of silhouetted planes flying in a "V" shape just like migrating birds.

'They'll be heading for the Clyde shipyards and factories,' she mumbled to herself. 'God help those poor folk up there.' I sat up and she perched on the edge of my bed again. The planes became tiny dots in the distance until they disappeared. Mrs Thornton caught her breath as a white flash flickered far away, then another followed by faint rumbling noises like those I'd heard coming from France when I was up the Plateau with Lollie. An orangey dome-shaped glow with bright red edges fringed with black formed in the distant sky where the planes had gone out of sight.

'Are they coming to get us next?' I asked.

'Noo don't be frightened, lass. Let's say a prayer for the people of Clyde and for our Vincent and Margaret.' We bowed our heads and put our hands together while she spoke softly into her fingers. I repeated 'Amen' when she had finished and she tucked me in, kissed me on the forehead, pulled the curtains, and left the room.

The next morning Aunty Beth came into the house red-faced, puffing and wheezing as she flopped down into a chair at the kitchen table with Mrs Thornton. I was up early and we were waiting to go out for the school bus. Mrs Thornton poured some tea for Aunty Beth and asked her what she was so flustered about.

'Och Mrs T, them German planes attacked oor city again last night. They dropped them stick-bombs near tae George Square. Now they're sayin they reckon the bombs didnae hit wit they shoulda, bit the auld corner buildings in Ingram Street ahn' Queen Street wiz hit bad. A five hundred poond bomb even fell doon oan HMS Sussex that wiz in fer her damage-fixin' next tae Yorkhill Quay bit thank God it didnae go off.'

'Och, you drink your tea Beth while I take Dorothy to the bus,' Mrs Thornton said as she saw the frightened look on my face and hurried me out of the room.

'Will the Germans come to bomb our house?' I asked as we walked along.

'Don't worry Dorothy, you'll be safe here out in the countryside,' she said and patted my shoulder as the bus drew up beside us. I climbed aboard and ran to sit beside Debbie to tell her all about the bombing.

11

News of my family

The months passed and the bombing raids mostly seemed to ignore Glasgow and go somewhere else. Autumn arrived. The leaves on the trees turned orange and red and some were curled and golden. They were tossed around in gusts of wind and then settled in big piles on the lawn waiting for Mr. Jack to rake them up, but he was kept busy in the orchard and vegetable gardens behind the house producing food for our table. I was back at school and we did gas mask drills where we had to suck up a piece of paper onto the snout and make it stick there to check it was working then wait until the teacher raised her hand before we could take them off. Each day we would have practise air raids and line up quickly in front of the school then walk in twos to the school shelter behind the playground. Apart from these events we had normal lessons and I tried Scottish dancing, which was fun but hard to learn. I was accepted now and all the girls were my friends. At times we almost forgot about the war. At playtime we chased each other playing tag or my friends skipped in and out of the swinging rope that I happily turned for them.

Mrs Thornton was standing with Kenny in a downpour of rain as I climbed down from my school bus. She was holding an open umbrella and we huddled beneath it and ran indoors. Inside we sat at the large scrubbed wooden table in the kitchen beside the shiny black cooking range that warmed the room. The usual smell of baking bread filled the air and Kenny was curled up on the hearth close to the range. Mrs Thornton poured me a glass of milk and pushed a plate with some shortbread biscuits on it in front of me.

'A letter came from your mother this morning, Dorothy. It was addressed to me but would you like me to read it to you?' She took it from her apron pocket. I was excited to hear any news of my mum and dad, and especially my brothers and sisters, so I eagerly nodded.

'*Dear Mrs Thornton,*' she began, '*The Red Cross wrote to the Channel Islands Refugees Committee in London for me and have found out that you have my eldest girl Dorothy up there with you. But they haven't found where my Edna is staying. Dorothy was supposed to be looking after her sister Edna but The Red Cross said they are not billeted together as I said they was to be. Me and my younger ones were sent to Stockport where we stayed for a bit in the Stockport Sunday School hall then we were sent up to Halifax but we couldn't find a place to live so we've ended up back here in Stockport not far from my step-mother Grace. I hope Dorothy is behaving herself tell her that we miss her and we'll see her again soon but to be good until then and thank you missus for looking after her. Signed Mrs Dorothy May Ogier. P.S. please could you find out where my Edna is for me thanks my address is 48 Edgerton Street Stockport.*'

When she read that Nunoos was lost because I hadn't looked after her I felt scared for what had happened to her and a sadness swept over me. My throat closed up and tears began rolling down my cheeks because I really missed her and the rest of my family. Mrs Thornton leaned over and stroked my hair and passed me her hanky.

'You'll tell my mum that Nunoos isn't lost and that she's with a nice family, Mrs Thornton, won't you?' I asked wiping away my tears.

She patted my hand. 'We'll do our best to find just who that family is and where they are so we can let your mother know, so don't you worry, lass. Noo away and get changed out of those school clothes and you can write back to your mother.' I felt happier and ran upstairs.

'What should I write?' I asked her later as I sat again at the kitchen table. The bread was sitting on a cooling tray and the smell reminded me of Trinity Bakery at the top of Mansell Street off Trinity Square in Guernsey. Sometimes Dad would make a traditional Guernsey "Bean Jar" with pig's trotters, beans, carrots and onions and send us down to the Trinity Bakery where they would put it in the oven after they had finished baking the bread. He would have to write "Ogier" on the brown paper tied on top with string (since the bean jar lid had been broken in one of their rows) so there wouldn't be a mix-up because lots of other people in the town took their bean jars to the bakery too. The next day we would wheel it home in the pram, all hot and smelling of pork. We would buy a loaf of bread at the same time and fight over who would carry it because whoever carried it would break off the corners of the warm crusty loaf and eat them. Once Lollie got a good clout when she presented Mum with a loaf with no crusty ends and not much middle left.

'You could tell her how you are; she'd want to know that, Dorothy.' Mrs Thornton interrupted my thoughts.

'All right, and I'll tell her about you and Margaret and Vincent and Kenny and…'

'Well, put pencil to paper, lass – she cannot hear you!' '*Dear Mum,*' I wrote slowly, holding my pencil tightly, my tongue poking out of my clenched lips as I shaped each letter in my best writing. '*I live in a nice house with a lady called…*'

'How do you spell "Mrs Thornton",' I asked sucking the top of my pencil. She spelled it out to me letter by letter and I wrote it down. '*…Mrs. Thornton and we have a little dog named Kenny the lady has a grown up son called Vincent and a grown up daughter called Margaret they are very nice to me.*' I kept stopping to ask her for help with name spellings and she patiently spelled them out for me. '*I am allowed to ride Margaret's bicycle and I go to a nice school where I have two friends named Kate and Debbie. I'm sorry I lost Nunoos when we were on the boat but the lady says that she is with a nice family and she will try to find her.*' I read out aloud what I had written and asked what else I should write.

'You must send your love to your family like you do in your prayers, Dorothy,' she reminded me.

'Oh yes.' '*I send my love to all my family, love Dorothy.*'

'That's very good, I'll write to your mother later when I have some news about your sister and put your letter in with mine, then we'll send them, lass.' I nodded.

It wasn't until just before Christmas that we heard from my mum again. Mrs Thornton had put her onto the Glasgow Channel Island Society to help find my sister. This was a group formed by Channel Islanders who had been evacuated to Glasgow and they regularly got together to learn any news about the Islands – now that they were occupied by the Germans – and they also organised social gatherings and outings for evacuees and their children. Mrs Thornton passed me the letter to let me read it. Slowly I read it out aloud to her,

'Dear Mrs Thornton, Thank you for your letter telling me about them people at the Glasgow Channel Island Society I have sent them a letter to see if they can tell me about whose looking after my Edna. Please give this Christmas present to Dorothy and tell her that her brothers and sister miss her and send their love and to be a good girl. Signed Mrs Dorothy May Ogier'

I couldn't stop the tears from flowing when I read that they missed me because although I lived with nice people I wished I could play with my brothers and sisters. I sniffed back tears as she showed me a small package that was wrapped in crumpled brown paper and tied with string. In big black letters that partly disappeared in the paper folds was written "TO DOROTHY HAPPY CHRISTMAS LOVE FROM MUMMY AND DADDY" and on the other side was Mrs Thornton's address.

'Wasn't that nice of your mother to send you a present, lass, I'll send this off to Father Christmas and see that he brings it for you when he calls here at Christmas. Shall I do that, Dorothy?' I looked at the little package and thought it looked scruffy and wasn't really excited to know its contents as my mind flashed back to Christmases past. I think Father Christmas used to pick up our toys from the Red Cross because they were never new. Once Little Cliffy got a wooden cart with a crack in the wheel, I got a doll with one eye that didn't open, and we always seemed to get big wooden jigsaws with the last piece missing. I smiled at Mrs Thornton and thought to myself: I bet she would never have let Father Christmas give Vincent and Margaret old mended toys; she would have made sure he brought them shiny new ones from his toy shop. That meant I would get new presents too this Christmas if I stayed here. She smiled at me and I smiled back and handed her the parcel.

12

Christmas in Glasgow

At school we had a Christmas party and danced the Gay Gordons. We hung paper chains around the walls and played games in class for the last two periods instead of doing lessons. We were given sweets, exchanged home-made greetings cards and wrapped up the knitted squares that we'd made in our sewing lessons for the teacher to send to a place where I think they would be made into blankets for the armed forces. When the final bell rang we said our "goodbyes" and ran away from the building cheering.

The following Sunday I went to our village church with Mrs Thornton for the Carol Service and we listened to the choirboys all dressed in red and white robes with frilly collars making high-pitched sounds from their rounded mouths. During the holidays we took the bus to town and did some Christmas shopping for Vincent and Margaret in the big store called Lewis's. I was sent to the far end of the toy department to join the queue of children waiting to tell Father Christmas what they wanted from him. I had already written a letter to him telling him what I would like and given it to Mrs Thornton to post but I told him anyway as he sat me on his knee and mumbled at me through his long white curly beard. I didn't really understand a word he said except 'Happy Christmas, lassie' as he lifted me down. I pushed my way through the crowds back to where Mrs Thornton was waiting.

People were calling to each other across the crowded store shouting 'Happy Christmas!' Their arms were loaded full of bags and packages and everyone seemed to be happy. Mrs Thornton met a lady who was an old friend and she asked her to keep an eye on me while she went to buy gifts. The woman smiled at me and held out her hand so I slipped my hand into her silky glove. She was wearing a long thick shiny fur coat and a fur hat, and around her neck was a strange furry animal, its body hanging over her shoulder. I tilted my head and leaned back to look at it. Its head was small and it was snarling at me with sharp pointed teeth as Kenny did when I tried to pull a rag out of his mouth. Its shiny little black eyes stared back at me. I wanted to touch it to see how it felt even though I was a bit frightened of it.

I lifted my arm slowly towards its hanging front leg and reached out with my finger to touch the tiny paw with needle-thin curled claws. I was holding my breath. My finger was almost touching the silky brown fur. I could feel my heart thumping in my chest. 'Go on... a little closer,' a voice in my head told me. I half-closed my eyes, screwed up my face and my throat tightened as I gently stroked the paw. It felt hard and cold. The lady let go of my hand and threw her arm up to wave to someone she knew and suddenly the snarling head flew at my face. A wall of fur swished past me knocking me off balance. Razor-sharp claws leapt towards me and its cold, hard, nose dragged across my cheek. I screamed and jumped clear of it. Like a flash it came back at my face, teeth bared, black eyes glaring. I crouched down and as I looked up its head jerked upright and stared straight at me. Then it flopped down once again and rested on the lady's back after she had lowered her arm. She'd heard me scream and gave me a puzzled look. I smiled nervously up at her and she took hold of my hand again. The lady she'd frantically waved to rushed over to greet her and they began to talk excitedly, often interrupting each other. I carefully moved around and stood in between the two women so that the scary animal couldn't get me again.

Mrs Thornton appeared from the crowd with two wrapped parcels and joined us. The other ladies asked her about Margaret and Vincent and me; they admired my lovely red coat and asked if I'd seen Father Christmas. I smiled shyly and nodded.

'Why is that lady wearing a scary animal over her coat. Mrs Thornton?' I asked after we'd left the other two ladies.

'Och, that's just the fashion, lass. Did it frighten you?'

'Yes, it really did! It tried to bite me when the lady swung around and I had to duck down.'

'Och, dear, I don't think it was alive,' she said and laughed. I wanted to tell her it really was but knew I shouldn't answer back.

'Why did you buy presents for Margaret and Vincent? Won't Father Christmas bring them a present?' I asked.

'Och I have to send them to him, lass, so he can deliver them on Christmas day.' We tried to cross the street, which was bustling with shoppers and servicemen. I stepped forward and Mrs Thornton tugged me back as an army lorry with huge wheels and tyres drove across our path. Soldiers sat in rows on benches in the back and they returned friendly waves to people. I pointed up into the sky above the town where big shapes that reminded me of elephants floated, held in place by long strings.

'What are those big things up there, Mrs Thornton?' I asked.

'Those are barrage balloons lass, they are floating up there to protect the town from low-flying enemy planes.'

'They look like big elephants. Will they frighten away the planes?'

'Aye, I expect they will, lass,' she laughed.

We weaved in and out of the window-shoppers blocking our way until we reached the Buttercup Dairy, next to the fishmongers on Great Western Road. Mrs Thornton was very friendly with the shopkeeper Miss Manson, who had been there for years, and while they chatted away I walked around the shop examining the shelves. There was Buttercup tea piled into a pyramid shape, fresh eggs, tinned fruits, and all sorts of neatly stacked jars and packets of things I didn't recognize. Eventually Mrs Thornton stopped talking to Miss Manson, made her selections from the shelves, returned to the counter, bought some butter with her ration book, and put everything into her shopping basket with her parcels.

Later at home I passed her the groceries as she stacked them in the larder. On the top shelf there were rows of big glass jars containing bottled fruit and others with pickled vegetables squeezed into them and all neatly labelled. I had never seen so much food. The homemade Christmas cake and mince pies were kept in pretty round tins with painted scenes of Victorian children dancing in a large circle in a snowy street lined with bow-fronted shop windows, their sills laden with snow.

Mr Jack had been fattening up a goose for Christmas dinner. It lived next to where he kept the laying hens behind the big shed and it hissed and flapped its wings at me and Kenny if we got too close to it. Maybe it knew we would eat it for Christmas and was angry with us. Mrs Thornton hummed Christmas carols as she waited for the kettle to boil on the range. Kenny tilted his head as he looked up at her and when she glanced at him he sat up and begged in the hope of a treat. It would be Christmas day in four days' time and I was bursting with excitement. Vincent and Margaret would be here and Mrs Thornton was excited too – I could tell.

Aunty Beth was full of chatter and songs as she busied herself cleaning the coal range the next morning, brushing out the flues and scraping the soot from the back and sides of the oven. She swept up the soot and ashes, wiped the dust from the top of the stove, and then polished it with blacklead mixed with turpentine. She puffed and her round cheeks reddened as she rubbed in little circles and when she'd finished the range was black and gleaming.

'Wit aboot that, lass?' she said, standing back admiring her work.

I looked up from my favourite place sitting at the big scrubbed table. 'It looks really shiny like new!' I replied, and she gave a satisfied smile.

I'd learned quite a bit about the war and bombings from Aunty Beth, who would be full of the latest news of raids on Glasgow and other parts of Britain. She would blether away to my foster mother and get so angry and disgusted at the Germans she would sometimes forget to "mind her language" in front of me, as Mrs Thornton had once or twice had to remind her. I'd heard far worse from my own mum's lips, I often thought to myself. Once the range had been fired up again the room was warm and the smell of baking soon filled the air. The weather was colder than I'd ever known it to be in Guernsey and when I had to take Kenny outside to do his business, I wore not just my coat but ankle boots and thick woollen socks, a warm knitted bonnet that tied around my chin and mittens to stop my fingers from going numb. We never stayed outside for long and Kenny was first to the door to go back inside to our warm place by the range. There had been more raids on Britain around Christmas and the Germans had bombed most of the major cities. Aunty Beth was talking about it to Mrs Thornton – she told her that the folk in Manchester had been hit really hard with many killed, but then she lowered her voice to a whisper and asked Mrs Thornton if that was where my family were.

'Och hush noo, the wee lass will hear you,' whispered Mrs Thornton. I tried to picture my mum and sister Pamela and my brothers Little Cliffy and Leonard all killed but I couldn't remember their faces and I didn't know what people who'd been killed looked like anyway. Mrs Thornton didn't mention the bombing in Manchester that night as we sat and listened to Christmas carols on the wireless before she put me to bed. She read me the story of Mary and Joseph and the birth of Jesus in a stable from a children's Bible stories book of Margaret's which had lovely pictures in it, then she gently kissed me goodnight. As she reached the door she turned to me and reminded me not to forget to ask God to look after my family when I said my prayers. I clasped my hands and closed my eyes and did as she had asked.

Christmas Eve. Margaret and Vincent were coming home today and the house was buzzing with expectation. Mrs Thornton had her hair neatly crimped and was wearing one of her best dresses and she put my hair up into two bunches with long red ribbons hanging down my back. I was wearing my dress with little red roses and a white cardigan, white ankle socks and little red slippers because we were inside. I skipped down the stairs to Kenny who was waiting for me at the bottom. Even he had been bathed and he looked pure white and bristly. I was so excited I even forgot to stay close to the staircase wall so that Grandfather's eyes couldn't look down at me from the picture. I bent down and patted Kenny and skipped into the kitchen to look for Aunty Beth. She was up to her elbows in flour, kneading dough and she puffed, then wiped her forehead with the back of her arm leaving a band of flour over her eyebrows. I giggled and pointed to her forehead.

'Och, lass, yer frock is bonny,' she smiled as she lifted her apron to dust off her brow.

'Mrs Thornton bought it for me,' I replied, holding out the skirt and twirling for her. My breakfast had been set on a tray for me. It was porridge and toast with jam and a glass of milk 'for your growing bones' as Mrs Thornton had said many times. I pulled up a chair and watched Aunty Beth concentrating hard on the mound of dough that she pushed this way and that, knuckling and rolling it with her floury hands, and I could smell the yeast. I finished my breakfast, lifted my napkin and dab, dab, dabbed away the milk from my top lip. Kenny and I went out into the garden to torment the goose and run away when it chased us. The ground was covered in a layer of frost that sparkled in the weak sunlight. Mr Jack was outside the hen house scattering food scraps and Mrs Thornton was standing alongside him in rubber boots, a heavy coat, hat and gloves. As she spoke steam appeared out of her mouth then disappeared. They were nodding towards the goose that I had named "Goosey Goosey Gander" after the nursery rhyme. She waved to me and I ran to her with Kenny at my heels.

'Help me with these, lass, and we'll go back inside where it's warm,' she said, passing me a cane basket of eggs with dirty shells that Mr Jack had collected for her. She carried another basket laden with vegetables and followed us through the back door that led directly into the kitchen. Aunty Beth came through from the hall with a big grin on her face and behind her stood Margaret still in uniform with her arms full of parcels. She flashed a smile at me and then at her mother. Aunty Beth took the parcels from Margaret, who reached out to her mother and hugged her. Kenny jumped up and down, twisting around her legs and barking like mad.

'Hello Dorothy,' Margaret said and held out her arms to me after she had released her mother. She sat me on her knee and patted Kenny who had his paws on her thigh.

'I might have something for you here, Dorothy. Close your eyes,' she said, taking something from her pocket and squeezing it into my open palm.

I opened my eyes. 'My special favourite, Fry's chocolate, thank you, Margaret.' I unwrapped it and broke off a piece for Kenny.

'I know, special chocolate for a special lass – that's why I chose it for you. I must go upstairs now to freshen up and change out of this uniform,' she said as she kissed my cheek and set me down from her lap. Kenny had wolfed down his piece of chocolate and was in a sit-up-to-beg pose but he'd had his lot. The rest was mine. I offered some to Mrs Thornton but she smiled and shook her head, so I bit into the dark thin chocolate and sucked out the sweet white sticky filling that clung to my teeth.

'Och, I nearly didn't get leave what with the raids, but another lass owed me a shift for covering for her one night when she had a dancing date at the Barrowland Ballroom, so she's doing my duty,' Margaret told her mother as we set the table in the dining room for dinner later that day.

'Och, I hope our Vincent can get home – he should be here too by noo,' Mrs Thornton said as she handed me the cutlery to set out on the table. The parcels had disappeared from the kitchen, but they were talking so much I didn't want to interrupt them to ask where they had gone.

A vehicle door slammed outside and we all rushed to the door to see Vincent climbing down from an open lorry carrying a canvas sack over his shoulder. He banged on the lorry door with the side of his fist and shouted something to the driver.

'A Merry Christmas to you too,' came the cheery reply as the lorry drove off. It was getting dark, although still only late afternoon, and heavy clouds threatened a white Christmas. Vincent's peaked hat covered his face as he came up the steps. Kenny was first to greet him but as he reached the door he dropped his sack and wrapped an arm around his mother, circled Margaret with his other arm and they stood there for what seemed to me to be a long time before turning to go inside. In the light of the hall I looked up at Vincent, whose face was thin and tired looking, his smile not quite so big as before. I closed the door behind him and followed the embracing threesome into the dining room where I carried on with positioning the cutlery. It gleamed in the candlelight as I lined it up on each side of the tablemats. There was a rounded spoon for soup and a dessertspoon as well as two knives and two forks, one smaller than the other, which had to be placed correctly and used for different courses. Mrs Thornton had shown me lots of times how to place them. I stared into the shiny hollow of a dessertspoon at the strange reflection of my face that looked all misshapen and ugly and I poked out my tongue and screwed up my nose.

'Be careful the wind doesn't change,' Vincent laughed as he came towards me reaching out to pick me up. 'Where's my welcome home hug, lass?'

'Merry Christmas!' I laughed as he held me tight and spun me around before lowering me to the floor.

'Away noo, and get washed and changed for dinner, son,' Mrs Thornton ordered and he patted my shoulder and headed upstairs.

'He's looking drawn and weary, hen – I'm worried about him,' she whispered to Margaret.

'He'll have flown a lot of sorties lately, Mother. It's been hard on our boys to see so many of their friends' names wiped off the board on their return, or sometimes to see them shot down without parachuting out,' Margaret replied in hushed words.

'What next?' I said loudly to remind them I was still there. They stopped talking and smiled at me, but Mrs Thornton only half smiled as though her mind was elsewhere. I stood with my hands clasped behind my back awaiting praise.

'Good lass, you've done that well,' Mrs Thornton called to me from behind Margaret. 'Noo take Kenny outside for you know what before we have dinner.' I think she wanted to talk some more about Vincent without me overhearing.

Kenny was in the hall where he'd been chased out of the dining room because he shouldn't have gone in there and he followed me and waited while I wrapped up against the cold. Outside it was dark. I waited at the top of the steps for Kenny, who knew what was expected of him – he trotted off and returned in a short while and sat quietly at my feet. Back inside, the heavy curtains had been pulled for blackout and the lamplight and flickering candles on the table filled the room with a warm glow as we all sat down for the homecoming dinner. Margaret insisted that her mother remain seated while she served and Vincent carved a mutton joint. Margaret asked me what I was hoping Father Christmas would bring for me, but before I could answer Vincent told me I'd get a present only if I'd been good and Father Christmas would know if I'd been good or naughty, but he was sure his mother would have written and told Father Christmas that I'd been good. He winked at Mrs Thornton who reminded me that I must be sure to get to sleep early so that I would be asleep when he came on his sleigh. It was as though they were just as excited as me. We ate and talked and dabbed with our napkins until I was so eager to get to bed and make Christmas come quicker that I stretched and yawned, remembering – a bit too late – to cover my mouth with my hand as Mrs Thornton had shown me. Vincent laughed at me and his face looked pinker and happier now.

'Off you go to bed, lass, and I'll come up to read you a bedtime story shortly,' he grinned as he jerked his thumb upwards.

Displaced Donkeys

'Don't forget to pray for your family, Dorothy,' said Mrs Thornton. I nodded and rushed upstairs. After I had said my prayers and snuggled underneath the soft eiderdown with Thomas, Margaret's teddy bear, the door quietly opened and Vincent crept in. He sat on the edge of my bed and read to me, by candlelight, a story about a boy who had a magic goose which people got stuck to if they tried to steal it. It was a short story but every time another person got stuck to the goose in the story Vincent laughed, as he showed me the picture in the book, and we laughed together. He kissed my forehead and left the room and I clenched my eyes tightly shut in case I was caught wide awake by Father Christmas and he wouldn't leave my presents.

The next morning I awoke early, climbed out of bed and pulled back the curtains to see something I'd never seen except in picture books – a blanket of white snow covering the fields and hedges. Everything was soft and white, all the angles and sharp edges gone. At the bottom of my bed a red and white Father Christmas face beamed at me from a large knitted sock that was draped over the foot of the bed. I rushed over and began to feel inside for my presents. The first I pulled out was the crumpled brown package from my mum. I threw it aside thinking it would probably be an old mended toy and felt inside the knitted sock for new presents but it was empty and my heart sank. I climbed back under the warm bedclothes and looked at the crumpled package. Slowly I picked it up and began to peel back the wrapping paper. A painted wooden tube shape broke through the paper and fell onto the bed – it was one of the handles of a skipping rope. There was also a colouring book and crayons. Father Christmas must have recognised me and remembered when he saw me asleep what kind of presents he used to give me in Guernsey and that's why I don't have any nice new presents, I thought. I fingered the skipping rope and spoke softly towards the snowy scene outside of my window. 'I don't like skipping, Father Christmas. I know I should have told you at the big store in Glasgow but I forgot. But it's okay: I like colouring, so thank you for those.' The house was quiet and I suddenly felt lonely; tears began to well up in my eyes and spill down my cheeks. I wanted to be with my sisters and brothers in our shared bed tearing the paper from our own presents and eagerly waiting to see what presents the others had got from Father Christmas. I wanted to watch Nunoos jumping up and down full of excitement on the bed and showing everyone her present. I wanted to be with the others running into our mum and dad's bedroom to show them what Father Christmas had brought us. I wanted to hug and kiss my dad and to see a big smile and a look of surprise on my mum's face when I showed her my present.

The door opened. It was Margaret in her dressing gown. She rushed to my bed, put her arms around me and gently rocked and hushed me as I cried.

'Noo what's all this about, Dorothy? Tell me what's upset you.'

'I miss my sisters and brothers and my mum and dad, Margaret. I want to go home to Guernsey,' I sobbed into her chest.

'What have you got here, a skipping rope and a lovely colouring book?' she said, trying to distract my attention.

'I don't like skipping, but I forgot to tell Father Christmas so he didn't know,' I sniffed back my running nose.

'Och here, Dorothy, blow your nose.' She offered me her hanky. I took it, buried my face into it and sobbed.

'Well now perhaps Father Christmas thought you were about to wake up when he called on you so he had to leave your room quickly so you wouldn't see him. I think that maybe he's left you some more presents downstairs under the tree with ours.' I looked up into her smiling eyes and I swallowed hard and blew my nose.

'Can we go and see?' I leapt out of the bed and she stood and took my hand in hers.

'Yes let's do that,' she laughed and led me from the room.

We hurried down the stairs and across the hall to the parlour room. Margaret pulled open the curtains and we looked out at the snow-covered garden, it was like a Christmas card scene. The room was flooded with early morning sunshine, the baubles on the Christmas tree glinted in the sunlight and beautifully wrapped presents tied with ribbons were piled around its base.

'Wait while I call Mother and Vincent, and no peeking, Dorothy,' she laughed as she left the room. I knelt down by the tree and wondered which presents were for me. Soon they all came into the room wearing slippers and nightclothes underneath their dressing gowns. Vincent rubbed his hands together.

'Och its cold in here, wait while I light a fire. Away and get dressed, all of you, and when you come down it'll be warm in here,' he ordered. I ran ahead upstairs and hurriedly put on my best dress and cardigan and shoved on my slippers, leaving my hair hung loose and tangled from sleep. I ran downstairs and into the room where Vincent was standing over the fireplace staring into the yellow wisps of flame that flickered and grew brighter and stronger as they pushed up through the kindling that crackled as it burned. He didn't know I was there. I could see he was deep in thought. He didn't blink and he looked sad. I stood still as I wasn't sure if I should disturb him.

'Och you're back already Dorothy.' He suddenly looked up towards me and smiled. It was a gentle smile that turned into a broad grin at my impatient glances between him and the presents.

'When can we open the presents?' I asked eyeing the biggest ones and wondering if one of them was for me. Just then Margaret and Mrs Thornton came into the room fully dressed and arm in arm.

'Somebody around here has no patience,' Margaret laughed as she knelt down beside the tree and Vincent sat beside his mother in the comfy armchairs.

'This one is for you, Dorothy.' She pulled out a big present from behind the tree and they watched as I eagerly began to tear at the wrapping paper. A wheel gave me the first clue as I ripped away the paper, then a hood and curved handlebars – it was a doll's pram, shiny white with a black hood and canopy. Father Christmas had remembered what I'd asked for. I wheeled it back and forth and it glided smoothly. I thought of Mum's pram that I had pushed my baby brothers around in, shabby and black with the handlebar up near my shoulders and the hood that I couldn't see over and the squeaky wheel.

'It's so posh and new. Can I go and get your doll and put her in it, Margaret?' I pleaded, rocking the pram the way I'd seen Mum do when she was shushing Leonard to sleep.

'Let's everyone open our presents first, lass,' Margaret said. I was soon unwrapping a big fully dressed doll of my own with a white dress tied around the waist with a wide red band and little socks and shoes and long black wavy hair like mine tied in a red ribbon.

'She's so pretty, Margaret. I'm going to call her Peggy because it means Margaret – a girl at school is called that but really her name is Margaret.' Margaret smiled.

Next I unwrapped a spinning top, a jigsaw puzzle, a paper fan, a game of snakes and ladders, another colouring book, a story book and a lovely pink silk and lace party dress with a wide pink ribbon sash belt. I was sitting amongst wrapping paper and toys unable to believe that anyone, let alone me, could get so many presents from Father Christmas. Vincent, Margaret and Mrs Thornton had all exchanged gifts and kissed and hugged and I ran to hug each of them in turn.

Vincent swept me up into his arms and said, 'Are you happy, wee sister?'

'Oh yes, this is my best Christmas ever,' I laughed.

Mrs Thornton told Vincent he should go and get dressed while she and Margaret prepared breakfast, and she told me to pick up all of the paper and separate the ribbons then put the paper aside. I noticed that they had carefully unwrapped their presents and smoothed out the paper so it was hardly damaged or crinkled, but I had torn most of my wrapping to shreds in my excitement. From the kitchen the smell of frying crept up my nose and I followed it. Mrs Thornton handed me a small package and asked me to give it to Kenny who was curled up in front of the range on his blanket. He heard her say 'Kenny' and his ears sprung up, his tail twitched and as I leaned down to him he jumped up and licked my face. I peeled off the paper, just as curious as he was to see the contents, and found a thick yellow doggy bone. After breakfast Vincent and I wrapped up in our hats, coats, gloves and boots and took Kenny outside to see the snow.

'We don't have snow in Guernsey but I've seen it on Christmas cards,' I told Vincent as we trod carefully down the steps from the front door and into the garden.

'Och, snow is fun, Dorothy, you'll see.' I watched Vincent scoop up a handful of snow and round it into a ball in his hands then without warning he threw it at me. I lifted my arm to fend it away and it splattered on my coat front. I stared down at my coat and then up at him – he was grinning like a naughty schoolboy. 'Gotcha,' he laughed. Then I realised it was a game and reached down to make a snowball to throw back at him. The soft snow grew harder as I squeezed and rounded it in my palms then I flung it at Vincent who was bending down making another.

'Good shot Dorothy, you got me!' he laughed. I threw another then another until my arm ached. Kenny yapped, jumped about and chased back and forth between us after the flying snowballs.

'Now we'll build a snowman,' Vincent announced, brushing down the glistening lumps of splattered snow from his coat. He ran indoors and came out with a carrot and an old hat. He started to build a big snowball then asked me to help him to roll it and as we rolled it the ankle-deep snow stuck to it and it grew bigger and rounder. When we stopped rolling it he straightened up and said 'There now, that's his body, now we do the same but a bit smaller for his head, lass.' We soon had another ball which he lifted on top of the body and pressed down firmly.

'Go and find some stones, lass: we need a good few – about ten I reckon.'

I ran around to the back of the house where there was a stony path and scraped the snow away until I could see the stones and counted ten into my pocket. When I returned to Vincent he was clapping his gloves together and as he shouted to me to hurry a steamy cloud followed his words. 'Now we give him a face and make him real. Let's start with his eyes – push a couple of wee stones into his head, not too close together now.' I gave the snowman eyes and made a wide smiley mouth using a row of stones, and the rest became his buttons in a line down his fat body. Vincent pushed the end of the carrot into the snowman's face to give him a pointy nose then handed me the hat. 'Here's the final touch, lass: put on his hat and he's done.' I placed the hat carefully on his head and stood back taking hold of Vincent's wet glove.

'Cor, my first ever snowman, what shall we call him?' I asked.

'That's for you to decide, lass,' he grinned.

'Let's call him Snowy,' I said and he smiled.

'I can't feel my fingers,' I said taking off a glove and sucking my fingertips.

'Me neither, lass, let's away inside for a hot drink.' Kenny had been sitting on the doorstep for ages waiting to go inside. We had a race to the steps and I won.

The house was warm and Christmas carols rang in the air from the crackling gramophone player. The smell of roasting goose floated through from the kitchen where the women of the house busily prepared our dinner. Once the food preparations were done they all sat and listened to the King's speech on the wireless – he talked about the war and they became serious and looked at each other with sad faces. Margaret jumped up after the speech and asked if I wanted to play snakes and ladders and Vincent joined in. Then when they all went to check on the goose I put Kenny in my pram and pushed him up and down the hall. At dinner the crystal cut glasses on the dining room table glittered in the candlelight, and the gleaming silverware and the cutlery that I had carefully lined beside each place setting with a neatly rolled napkin in its ring made everything look organised. Margaret appeared with a soup tureen and carefully ladled the steaming vegetable broth into our bowls. After the soup course was finished yet another course appeared – boiled salmon with egg sauce – and then the huge golden goose on a great silver platter surrounded by crispy roasted potatoes and another platter of winter vegetables from Mr Jack's garden. We clinked our wine glasses together – mine filled with lemonade – and drank a toast, first to each other then to the King and Queen, Churchill and those fighting for our freedom and the end of the war. Vincent carved the goose. The smell from it made my mouth water as Margaret placed a selection of vegetables on my plate. As the candle wax softened under the burning flame and rolled down the silver candlestick into a cold solid bubble at its base, I glanced at Mrs Thornton. She was smiling tenderly at Vincent who was laughing at Margaret's protests about the amount of goose he was serving her. I pictured Goosey Goosey Gander hissing and chasing Kenny and me away from her pen and didn't feel sad about eating her at all. I cleared my plate.

Margaret cleared her plate too despite her protests and then we had plum pudding and my piece had the sixpence in it and they all cheered as I held it up. Later, as I was put to bed Mrs Thornton reminded me to say a prayer for God to look after my family. I'd completely forgotten how sad I'd been that morning about missing them, so I lay there and tried to picture their faces but I could only see Nunoos' happy singing face. Where was she? Tomorrow I'd ask if she could come and play with me so I could show her all my lovely presents. I recited the prayer as I had done every night with my palms pushed together and my eyes tightly shut, and then, exhausted by the day, I sank into a deep sleep.

Boxing Day was fun too. Margaret and Vincent played hide and seek with me but Kenny kept coming to give me away. Mrs Thornton played the piano and we sang Christmas carols. There was a huge ham joint and lots of cold meat and pickles for lunch with mince pies and cakes but I struggled to eat very much. Vincent was slumped into the armchair listening to the wireless after lunch and Margaret was reading in the other armchair as I kneeled down beside Mrs Thornton. She too was reading on the sofa and smiling to herself.

'Can my sister Nunoos come and visit to play with me?' I asked.

'Och I'm sorry, lass, we don't know where she's staying,' she replied folding her book into her lap and placing her hand over mine.

'But you said she was with a nice family.'

'Och I'm sure she is but I wouldn't know how to contact her just now – it's difficult with the war and all, you understand?' Margaret quickly came to her mother's aid and sat beside her then pulled me towards her.

'I know what we'll do, we'll do our best to find her as soon as the holidays are over and everyone is back at work Then when we find her and the family she's with we'll ask them to bring her to visit. How will that be?' I nodded and I believed her.

'Now fetch your book, Dorothy, and we'll read a story,' she chirped. I was soon distracted and the moment passed.

13
My birthday party

It was February 1941 and I'd heard no more about Nunoos from Margaret or Mrs Thornton, and I somehow sensed that it wouldn't be good to keep asking about her. The snow had long ago melted, taking Snowy with it and leaving behind just an old hat, a withered carrot and some stones, yet the weather still seemed really cold to me.

'It's my birthday this month and I'll be eight years old on the twenty-fourth,' I proudly announced to Aunty Beth, who was plaiting my hair before school.

'Well noo ah think we'll have tae have a wee party for ye ahn ye friends,' she said looking up at Mrs Thornton who had walked into the bedroom with a clean yellow ribbon for my hair.

'Cor I've never had a birthday party. Please can I have Debbie and Kate and can we have Lollie and Nunoos too?' I jumped up pulling the plait from Aunty Beth's hands.

'Keep still Dorothy, while Beth does your hair.' Mrs Thornton passed the ribbon to Aunty Beth, giving her a quick frown. 'We've got a couple of weeks until your birthday, so we'll see what we can do.' At school I told Kate and Debbie about my party and was surrounded by eager hopeful faces in the playground wanting to know when and where. The clanging hand bell signalled the end of playtime and they all hovered around me – breaking away only when we lined up at the door to return to class.

Three days before my birthday party Mrs Thornton explained to me, on our way to the school bus stop, that she had been in touch with the authorities responsible for the evacuees' arrival and billeting arrangements. She told me they were going to do their best to find Nunoos' and Lollie's carers and inform them about my party. And she reminded me that I could ask only a couple of school-friends to my party because she was getting a little too old to cope with lots of children. At school, I told the other birthday party hopefuls that I was allowed to invite only Kate and Debbie.

They accepted this with a disappointed shrug because it was a grown-up's say-so.

'You have a parcel, and a letter came with it, Dorothy,' Mrs Thornton announced when she and Kenny met me that afternoon at the bus stop. She could see I wanted to run to the house to see what it was. 'Off you go, I'll catch up with you inside.' Kenny raced after me as I charged up the drive. The parcel was on the kitchen table wrapped in brown paper tied with string and a loopy bow. It wasn't a very big parcel – I squeezed it and it was soft. Mrs Thornton came puffing into the room and sat down resting her arms on the table.

'Do you think it's a birthday present for me?' I asked shaking the parcel next to my ear.

'Well lass, perhaps we should read the letter that came with it first and we may find out. You see the parcel is addressed to you and the letter is written to me, but it's not your mother's writing on the envelope.' She lifted her glasses from her chest, where they rested supported by a gold chain around her neck, and placed them on her nose as she read the envelope.

'I wonder who it's from – can you read it now please?' I begged. She pushed herself up to her feet and left the room but quickly returned with a shiny brass dagger-shaped letter-opener, which she used to neatly slit the top edge of the envelope. She opened the folded letter and quickly read the two pages. Her smile disappeared and she dropped her chin downwards and covered her mouth with her free hand. I tilted my head and looked at her, I was bursting to ask who had sent it but I somehow sensed I had to wait for her to speak first. Finally she lowered her hand and looked up at me.

'It's from your father, Dorothy. He wants me to send you back to be with your mother and the parcel is a present from him for your birthday.' She tried to be cheerful again but I could see her eyes were sad. My thoughts raced. Memories of my dad filled my mind and I conjured up the image of him in uniform, smiling, in the silver picture frame in the room next door.

'Is he going to come and fetch me today?' I asked, excited about seeing him again.

'No lass, he wants me to send you to Manchester on the train, but that will take time to arrange.'

My birthday party

'Does that mean I won't be able to have a birthday party?' I wanted that party so much and now maybe my dad was going to spoil it and take me away.

'Och of course you'll have your birthday party, Dorothy, and we'll make it an extra special one, won't we Kenny?' She threw her arms around me and hugged me tight, then turned and hid her face from me as she leaned down to pat Kenny, who wagged his tail and sat up to beg for a treat. I took my hanky from my pocket and held it towards her.

'Please don't cry. I'll come back to visit you often, I promise.'

'Of course you will lass, of course you will.' She was smiling now as she turned and stroked my head.

'Can I open my present now?' I asked, pulling at the string and glad that she was happy again.

'I think you should wait until your birthday, lass. Now you go and change out of your school clothes.' She patted her eyes with her own neatly folded hanky and took the parcel from me. In my bedroom I hung up my school clothes, pulled on the warm cable-knitted dress that she'd made for me, and buttoned up a cardigan. On the chest of drawers Margaret's doll Rosemary and Thomas, her threadbare teddy, sat hidden behind my new toys, books and games. I'd tucked my doll Peggy into Margaret's doll's crib beside my bed. In the wardrobe my shoes were lined up in a neat row at the bottom and lots of pretty "Shirley Temple" dresses were squashed onto the short rail hanging above. The pink silk party dress that Mrs Thornton had bought for me at Christmas was hanging ready for me to wear for my birthday party. This felt like my room, not Margaret's. I liked being here as I was special in this family and yet still I felt a sense of excitement that I was going to see my dad and mum and brothers and sisters again.

'I'm going home to my family after my birthday party,' I announced as I knelt down and peered at the Grandfather portrait from the safety of the landing banister rails. His glassy eyes stared at me from his thoughtful looking face and I tried hard to stare bravely back but I was still afraid of his stern look. I slipped carefully down the stairs beneath Grandfather and went into the kitchen to find Kenny and Mrs Thornton. She was at the table writing a letter and she kept stopping and screwing up the sheet she'd been writing on and starting again.

'Can you please take Kenny outside for you know what, lass?' she asked, barely lifting her head.

'Do I have to write a letter too?' I asked as I beckoned Kenny to come.

'Yes of course, if you like, I'll put it in with mine to your father.'

'Does he live with my mum now?'

'No he's with the Royal Artillery, lass.' She sniffed and blew her nose.

Later I wrote to my dad:

> *Dear Dad, Thank you for my birthday present but I don't know what it is until my birthday. I am going to have a real birthday party with a cake and candles to blow out that Aunty Beth is baking for me and Nunoos and Lollie are coming so are my friends from school. Mrs Thornton is a nice lady and she is writing you a letter too. Yours truly, Love Dorothy"*

My birthday had come at last. I was up dressed and downstairs in such a hurry that I ignored Grandfather on the way. As I rushed into the kitchen, Aunty Beth was slowly stirring a pot of porridge which bubbled and plopped over the heat.

'Happy birthday, wee Dorothy!' Aunty Beth shouted, holding open her arms. I ran and hugged her, and I could smell the yeast on her pinafore. 'Sit yersel doon ahn get this porridge into ye, lass, then ye can hiv ma present.' I wolfed down the porridge and gave myself hiccups, so I drank a glass of milk to make them stop but it didn't work. I dabbed my milky upper lip and eagerly waited.

'Here lass.' She handed me a small folded piece of tartan material wrapped in a ribbon. My fingers pressed and explored the square shaped packet and as I opened the fold I flashed a big smile at Aunty Beth.

'Cor, clothes for my doll – thanks Aunty Beth.' I held up a doll's size tartan Scottish kilt between fingers and thumbs and there was also a hand-knitted waistcoat in red with a matching red beret.

'Ah made 'em special fer ye doll, lass.' She was grinning proudly.

'I'll go and put them on her straight away,' I said sliding down from the chair.

'No, you don't have time now – we have to go for the bus.' It was Mrs Thornton coming into the room holding my coat and hat. 'You'll have plenty of time for your presents at your party this afternoon after school. Hurry now!'

The bus was waiting near the front gate today and the driver lifted his cap to Mrs Thornton as I climbed aboard. I joined Debbie on the back seat and we waved to her through the rear window. When she was out of sight we sat down and I wiggled my legs over the edge of the seat with excitement.

'Aunty Beth made my doll Peggy a Scottish outfit and I'm getting more presents later, I'm going to have the best birthday party and Lollie and my sister are coming too.' I chattered away all the way to school and Debbie seemed just as excited as me. It was the longest school day I could remember. I watched the hands on the white face of the classroom clock crawl from hour to chiming hour until finally it was home time. The bus seemed to me to crawl along really slowly as we headed home for my party. Debbie and Kate were seated on each side of me clutching paper bags containing their party dresses and my presents.

'What have you got me for my birthday,' I asked grinning at them.

'It's a surprise – you have to wait for the party to see,' said Debbie.

'Aye that's right,' said Kate.

'I bet my sister and Lollie will be waiting for the bus with Mrs Thornton and Kenny,' I said to them as we grew nearer to our stop, and moments later we were climbing down from the bus to a smiling Mrs Thornton and Aunty Beth. Kenny was pulling on his lead to come to me but for a moment I stood still and wrestled with the thoughts rushing through my head... *oh why aren't Nunoos and Lollie with them? I know why, I bet they are hiding inside to jump out to surprise me. But what if they haven't found them? Perhaps they're just a bit late and they'll turn up soon.* At this last thought I started to feel happier again.

'Dorothy, what are we standing here waiting for?' asked Debbie who nudged me and nodded towards the women. Kate cocked her head sideways and glanced from me to Debbie and back to me.

'Oh nothing. Let's go inside, c'mon,' I said to Debbie and linked arms with them both as we ran to the waiting trio.

'Let's hurry inside. Beth has been busy making lots of sweets and treats for you all, and we're going to have a lovely party,' Mrs

Thornton announced and we all cheered. We poured into the kitchen where it was warm and still smelled like cake baking. The table was piled with plates of buns, tarts, biscuits, individual trifles and little paste-filled triangle-shaped sandwiches. I reached for a tart. Mrs Thornton tapped my hand gently.

'Away upstairs and change out of your school uniforms into your party frocks first, Dorothy. Take Kate and Debbie to your room, quickly off you go,' she ordered cheerily.

'Isn't your sister coming, Dorothy?' Kate asked as she tied the shiny pink ribbon at the back of my party dress.

'Yes she is and so is Lollie my cousin. I'll ask Mrs Thornton what time they're coming when we get downstairs.' We admired each other's frocks and did a twirl for each other before heading downstairs. They followed me as I kept close to the wall on the stairs under the Grandfather picture just as I had shown them on the way up, although Debbie had shrugged and told me I was being silly as it was just a painting.

'When are Nunoos and Lollie coming?' I asked Mrs Thornton when we were seated at our set places around the table. Aunty Beth poured some lemonade into our glasses and glanced nervously at Mrs Thornton.

'Well we don't know for sure lass, but you do know that we've asked the authorities to find them and tell them about your party, don't you? We'll put some treats aside for them in case they come a little late.' She patted my head and smiled. We tucked into the food and Aunty Beth presented my birthday cake with eight candles flickering. Everyone sang *Happy Birthday* to me and I blew out the candles. Next I opened my presents from Kate and Debbie. Kate's was a bag of home-made fudge her mother had made. Debbie gave me a doll's pram blanket that she'd knitted out of scraps of her mother's wool. I took my dad's present from on top of a small pile at the end of the table and carefully untied the string. It was a dark blue dress made of linen with white buttons down the front and short puffed sleeves. I held it up against me but the material was limp as it rested on the full skirt of my party frock. I quickly folded it and put it on the empty chair beside mine. I started to screw up the wrapping paper and a folded piece of paper fell into my lap. I opened it and read, '*Happy Birthday to my best girl. Love from Daddy.*'

My birthday party

'That's a nice wee frock frae ye da, Dorothy,' said Aunty Beth. I nodded to her and smiled but couldn't speak and I fought back tears. I was feeling a bit disappointed with the dress and with my dad for choosing it, but at the same time I was wishing he could have come to my party and brought Nunoos and Lollie with him.

'What else have you got?' Kate asked, ignoring the dress.

I unwrapped the other presents. Vincent had sent me a storybook, and Margaret a cardigan in soft white wool with pearly buttons, and Mrs Thornton had made me a blue and white sailor style frock with a white bib embroidered with an anchor.

'Och I love that sailor frock,' Debbie cooed.

'Och it's really pretty, Dorothy,' Kate agreed.

I held it against me so they could see it better and noticed a gentle smile of approval on Mrs Thornton's face as I twirled in front of them.

'Thank you Mrs Thornton, I love it!' I said.

After we'd eaten, Aunty Beth joined in our game of hide-and-seek around the house and Mrs Thornton played the piano for musical chairs. Then she was the judge of our game of statues. It was beginning to get dark outside when Debbie's dad arrived in his car to take her and Kate home and he offered to drop off Aunty Beth on the way. I waved goodbye to them on the steps with Mrs Thornton and Kenny. She said she was feeling tired and asked me to read to myself before going to sleep. I read for a while and afterwards I prayed for God to look after my family wherever they were, as usual, but I also asked Him why He couldn't have found them and told them about my party because He could see everyone from up in heaven. I waited for an answer – for a gentle, kind voice to come into my head or fill the room – but there was only silence.

14

Leaving Glasgow

The following week Mrs Thornton was flustered when she met me at the bus stop with Kenny. She grabbed my hands in hers and spoke hurriedly. 'Dorothy, Margaret will be here soon, and she'll be coming with us tomorrow morning to the station in Glasgow where we'll put you on a train back to your family.' I was happy at first but suddenly I thought about my friends Kate and Debbie and my classmates.

'But I won't be able to say goodbye to my friends if I don't go to school tomorrow.'

'I'm sorry lass, but it's all been arranged, much sooner than I thought, by the Red Cross. They sent a nurse to our house this afternoon – she's going to meet us at the train station and accompany you on the trip.'

'What about Nunoos and Lollie? Are they going back with me?' I asked.

'Och Dorothy, I really don't know the answer to that as I've heard nothing about them at all, but we have a lot to get organised so hurry on up inside the house noo.'

'Is Vincent coming to the station too?'

'No lass, he's not due any leave for a wee while yet.' We climbed the steps and headed for the warm kitchen where a plate of shortbread and a glass of milk were prepared for me on the table. As I nibbled on the shortbread I could smell a meaty stew simmering on the range. The windows were steamed up like frosted glass and Kenny had curled up in his favourite spot on the hearth. He rested his chin on his crossed front legs and eyed me carefully so he would be ready to jump up and play when I called his name. I was going home to my real family, I thought, smiling to myself, with brothers and sisters to play with every day and I wished I could take Kenny with me but knew I couldn't. Mrs Thornton came puffing into the room – her faced was flushed and she went to the pot of stew, carefully lifted the lid with a cloth and gave it a stir with a long-handled spoon. I could almost taste it as the smell of herbs and onions floated out of the pot.

'When is Margaret coming?' I asked.

'Och she should be here before dark, lass, but we must make a start on packing your things before dinner. Hurry now and change out of your school clothes.' I left my nibbled shortbread, drank down my milk and slid from my chair. Slipping quickly underneath Grandfather I ran upstairs into my room. All my dresses were laid on the bed except for the warm cable-knit one Mrs Thornton had made, which hung in the centre of the empty space in the wardrobe. The chest of drawers' top had been cleared of my toys and Rosemary the doll and Thomas the teddy with his lop-sided smile looked back at me with lifeless stares. In the corner of the room a grey metal box that looked like a pirate's treasure chest with handles at each side and a rounded lid, was partly packed with my games and books. The crib was empty. My doll Peggy was half-hidden beneath my frocks on the bed. I took off my school uniform and, unsure where to put it, I hung it in the wardrobe in the place of the cable-knit dress that I'd taken out to wear. I pulled the dress down over my head and stared out through the window, past the neat rows of Mr Jack's vegetable garden and across the grey wet fields edged with dark naked trees with spidery branches. The sky was heavy with black clouds and in the distance the rain escaped from them and fell to the ground in a grey misty curtain. I could hear Margaret's voice as she came up the stairs.

'Are you up there, Dorothy?' I turned as she walked into the room and held out her hands towards me. 'I hear you're leaving us to go back to your family, Dorothy. We'll miss you lass, but I'm sure you're really excited about seeing your family again, aren't you?'

She took my hands into hers and stood me in front of her as she sat on the bed. Her mouth smiled at me but her blue eyes looked watery and sad. I looked around the room and then into her sad eyes. 'Don't be sad Margaret, you can find another girl to have my room and you can read her stories and she can play with Kenny and ride your bike.'

'Perhaps, we'll see, but right now we have to get you packed before dinner, so let's get started lass.' She glanced upwards, blinked, and stood up. I emptied the drawers of clothes, passed them to her with my shoes and she packed them into the trunk. Finally she carefully folded my dresses – the last was the sailor dress – and laid them on top.

'Can I wear my sailor dress tomorrow?' I asked.

'Och hen, it'll get really dirty on those trains so you should travel in your school clothes. Now I must change and get ready for dinner.' She closed the lid of the trunk. 'I'll see you downstairs,' she said then quickly left the room.

The stew was delicious but they just pushed it around their plates. I asked for seconds and Mrs Thornton gave me a sad smile as she served it up. They were both strangely quiet.

'You'd better get to bed early, Dorothy, you have a big day ahead tomorrow. I'll come up to read you a story shortly,' Margaret said after we'd finished our dinner.

I left the table and kissed Mrs Thornton on the cheek and then Margaret. I thanked them for my dinner and walked slowly upstairs wondering why they were behaving so differently. Margaret came up and read me a story and when she'd finished she leaned over me and kissed my forehead.

'We're going to miss you, Dorothy,' she whispered. 'The house will seem empty for Mother without you, and Kenny will miss you too – we have all grown very fond of you.' Her eyes misted up and she took out her hanky.

'Please don't cry, Margaret,' I said, and I threw my arms around her and buried my face into her warm sweet-smelling neck. A feeling of sadness like I have never felt came over me and tears filled my eyes and plopped down onto her shoulder. She held me close and shushed me until my tears had stopped and gently she released my arms from her neck and tucked them under the bedclothes.

'You get some sleep now, Dorothy, I'll see you in the morning, and don't forget to say your prayers. Goodnight lass.' She walked away and stopped to look back at me when she'd reached the open door. 'Sweet dreams,' she smiled.

'Goodnight Margaret,' I sniffed. She had turned out the light and I stared at the ceiling in the darkness – confused at my sadness and unsure if I wanted to go to my family or stay here. I closed my eyes, pressed my fingers together and whispered my prayers. In my mind I could clearly see my dad's face smiling at me from the silver framed photo, then I could see my whole family greeting me with waves and happy smiles outside our house in Pedvin Street as I drifted into sleep.

The next morning everyone was rushing around. Margaret shook me awake and told me to hurry and get washed and dressed. She pulled open the curtains, laid my school uniform on the bed, put the cable-knit dress into the trunk beside the sailor dress, and then hurriedly left the room. Downstairs, breakfast was ready. A bowl of steaming porridge was waiting for me alongside my glass of milk. It must have been really early because Aunty Beth wasn't there yet and she usually made my breakfast. Mrs Thornton was wearing a dark blue knitted twin-set costume with a pearl necklace and her hair looked crimped and neat as she swept into the room behind me.

'Hurry now lass, the car is outside waiting and Mr Jack has gone upstairs to get your trunk. We have to get to the station very early this morning to catch your train to Manchester.'

'Where's Aunty Beth?' I asked.

'Och lass, she doesn't know you're leaving because she'd already gone home when the Red Cross nurse came to tell me. It's all a bit sudden for us all.' She was wringing her hanky between her fingers. After breakfast I went into the hall where Kenny was scratching inside the front door to get out. I opened it and he jumped up at me wagging his tail as I bent down to pat him. I saw my doll's pram in the hall near the back door. I hurried back into the kitchen.

'Can I take my pram please, Mrs Thornton?'

She hesitated and leaned over to place her hands on my shoulders and look down into my face.

'It would be in the way on the busy train, Dorothy, but when you get home safely you write and tell me and I'll have it sent down to you – would that be all right?' I nodded, unable to hide my disappointment, and she stood up and stroked my head. 'Och we haven't done your hair. Sit down here, lass, while I get your hairbrush.' I slumped into the chair. The brush strokes were slow and gentle as she lifted my hair and pulled the brush underneath to free any tangles. Carefully she twisted the strands into two plaits and secured the ends with yellow ribbons, and after she'd put down the brush she stood still and quiet for a moment. I turned to look up at her.

'Och I'm really going to miss you so much, lass. Come here.' She held open her arms and I stood up and fell into them, holding her tight and not wanting to let go. We stood wrapped around each other in silence until Margaret came into the room.

'Mr Jack has put the trunk in the car and he's ready for us Moth…' she broke off and put an arm around her mother's shoulders and the other across my back. 'We have to be strong. It's the war – it's hard on everyone. Jack is waiting, Mother, we must hurry to catch that early train.' She went into the hall and came back with Mrs Thornton's fur coat and my hat, coat, gloves and shoes and under her arm was tucked my doll dressed in the Scottish clothes that Aunty Beth had made for her. Once Margaret had helped me into my coat she passed me Peggy and held open her mother's coat. We all put on our hats and moved to the door and Kenny trotted behind us wagging his tail. 'You must stay here, Kenny,' Margaret ordered him back into the kitchen and he skulked back to his place by the hearth. I ran back to him and knelt down to stroke him.

'Goodbye Kenny, be a good doggy and don't forget me, will you?' He sat up and licked my chin, his tail wagging again.

'Dorothy, we must go now – you stay, Kenny!' He lay down again, dropped his head onto his front legs and raised his eyes towards me. I stood up, gave him a weak wave and joined the others at the front door. I turned to look up at Grandfather's portrait and his glassy stern stare looked back at me. Goodbye to you too, scary Grandfather. We stepped out into the cold February chill. Mr Jack was holding the car door open and the others were already inside waiting. I ran and climbed into the back with Mrs Thornton. Margaret was in the front. Our gas mask boxes were lined up along the back window. Soon we were driving down the driveway and out into the lane, past the bus stop.

'I haven't said goodbye to my school friends, so how will they know I've left?' I asked Mrs Thornton. She smiled, handed me a notebook and a pencil and told me to write a little note to Debbie and Kate and she would see that they got it.

I spent the rest of the journey with my head down scribbling my farewell messages and in no time we had arrived at the station in Glasgow. Mr Jack pulled the car up to the kerbside and unloaded my trunk. He waved to a porter who came and threw it up onto his shoulder. Mrs Thornton asked Jack to wait there for them as we climbed out of the car and he nodded as he handed us our gas mask boxes. I turned and looked up into the craggy, lined face under his cap and smiled at him.

'Goodbye Mr Jack.' He smiled back at me, winked and patted my hat.

'Bye noo, take care of yersel', lassie.'

'Now Dorothy, we'll have no tears today as we are all going to be brave and say goodbye nicely – do you understand?' Mrs Thornton smiled as she held up her finger. We followed the porter who was weaving in and out of hundreds of people. Soldiers with rifles slung over their shoulders were striding out and laughing, maybe at a joke. There were others in thick army overcoats and women wearing fur coats with muffs to keep their hands warm. Some stood and talked and hugged each other. A sailor wearing a suit like my sailor dress dropped his heavy canvas kit-sack and stooped over, shielding his cigarette from the wind with a cupped hand, to take a light from another sailor. As we drew nearer to the platform the train was slowing to a halt. A strong smell of soot in the air made me cough. An echoing voice announced the train's arrival and where it had come from. I held on to Mrs Thornton's hand as the porter lowered the trunk onto the platform near to the train. Margaret went to speak to a station guard who pointed her towards a young woman dressed in a nurse's uniform and cape, surrounded by four children around my age or younger wrapped up in hats and coats and clutching bags and small cases. Margaret approached her and then came back over to us.

'That's the nurse who's going to accompany you to Manchester with those other children, Dorothy,' she said. I looked across again and the nurse waved and smiled. Margaret bent down to my level and held my chin. 'She'll take good care of you, don't you worry and soon you'll see your family again.' She gave me a hug and lifted me up level with her mother who brushed her lips softly against my cheek.

'Goodbye hen.' She smiled and Margaret lowered me to the platform.

'Shall I take that for ye?' The porter lifted my trunk and Margaret gestured towards the group of children and the nurse who were starting to climb up into a train carriage. We followed him and he stepped up into the train and loaded the trunk onto the shelf above the seat. Then he lifted me up and swung me into the open doorway where I stood clutching Peggy looking into the sad faces of my carers. A whistle blew and the nurse said something to Margaret and moved to get onto the train so I stepped back and returned to the open window after she had slammed the door shut. Slowly the train began to move, people on the platform called out and waved to the faces at the open windows, who waved and shouted back. As the train drew away tears stung my eyes and I called out to Margaret and Mrs Thornton.

'Cheerio, cheerie bye!' They waved and Margaret blew me a kiss and they became smaller and smaller until they were lost in the crowd of bodies with waving arms.

15

Together again

As we left the station the heavy black clouds dumped a downpour of rain onto the train and it blew into the window. The nurse told me to close it and sit down with the other children as she took my gas mask box and put it on the luggage rack with the others.

'Your doll is pretty. What's her name?' a cheery voice asked from behind me. I turned to reply and saw my sister Nunoos sitting with her rag doll on her lap. I leapt onto the seat next to her as she continued to speak. 'Mine's called...'

'Missy!' I interrupted. Her eyes opened wide as she looked at me, puzzled.

'How did you know that?' she asked and pulled her doll close to her chest.

'Don't you recognise me, Nunoos, I'm your sister Dorothy?' I took off my hat.

'Oh Dorothy, it's you! Where did you go? They tried to find you but said they couldn't and I thought I'd never see you again and I was frightened.' She started to cry and I hugged her as hard as I could and I laughed through my tears.

'Oh Nunoos, I've missed you so much.' She stopped crying and smiled at me. 'Here blow your nose.' I gave her the neatly folded hanky with embroidered flowers on the corner that Mrs Thornton had given to me. She looked at it and then at me, from head to toe and back up at my face.

'You look really posh. Did you stay with the King and Queen?' I shook my head and laughed.

'I've got some new shoes, look,' she said, and moved her toes up and down over the edge of the seat. Her shoes were scuffed at the toes but were the same style as my shiny black patent leather pair. Her white ankle socks were too big and the heel pushed out over the back of her shoes. She was wearing the same coat I thought she'd lost on the boat, but she'd outgrown it. The sleeves were short, showing her ribbed cardigan cuffs underneath and the buttons down the front strained to keep it closed. A grey knitted bonnet flattened her hair and was tied under her chin framing her face.

Everyone in the train compartment was quiet. I looked up at the twin boys of around six years who were seated facing us. Each wore an identical suit of jacket and shorts and long woollen socks, and their shoes shone with black polish. They were staring at us. A girl aged about eight was on the end of their seat by the window; she had fair hair pulled off her face to one side with a slide grip. She turned her face to look out of the window as my eyes met hers. The nurse had placed her book on her knee and was also watching us and smiling. I glanced at her and she nodded at me and then quickly explained to the other children.

'Dorothy and Edna are evacuees from Guernsey – they're sisters who haven't seen each other for a long time – now let's read and leave them to talk.'

She passed the boys a *Beano* comic each from a large bag beside her on the seat and they opened them up to hide their faces and giggled behind them.

'Where's Lollie?' Nunoos asked, wiping her tears on her sleeve and sniffing deeply as she handed me back the hanky.

'She was taken to live with a lady and man in Glasgow but I don't know where she went. We left the hall on the same day and I went to stay with a nice family named Thornton. So what happened to you?'

'I couldn't find you on the boat or in the big building by the harbour so my teachers took me in a train to Glasgow too but it must have been a different Glasgow to your one. We were put in this hall where we slept on camp beds and in the daytime we cleared our beds away to have our lessons with an old lady teacher. After about a week people came and took children away to their houses.'

'Did someone take you?' I interrupted.

'Not at first but a nice young lady called Margaret came and sat with me and started to visit me sometimes. She bought me puzzles and colouring books but said she couldn't take me to live with her because her mum was an invalid.'

'My lady was called Margaret too. So did you stay in the hall the whole time, and were you all on your own?' I asked.

Together again

'No, there were a few of us who didn't go to homes, but this lady Margaret started to bring her boyfriend with her and they sometimes took me out to the park. He was nice to me, and one day they took me to town and bought me these shoes. I was so chuffed I didn't want to take them off.'

'What about Christmas – did you stay in the hall then too?' I was starting to feel sorry for her and remembered what Lollie had said about being left behind and not being picked by anyone.

'No, I was at Margaret's mum's house; it was just across the road. She'd been taking me there for my tea every day for a long time by then, and back to the hall to sleep, but she said her mum said I could stay with them after all. We had nice food and I had a new doll from them with curly hair and a blue dress and white shoes. I danced and sang for her sick mum and she smiled and clapped – it was fun.'

'Where's your new doll then, why have you still got Missy?' I teased.

'Because I love Missy; she's from my mummy and daddy.' She hugged the doll with thick strands of black wool for hair and a flat knitted face and she kissed her.

'They put the other doll in my bag,' she said.

'Didn't you ever go to a proper school?' I asked.

'After a few weeks we were sent to the proper school with the other kids. There were some older ones that someone said were from Guernsey but I didn't know them and they didn't talk to me. I used to walk to school and back on my own: it wasn't very far, just down a couple of roads. Sometimes when I was skipping along singing songs I learned in Guernsey a nice man would stop me and call me to his garden gate. He called me "Topsy" and used to give me a carrot, I think he must have been a farmer.' She shrugged and grinned. She had grown new teeth and had a little gap between the two at the front. We spent the journey swapping stories about our lives in Glasgow.

The train stopped at stations along the way and soldiers who passed along the crowded corridor opened our door searching for an empty seat. Their cigarette smoke drifted in from the corridor and the smell hung in the air even after they'd closed the door.

Displaced Donkeys

The nurse called herself a Journey Nurse and told us as she fed us with sandwiches and lemonade that she'd spent most of her time during the war so far on trains, accompanying children away from or back to their homes. After we'd eaten the twin boys fell asleep and the girl rested her head against the window and closed her eyes. Nunoos' eyelids were drooping slowly. I put my arm around her shoulders and she gradually slid down my chest until her head was in my lap and she was asleep. I rested my head back against the seat and thought about Mrs Thornton, Margaret and Kenny and I pictured them telling lovely Aunty Beth in her apron with floury hands that I had gone to be with my family. I felt sad but eventually the rocking motion of the train lulled me to sleep.

'Wake up children! We're here at Manchester Station.' The nurse shook my shoulder and Nunoos lifted her head and rubbed her eyes. The girl at the window – who'd told Nunoos when we were eating our sandwiches that her name was Mary – buttoned up her coat then reached for her small case from the rack above her seat. The twins took their folded caps out of their pockets at exactly the same time, stood up, and then put them on their heads at exactly the same angle. As the train slowed to a stop, the nurse passed us our gas masks. She handed Nunoos her bag and the boys their cases but she left my trunk on the rack. A man in uniform opened the door to the platform below and the nurse asked him to lift my trunk down for her. When he'd put it down on the platform we all gathered around it waiting to be told what to do next.

'Mary!' A woman came running towards us waving her arms. Mary burst into tears and ran towards her mother. There were lots of people craning their necks to see past each other and into the open carriage doors. After Mary had gone with her mother a man dressed in a smart pinstriped suit with a briefcase and wearing a bowler hat came towards us. 'Father!' shouted one of the twins and grabbed his brother's hand. They ran to the man who put down his case and swept them both up into his arms and kissed each of them on their cheeks. He came over to thank the nurse, then put his briefcase under his arm so he could carry their cases. As they walked away the boys clung on to his sleeves and gazed up at him with big grins on their faces.

'Everyone is leaving the platform and it's getting late – I wonder where your mother is,' said the nurse looking at her watch. I sat on my trunk and shifted across so that Nunoos could sit down beside me.

'Mummy is going to come, isn't she Dorothy?' she asked, still half asleep, and before I could answer we heard a woman shouting at some children.

'Mind you keep away from those rails! Get yer Cliffy – keep in line!' It was our mum. She was striding up the platform with her coat flapping open, pushing the old black pram. She had a piece of string tied around her waist and at set distances along the length she had also tied it around the waists of our sister Pamela and Lollie's sister Barbara and tied at the end was our brother Little Cliffy, who had tried to wander towards the train tracks. They were all running behind trying to keep up with her. Their winter coats looked shabby and their grey woollen socks had lost their stretch and rested in folds around their ankles over their scruffy worn=out boots.

'Mummy!' Nunoos shouted and she set off towards our mum with her open arms lifted and Missy dangling and jerking about in her raised hand. My heart sank as I looked at this scruffy woman with her grubby kids. I wanted to go straight back to Mrs Thornton, who was clean and respectable with nice clothes and a gentle voice.

'Go to your mother, Dorothy.' The nurse nudged me in the back and I stumbled forward. Mum had lifted Nunoos up and was showing her to the other children who were smiling at her. I slowly walked up to them and waited to be noticed. Mum turned towards me and put Nunoos down.

'By Christ! Take a look at you, Dorothy, quite the little lady aren't you? Those people you were with must have been posh!' The others came and stood around me and looked me curiously up and down.

'Can someone get my trunk please Mum?' I said trying to take the attention from me to something else. I pointed to where the nurse was standing.

'How the bloody hell am I going to carry that big thing home? We've got to catch a train to Stockport yet. What's in it anyway?'

'My clothes and toys,' I said, 'from the Thorntons.' She thought for a minute then lifted Leonard out of the pram and took my doll and passed it to Pamela.

'Hold that doll,' she said to her, then pushed Leonard into my arms. 'You can carry him for me.' She strode towards the nurse with the empty pram with the squeaky wheel. My sister, brother and cousin were all staring at me curiously, but their expressions switched to surprise as the string suddenly pulled tight and they were dragged stumbling after her.

'Yer, can you help me with this, my girl?' she shouted to the nurse, who nodded at her and together they heaved the trunk into the pram. Mum came back dragging her brood and I turned to wave goodbye to the nurse, who smiled and waved back. I tagged along behind the snaking line of children with my brother in my arms. He tilted his head and eyed me warily. Nunoos skipped along happily as she held on to the pram handle beside Mum and told her all about her lady Margaret and proudly showed off her shoes. Near the station end of the platform Granny was seated on a wooden seat. Lollie was pointing us out to her. She left Granny and ran up to me with a big grin on her face. She stopped and stood in front of me and slowly looked me up and down.

'You look posh. Was that lady who took you really rich then?'

'I don't know, but they were really nice to me. Why didn't we see you on the train – were you in another carriage?' I asked.

'Nah I've been in Stockport ages me, my mum sent for me after she got here and found a house for us.'

'Why didn't our mum send for us when she got a house?'

'I dunno me, anyway it was your dad that made her find you and send for you and Nunoos to come back and live with her.'

'Where's my dad, does he live with us in Stockport too?'

'Nah, but sometimes he gets a forty-eight hour pass and visits your mum.' We reached Granny who had fallen asleep again as she used to in Guernsey. Mum was shaking her shoulder roughly and shouting at her.

'Bloody hell Grace, not now! I've got to get these kids home and get some food rations for their tea: wake up!' Granny opened her eyes and squinted through her spiralled lenses.

'Did I drop off again?' she asked peering around at us all through her little piggy eyes.

'Yeh Granny,' the kids all chimed. I noticed that they spoke with a twang of an accent that I'd never heard. We wandered along to the train for Stockport and Mum untied the string from the others and stuffed it into her coat pocket as we climbed aboard. The porter lifted the trunk onto the luggage rack and Mum folded up the pram and untied the big box tied onto the handle and put it on the luggage rack.

'What's in that box?' I asked Lollie.

'It's a special gas mask for babies and toddlers,' she replied. I sat next to Lollie and as the train pulled away Leonard started crying so Mum took him from me. Lollie told me all about Stockport, her school, the teachers and the other kids in her street. She asked me about my time in Glasgow and asked if I was speaking Scottish because I sounded strange. I told her she sounded strange too. Then I told her about living in Glasgow and she listened open-mouthed. When the train arrived at Stockport we woke up Granny again. We were all weary and hungry when we got out at the station but we still had to walk to the house and I had to carry Leonard again. Nobody spoke as we trudged along in pairs behind Mum. Suddenly she stopped outside a corner grocery shop and turned to me.

'Did you bring your ration book with you, Dorothy?' she asked. 'And have you got yours, Nunoos?' she held out her hand. Nunoos shrugged her shoulders so Mum took her bag and rummaged through until she found it, then quickly she flicked through it counting the coupons.

'Mine's in my gas mask box,' I said, lifting it off my shoulder.

She opened the box and took out the card – it was clean and looked unused. After turning a few pages she smiled. 'There's enough coupons in here for us to buy some nice things to eat, so we'll have a welcome home party for Nunoos and Dorothy. What do you say, kids?' They all cheered and followed her into the corner shop and I waited in the doorway as the old shopkeeper frowned and told them to wait for their mummy outside because his shop was too small. They piled out of the shop and pressed their hands and noses against the large taped shop window trying to see what Mum was buying for the party. She came out with a bag filled with surprise goodies for our party and we fell into line again and marched along with more energy and excitement. The cobblestone street was lined with identical houses built of soot-blackened red bricks. The small panes of their dirty windows were all taped against a bomb blast just like in Glasgow. Dark smoke curled up from the rims of their rooftop chimneys and mingled with the thick grey blanket of smog that loomed over them. I carefully sidestepped the shiny yellow lumps of blood-streaked gob-spit on the pavement that the others didn't even seem to notice.

'Here we are,' Mum announced as we arrived at what was to be my new home.

We were standing outside a house much the same as the others with taped-up windows. It looked like the houses I first learned to draw as a child except for the bricks. It had a front door with a window either side with four panes of glass each and another two windows upstairs above those. I couldn't see inside the windows as they were blacked out with material. It stood in the middle of a row of five houses in Great Edgerton Street and across the road were more terraced houses and far behind those were trees and sloping green hills. My sister Pamela opened the door and stepped into the dingy narrow passageway holding it against the wall for us to pass thtough. I stood on the doorstep and noticed for the first time the sores around her mouth and nose and she saw me staring and covered her mouth with her hand. Barbara pushed me from behind.

'Hurry up, get inside! I'm starving hungry.'

She looked at Pamela covering her mouth. 'She's got impetigo . She caught it from me. I had it last month but it healed up quicker than hers because I didn't pick the scabs off like she does.'

'Shuddup you, I don't pick them, so there.'

'Yes you do: I seen you when you didn't know I was looking, so there.' Granny clipped the back of Barbara's head and told her to shut her mouth and get inside and I got a harder shove in the back.

'That was your fault she hit me because you were too slow, silly bitch,' Barbara scowled. We all crammed into the tiny living room where the curtains were pulled open from a window that overlooked the back yard and waited for Mum and Granny to come in with my trunk. They swore and puffed as they lifted it out from the pram and into the middle of the room where they dropped it and stood up.

'It looks like a treasure chest that the pirates have, eh Mum. Can we see inside it?' Lollie was asking Granny.

'Is it locked? Does she have a key?' Granny asked Mum.

'It's in my pocket,' I said pulling it out and holding it up. Mum took it and knelt down beside the trunk to put it into the lock. I glanced around and everyone in the room was stooped over it, their eyes wide, mouths open like greedy pirates. Mum lifted the lid and flipped it wide open. She fingered the cable-knit dress that was laid on the top beside my new sailor frock and looked underneath at the silky pink party frock.

'Did that family buy you this, Dorothy?' Mum asked looking up at me.

'Yes and there's lots more nice clothes under that frock,' I boasted feeling really proud of myself. She held up the pink frock for all to see and Nunoos told me it was a really pretty dress and she wished she had a pretty dress like that.

'Does it still fit you?' Mum asked.

'Of course, I've only worn it once, for my birthday party,' I replied haughtily.

'Don't come the lady with me, you cheeky mare. You can share these dresses with your sisters,' she snapped, and began lifting them out one by one, and holding them against my sisters and cousins, all eagerly stepping forward to be measured. 'And don't forget to share your toys around too,' she warned me as she reached the games and books at the bottom of the trunk.

'Please, can I keep the sailor dress for me, I haven't even worn it yet.' I reached to grab it from the lid of the open trunk where the other clothes had been tossed into a pile. My face was burning with rage: these were my dresses bought for me! How dare she give them away, I thought. I hated her and everyone else in the room, I wanted to go back to Glasgow to be with nice people who spoiled me and loved me. She pushed the sailor dress and the other clothes back into the open trunk and closed the lid before she stood up and dragged it into a corner. Then she smiled and undid her coat buttons.

'We'll sort that lot out tomorrow. Now get your coats off and let's make some nice food for Nunoos' and Dorothy's welcome home party. You can lay the table, Dorothy. Pamela, show her where everything is. Make haste now!' I didn't want to take off my coat in case it got handed to someone else so I pretended I was still cold, though I didn't have to pretend for the room was really cold and felt damp.

'I'll light the fire and warm this place up,' Granny told Mum as she began screwing up paper and putting it into the grate.

'Here's the plates and cups; the spoons and that are in that drawer,' Pamela said as she tugged at a cupboard door that had been painted so many times it got stuck. Inside a stack of enamel plates was squashed in alongside assorted bowls and chipped cups that hung by their handles from nails along the edge of the top shelf. I thought about Mrs Thornton's dainty plates ringed with roses and china cups and saucers.

'Make haste Dorothy. Don't stand there daydreaming, you're under my feet girl,' Mum snapped.

'Help her get that table laid, Pamela. By Christ do I have to do everything around here?' I took down the pile of plates and followed Pamela back into the living room where wispy blue flames were licking through the lumps of coal in the fireplace. Granny had pulled the blackout cloth across the back window and the room was dimly lit. The table was a dark wood and splattered with paint spots and rings left from hot drinks. Pamela placed the plates around the outside edge and counted the bodies in the room on her fingers then counted the plates. I put the cutlery in the middle of the table: six tablespoons, four bent forks, eight knives and seven teaspoons. I'd emptied the drawer.

'Where's the rest of the cutlery?' I asked Pamela.

'S'all there is… just leave it there and we'll all take something, mostly us kids just use the spoons.' I thought about Mrs Thornton's shiny silver cutlery and sighed.

'Move yourself, make haste, you spread something on this bread.' Mum pushed past me holding a wooden board laden with sloping slices of thickly sliced bread and plonked it on the table.

Pamela rooted through the shopping bag and pulled out tins of treacle and sweetened condensed milk and handed them to me. I began hurriedly spreading dollops from each tin onto the slices then cutting them into neat little triangles. Pamela then went back to the cupboard and returned wearing a grin as wide as the impetigo sores around her mouth would allow without cracking open. In her hands was a tin with a snow scene and dancing children painted on the lid and sides. Oh cakes! I thought, remembering the tins in Mrs Thornton's pantry. Pamela put the tin in the middle of the table and the others swooped around the table like seagulls around a fishing boat.

'Yummy, I'm starving!' shouted Little Cliffy. He climbed onto a wooden bench at the table and shuffled along to make room for Nunoos, Pamela and Barbara. I sat down on one of the three chairs in the room, Lollie sat on another and after Mum had dropped Leonard into a highchair she sat down to feed him. We tucked into the sticky sandwiches licking our fingers as the treacle oozed out from the edges. Mum took a triangle for Leonard and examined it.

'Very dainty, I must say.' She held it up, stuck her little finger out, and pursed her lips. She put the sandwich on Leonard's tray then went back into the tiny scullery and returned with a large saucepan that she put over the heat on the range in the living room and stirred. She tilted her head to see if Granny, who was sitting in an old armchair by the fire, was awake, but she was snoozing with her bottom lip drooping and vibrating as she breathed out. When all the bread was gone Pamela grabbed at the tin and slowly prised off the lid as if she was a magician about to pull a surprise rabbit out of a hat. I was desperate to see this cake that was causing so much excitement in the faces of the other kids. I leaned across to look into the tin.

'It's only broken biscuits,' I whispered, feeling disappointed. All kinds of bits of biscuits rested among a pile of golden crumbs. I raised my eyebrows and Nunoos who was watching my face asked, 'What's in the tin Dorothy?'

'Biscuits, lots of yummy biscuits,' Pamela answered, tilting the tin to show Nunoos. We watched Pamela reach into the tin, grab a handful of biscuits and crumbs and put them on her plate. She passed the tin along and we all did the same, Little Cliffy clutching as many as his tiny fist could hold. I nibbled at a biscuit… it was soft and stale. Disappointed, I put it back on the plate.

'Yer we are, mind your hands,' said Mum as she carried the saucepan to the table and poured steaming custard over our biscuits. I watched Pamela stir her custard through the biscuits. Barbara crushed them with a spoon then stirred the mixture into a paste. Lollie just shovelled spoonfuls of the unstirred pile into her hungry mouth. Nunoos copied Lollie and I copied Pamela. I was surprised:

it tasted lovely and you couldn't really tell the biscuits were soft or stale, all mixed in with the custard.

'Empty plates and tired kids is what I see and it's time you were all in bed.' Granny had woken up and was heaving herself up from the fireside chair. She handed Lollie and Barbara their coats and told Mum she must get back to the boys who were looking after Delia as they would be hungry. I asked Mum if I could get my toothbrush and nightdress out of my trunk and she nodded as she cleared away the plates. There wasn't a bathroom upstairs, just two bedrooms off the landing and the toilet was in a shed outside in the back yard.

'Where's the bathroom, Pamela?' I asked.

'We don't have a room, just a tin bath like we had in Guernsey, remember?' I did remember now: it was starting to sink in. My family used to be poor and scruffy and we are still poor and this is real life and life in Glasgow was like a dream, just pretend, except it *was* real for me and I didn't want to be poor and scruffy any more. I didn't clean my teeth. I pulled my nightdress over my head and slipped into the double bed beside Nunoos who was in the middle. There was no top sheet and the blankets were itchy.

'There's a hole in the mattress and I keep falling down into it, Dorothy,' Nunoos whispered.

'That always happens to the one who sleeps in the middle,' Pamela laughed.

'Move closer to me Nunoos,' I said and I put my arm around her and pulled her into my chest.

She snuggled into me and as I held her in the silence I heard a scratching noise that seemed to be in the walls and above my head in the ceiling and under the bed.

'What's that noise, Pamela?' I whispered.

'It's the mice, Mum says this place is overrun with mice.'

'We should have Tibby here; she would catch them,' Nunoos said from under the blanket.

'Will they come into our bed?' I asked Pamela as I dragged the blanket tightly under my chin.

'I've never seen one on the bed yet,' she said.

I thought about my lovely soft eiderdown and my pretty bedroom and I cried silent tears until I slept.

In the morning I felt cold and wet, and my nightdress was soaked. I threw back the blanket and glared at Nunoos. Her eyebrows were knitted together and her bottom lip was pouted as she looked guiltily at me.

'I didn't know I'd wet the bed until I woke up, honest, Dorothy.'

'Don't you worry, I'll wash it out. You don't do that every night do you?' I asked.

'Not for a long time but sometimes it just happens. I'm sorry. I don't mean to do it.'

Pamela was already up and dressed and she popped her head around the bedroom door. 'Mum said make haste and get downstairs.' She looked me up and down and sneered. 'Did you wet the bed?'

'No, it was Nunoos,' I snapped.

'Please don't tell Mummy, or she'll give me a hiding,' Nunoos whined.

'Nah she won't. Little Cliffy does it and she doesn't smack him, but I'm not sleeping next to you from now on, that's for sure,' Pamela grinned.

16

A visit to the park

I had to gobble down bread and treacle and a cup of tea sweetened with condensed milk for breakfast, before being shoved out of the door with instructions from Mum to take the kids down to the park to get them out from under her feet. Pamela was to show me the way. We stood beside our doorstep wrapped up against the cold in our coats, hats and mittens. The thick dirty yellow haze of factory smoke that hovered around the rooftops thwarted the sun's effort to spread its warmth and light over the dull grey streets. Leonard was asleep in the pram, wrapped in a blanket, and Little Cliffy was holding the side of the pram handle. He was gazing up at me as if he was still unsure about where I fitted into his family. Nunoos was dancing on and off the kerb edge in her own little world tapping her toe and her heel and humming to herself.

'Follow me, it's this way,' Pamela beckoned as she strode ahead. We followed her. It was Saturday and the street was full of kids. Big sisters like me were minding the baby in the pram surrounded by their younger brothers and sisters. They weren't all going to the park like us: some were just playing in the street outside their houses. It wasn't far to the "Rec" as Pamela called the park – just along the road a bit and on the other side. Bare trees and low railings surrounded the play area. There was a big slide and two swings side by side with flat wooden seats and the chains fixed to the edges of the seats hung from a sturdy iron frame. Two small scruffy kids leaned against the frame with their hands stuffed into their pockets, waiting for a turn. Pamela and Nunoos slipped off their gas mask boxes, threw them into the pram and ran over to the slide to join a long queue of kids that started at the top of the steps and came down long past the bottom. An older boy was climbing up from the bottom scrawling circles onto the metal chute with a candle. I found a wooden bench seat near to the swings, pulled the pram alongside me and sat down. Leonard was still asleep and little Cliffy was taking off his gas mask box ready to join the others at the slide. I told him he was too small and he argued with me, claiming that he had been on it lots of times and that Pamela had always let him.

'Oh go on then, but stay with Pamela,' I sighed, taking his gas mask box and waving him away. I leaned back against the seat as I watched the kids judder down the slide, slowed by the candle wax. Soon they would polish it in with their coats and then they would fly down really fast – I knew this because I'd seen Ronald do this to the slide at Cambridge Park in Guernsey. By the time Pamela had reached the top she was smiling but her smile changed to a look of fear as she flew down and shot straight off the end to land flat on her back.

'Shuddup you,' she scowled at the two older boys who were standing near the bottom of the slide pointing at her and laughing. She got up and brushed the dirt from the back of her coat. When she looked up she saw Nunoos sitting at the top.

'Hold on to the sides!' she shouted, but it was too late. Nunoos had let go and her head flipped back and her legs flew up into the air. She screamed as she rammed feet first into Pamela at the bottom of the slide knocking her backwards and landing on top of her. Nunoos started to cry but as soon as she realised that Pamela was hurt more than she was she stopped and rolled off Pamela's body. The boys were bent over laughing and Little Cliffy ran over to one of them, kicked him in the ankle and then ran back to his sisters.

'Cor you saved me, Pamela, they made it too slippery and I was scared,' Nunoos said.

'I tried to tell you to hold on.' Pamela scowled, brushing her coat down again. I watched her take Nunoos and Little Cliffy's hands in hers and run towards me.

'Pamela and me skidded off the edge and those big boys were laughing and Little Cliffy kicked them, eh Pamela,' Nunnos blurted out.

'I know, I saw,' I replied.

'Are you all right Pamela?' I pointed to her chest. She rubbed it and nodded.

'I'm freezing cold. Let's play tag,' I suggested and they grinned their agreement and ran off shouting that I was "It". I knelt down beside Little Cliffy and told him to run away like his sisters and that I would try to catch him, but he mustn't let me touch him or he would be "It". He ran off and I left the sleeping Leonard and chased after them. We all took turns of being "It" and were soon warm and breathless, but I could hear Leonard crying so we ran back to the pram. We were feeling hungry, so we headed back along Great Edgerton Street to our house. Front doors opened along the terrace of houses as we passed along the street and other kids were called inside by their mums; I thought this must mean that the time when kids would have got under their mum's feet must be over now.

Inside our house the fire warmed the living room and Granny was sitting alongside it with the baby Delia on her lap. Pamela ran up to the fire and stood with her back to it to warm her legs.

'Don't stand there blocking the heat!' Granny shouted and slapped the back of Pamela's leg. Pamela let out a squeal, jumped clear and rubbed her stinging leg. Mum lifted Leonard out of his pram and changed him – he was still in nappies.

'Lay the table Dorothy, I've made some vegetable soup for your tea. And you can help her, Pamela.'

I'd got used to calling the midday meal "lunchtime" when I was living with the Thornton's and the evening meal "dinner" and now I had to call it "tea" again. It was nice soup – there were dumplings in it – and we felt full up afterwards. Lollie and Barbara came around, hungry, looking for their mum but our soup was all gone.

'When are we going to have our tea, mum?' Lollie asked Granny.

Granny pointed into the corner, 'I'm coming as soon as we've shared out what's in that trunk.' Mum heard her as she came back into the room after putting Leonard down to sleep. She went over to the trunk and pulled it away from the wall so she could open the lid. The kids all gathered around and one by one my pretty frocks were held up against them then pushed into their eager open arms. Mum put my sailor dress to one side. She glanced at the dress and then at me before smiling and tossing it at me. 'You can keep that one for yourself. By Christ, girl, they spoiled you all right. Now make sure you share out those toys and games,' she said, standing up.

'Why don't I keep all the toys and games together so everyone can play with all of them instead of just one each?' I asked, desperate not to have to give them away.

'As you please, but don't be selfish, that's all,' she said, not really interested. I emptied the chest and she dragged it outside into the back yard where it was to become a store for kindling wood. When we went to bed that night I put the clothes I'd been allowed to keep for myself into a drawer in a chest. The bedroom stank of stale piss. The blanket had been pulled back to dry the sheet but the window had been closed all day and the blanket was still damp, as was the mattress. I put on my spare nightdress and stared at the yellow-stained sheet.

'Let's take the sheet off and turn over the mattress. We can sleep on the blanket and fold the bottom up to cover us,' I said.

Pamela and Nunoos agreed and we stood on the edge of the iron bedspring frame and pushed and struggled to tip up the mattress but it kept falling back on top of us.

'This is no good: we're not strong enough,' moaned Pamela.

'All together now – push!' I urged and we got it up against the wall and bent over to grab the bottom edge. But then our feet slipped into the bedsprings and the wire cut into our ankles.

'Ouch! My foot is stuck,' Nunoos cried.

'Pull up now!' I shouted and put all my strength into lifting the mattress. We heaved and it slid down the wall and across the springs trapping us all underneath. Nunoos screamed, but we shushed her so Mum wouldn't hear and pulled ourselves free. We spread the blanket over the mattress, threw our pillows across the top of the bed and then climbed in and pulled the blanket up over us. 'There you are, that's better,' I said.

'Dorothy,' Nunoos whispered.

'What?' I said getting a bit fed up with her whining.

'There's a big hole in this side of the mattress too and I'm falling in it again.'

'Oh just go to sleep,' I snapped.

Pamela started to giggle and so did Nunoos and much as I tried to act annoyed and not laugh too, I couldn't stop myself.

Sunday morning and we slept in. The bed was dry – no mishaps during the night. When Mum shouted us down she told us to bring our dirty washing, so we bundled up the sheet and took it downstairs.

'Oh no! Not more pissy sheets. Who wet the bed?'

'It was an accident Mummy, I didn't mean to,' Nunoos said hiding behind my back.

'Yeh, I've heard that one before an' all. C'mon get yourselves fed and go outside to play – and you can take Little Cliffy with you,' she ordered. When we were outside Pamela suggested that we walk to Granny's house to play with Lollie and Barbara, so we followed her through the streets until we got to Manchester Road where Granny lived in a two-up, two-down that looked just like our house. We knocked on the door and Lollie opened it and let us in.

'Who's there?' Granny shouted.

'It's Dorothy and that come to play with us,' Lollie shouted back from the open door.

'I'm not having my house full of kids, so you can all bugger off and play outside.' We stood still and waited for Lollie to tell us what to do and she pulled a face and stuck out her tongue towards Granny who couldn't see her.

'I'll get my coat and call Barbara – wait here,' she said.

Lollie took us exploring up and down narrow winding streets and back alleys. A family dressed in their Sunday best hurried past us on the way to church. The parents ignored us but their two small boys with scrubbed faces and clean knees poked their tongues out at us.

'Same to you,' Barbara shouted after them, poking her tongue out. Their mother heard her and frowned at Barbara as she grabbed the boys' hands and yanked them along behind her. It started to hail – not just drops but really heavy hailstones that bounced high off the cobbled streets, then settled and spread into a bubbly white covering. It stopped as suddenly as it had started and a faint rainbow appeared in the sky, its colours faded out behind the heavy smog. Little Cliffy slipped his hand out of mine and ran into the street stamping his boots on the hailstones, and as they crunched under his feet he squealed with laughter. We all joined in until we had turned our patch of street back into shiny wet grey cobbles.

'I'm hungry – can we go home now?' Little Cliffy panted.

'Let's go to your house and play.' Barbara took Nunoos' hand in hers.

'We're not allowed to play in our house either,' I said to Barbara. I suggested that we go to our own houses and Lollie and Barbara agreed and ran off home. Pamela led the way and we walked home. It seemed further going back than when we came and we were all tired as I pushed open our front door. I heard a man's voice mumble something – it's my dad, I thought, and ran inside excited. I just managed to stop myself from running into the arms of a man who was standing in front of the fire warming himself like Pamela wasn't allowed to.

'Hello lass, you must be Dorothy back from Glasgow. Have you got Nunoos with you?' He winked at me then turned to Mum.

'She's pretty this one, Dolly,' he said. I lowered my head and looked at his shiny shoes, and then slowly my eyes travelled up the neatly pressed dark pin striped trousers and jacket. What was such a smart man doing in our home, I wondered – perhaps he's come to collect money for something? Pamela, Nunoos and Little Cliffy came into the room behind me and Little Cliffy ran up to the man with his arms outstretched.

'Hello Uncle Chalky,' he cried as the man swept him up and held him against his chest.

'Hello lad, what have you been up to, eh?' he asked looking over my brother's shoulder at Nunoos.

'I been squashing the hailstones,' laughed Little Cliffy.

'Very good lad, very good,' he said lowering him to the floor.

And then to Nunoos, 'Hello lass, you must be Nunoos.'

She stepped forward and gave him a big smile and he patted her head. I stepped back.

''S okay Dorothy, this is Uncle Chalky. He brings us nice things,' said Little Cliffy.

Uncle Chalky squatted down to our level. He smelled of some kind of spicy perfume and his cheeks were ruddy red and greasy with lots of holes in them like an orange. I didn't like his eyes – they were dark and sunken deep under his thick eyebrows.

'I've given your mum a little something for you all,' he said winking. Before he left he whispered something to our mum and patted her belly. She laughed and nudged him away, then she followed him to the door. He didn't stay for tea but he left Mum a packet of sausages and some chocolate for us to share, so I decided he was probably a good uncle after all.

Sunday night was bath night, the same as in Guernsey. We dragged in the tin bath from the backyard and Mum heated big saucepans of water to fill it. It was nice and warm in the bath beside the fire but when we got out and went to bed we were freezing and my hair was still damp.

'Does Dad ever come home to visit?' I asked Pamela.

'Yeh he came a few times before Christmas on a "forty-eight hour pass", I think he called it, and he brought us sweets and that.'

'I wish I'd been here when he came. Do you think he'll come again?'

'I want to see Daddy. When is he coming?' Nunoos chirped in. Mum stomped upstairs, threw her overcoat on top of our blanket and told us to get to sleep because it was school in the morning. I wondered if it would be okay to wear my Green Lanes school uniform even if it wasn't the same as the uniform at the new school. I wished my dad could see me in my smart uniform.

'You'll be in Lollie's class,' Pamela said as she snuggled into Nunoos' back to get warm, 'with Miss Peacock – she's a new teacher, really strict.'

Nunoos lifted her head from where it was tucked into my neck. 'Who will be my teacher?'

'Dunno, maybe Miss Blackburn but she's a really nice teacher,' Pamela replied.

'Go to sleep now both of you,' I said, remembering my friends Debbie and Kate and wondering if they'd forgotten me by now.

The next morning I felt shivery but my head was burning. I climbed out of bed and my legs felt weak beneath my weight. Mum came into the room, took one look at me and ordered me back into bed.

'You're going nowhere, my lady, you've got the flu – that'll teach you to go to bed with damp hair.' She sent Pamela and Nunoos downstairs to get dressed in front of the fire. I shivered and wrapped myself up in the overcoat but then I was too hot and threw it off. Mum came back into the room to get the overcoat so she could take Nunoos to school to introduce her to the headmistress.

'You stay there until I get back and then I'll make you some porridge and a hot drink,' she said buttoning her coat up to the neck. I nodded.

'Oh no, not porridge!' I said out loud after she'd gone, remembering how lumpy and undercooked Mum used to make porridge – it was always better when Dad made it. The outside door slammed and the house fell silent. Then I heard a man outside shouting something over and over and the clip-clop of horse hooves and the clattering of wheels on the cobbles. I ran to the window and pulled back the curtain.

'Ragbone! Ragbone! 'As got out for me?' A rough-looking man wearing a cloth cap and heavy woollen coat with the collar turned up shouted through the scarf wrapped loosely around his face. He flicked at the reins and the blinkered horse that pulled his cart, which was laden with old clothes and household junk, tossed his head and plodded forward. A door across the street slowly opened and a half-hidden woman in a dressing gown beckoned the man inside. I watched the horse to see if it would run away when he left it but it just stood still and we both waited and waited for him to come out. I came over all shivery, so I left the horse to wait alone and jumped back into bed and rolled myself up in the blanket. I lay there and listened to the echoing noises of wooden clogs pounding the street and voices shouting greetings in this strange accent that was still new to my ears. The door slammed downstairs.

'You can get dressed and come downstairs by the fire where it's warm,' Mum called up to me. I pulled on my cable-knit dress and a cardigan, some thick stockings and my slippers and pulled my hair into two bunches over my ears to keep them warm. Downstairs the fire was blazing and Mum was putting a bowl of steaming porridge on the table for me.

'Get that inside you – it'll warm you up,' she said.

'Is it lumpy?' I asked and screwed up my nose.

'Well pardon me if it is, your majesty,' she faked a curtsy.

'Cheeky mare,' she snapped and went to get me a cup of tea which she put down beside the porridge.

'Thank you,' I whispered. She tightened her lips to deny me a smile and knelt down beside the tin bath full of washing in front of the fire that flickered and glowed behind her back. I spooned the lumpy porridge into my mouth and studied her as she rolled up her cardigan sleeves and plunged her arms into the bath water to scrub the washing up and down the ribs on the wooden washboard.

I scraped my spoon around the empty bowl and licked out the hollow and then the back of the spoon until it was clean. I took my cup in both hands to warm my fingers. Mum's breathing got faster as she held up the sheet and inspected it then thrust it back into the soapy water for more rubbing. She hadn't glanced up at me – it was as though I wasn't there. She began to wring out the sheet from one end, twisting it one hand over the other and coiling it into a bucket, until the final twist when she sat back on her heels and looked up at me.

'Have you eaten it all?' she asked. I nodded.

'Are you cold?' I nodded.

'Come yer and sit by the fire,' she pointed to the fireside chair. I started to take my dishes to the scullery.

'Leave those, come and sit yer.' I climbed onto the chair and curled up with my hands tucked under my armpits. She stood up and went upstairs and returned with a blanket which she folded over me and tucked around my shoulders. I started to shiver and she put her hand gently over my forehead. She looked at me with concern and pushed a strand of hair away from my cheek, I wanted to hug her – no, I wanted her to hug me, but she straightened up and put her hands on her hips.

'You'll just have to sweat it out, Dorothy I haven't got any money for medicine.' She knelt down to her washing again. The fire had burned down and the glowing red embers had turned to grey as they cooled. She carried out the bucket-load of washing and pegged it up on a line strung between posts near the back door and the backyard gate. It was windy outside and as she opened the door I could hear the shouts of the rag 'n' bone man again and the clip-clop of his horse. The pram in the corner of the room moved and a small hand gripped the side. Leonard sat up, rubbed his eyes, and stared at me.

'Mummy!' he wailed. She came running in and the wind slammed the door shut behind her. She picked him up and swung him onto her hip and I noticed that she had a big belly again, which meant a new brother or sister. Later she emptied the bath water down the sink with a bucket and dragged the empty tin bath outside where she hung it by the handle on a big nail on the back wall of the house. The fire was nearly out.

'You'll have to go back up to bed now, Dorothy – I've got to go and join the queues for my rations so I've got something to feed you lot with.'

'Can't I stay by the fire – you could put more coal on it?' I asked.

'I've only got enough coal to warm the place for when the kids get home from school later. We're not made of money like those people you were with in Glasgow so you'd better get used to it, lady.' She pulled the blanket off and handed it back to me as she pointed upstairs. I jumped up and ducked clear of her free arm in case she followed me with a clout.

After she'd gone I stood wrapped in the blanket at the window overlooking the backyard. It was small and narrow with a path between the gate and our back door. Built against a wall to the side was our outside lavatory with a sloping tin roof and a wooden door with a gap at the bottom. Pamela's job was to tear the newspaper into small squares and push them onto a bent piece of wire that was fixed to the wall for us to use to wipe ourselves. The billowing sheets were flapping against the side of the sloping tin roof and the edges were getting brown from the rust. I looked down the row of backyards along our terrace. Shirt sleeves waved, trouser legs kicked wildly and frocks twirled and danced in the blustery wind. '*Monday's washing day…,*' I sang the rhyme to myself.

17

Starting a new school

A few days later I was well enough for school and got up with the others, feeling quite excited. I smoothed down my gymslip and straightened my hat as we walked up the street. Nunoos had been a bit quiet about school and I begged her to tell me if there was anything she didn't like about it as we walked ahead of our mum, who was pushing the pram and shouting at Leonard to get his arms inside the pram and keep his fingers away from the spokes in the wheels.

'There's this boy in my class and when we queue up to go into school from the playground he keeps kicking me in the back of my ankles and it really hurts,' Nunoos whined.

'Have you told the teacher?' I asked.

'No, but I told Mummy and she said to kick him back and don't be such a sissy, but he's bigger than me and I'm too frightened of him.'

'You should tell your teacher,' I told her.

'Mummy said I shouldn't tell tales,' she whispered. We approached the school gates and Pamela and Nunoos ran off to their classmates in the playground. Mum pushed the pram up to the main entrance and told me to wait with Little Cliffy and Leonard while she spoke to the headmistress about me. When she came back out she sent me inside and told me to wait by the headmistress's office. I found the office and waited outside twisting my finger. The door opened and a stern-faced woman held it open.

'You must be Dorothy.' Her features widened as she eyed me up and down in my smart uniform and she smiled at me.

'You'll be in Miss Peacock's class and I've sent for a girl to take you to your class. She shouldn't be long.' She shuffled some papers on her desk. I wasn't sure if I was supposed to answer, so I didn't.

'Come in Maude,' she called out to a gentle tap on the door. The girl who came into the room was wearing round glasses and a badge that read 'Prefect'. She showed little interest in me but smiled at the headmistress, who scribbled something on a piece of paper and then looked up at her. 'This is Dorothy – an evacuee. Take her to Miss Peacock's class and give Miss Peacock this note.'

She handed the note to Maude, who looked me up and down and said, 'Yes Miss Mallory,' then to me, 'Follow me.' I followed her down the corridor to my new classroom. She knocked on the door that had glass panes in the top half and I peeped into the room at all the curious faces that followed the teacher to the door.

'This is an evacuee. Miss Mallory said to bring her to your class,' Maude explained in her broad Lancashire accent to Miss Peacock and handed her the note.

'Thank you Maude, you can go back to your class now.' Miss Peacock beckoned me into the room. 'You can sit there next to Vera Crowthorne.' She pointed to an empty seat at a double wooden desk with a sloping lid at the front of the classroom. Vera shuffled along to make room for me. She smiled at me, baring her buckteeth, and looked me up and down. I slid along beside her but not too close.

'Pay attention class!' Miss Peacock was peering over the glasses that pinched the end of her beaky nose. We all sat bolt upright. She pointed with a stick to a map of Great Britain that was pinned to her blackboard.

'As I was saying earlier, this is Scotland,' she turned to look at the map. 'Now does anyone know what we call a person from Scotland?' Hands shot up around the room reaching high to get her attention.

'Well Clitheroe, stand up and tell us.' She pointed her stick at a boy at the back of the class.

'A Scot, miss, my granny told me that, she's from Fife,' he grinned.

'That's correct, Clitheroe, now sit down,' she said. Vera kept scratching her hair and I shifted away from her in case she had nits. She sniffed and dragged her cardigan sleeve across her nose leaving a clear slime on the matted wool and, noticing my look of disgust, she wiped her sleeve down the back of her cardigan and smiled at me. It was a desperate smile: I could tell she wanted to be my friend. I bet she has no friends, I thought, forcing a smile back at her.

'And what about a person from Wales, Vera Crowthorne?' Miss Peacock was leaning right over our desk. Vera jumped and stood up.

'A W-Welshman, m-miss,' she stammered.

'That's correct: now pay attention.' She struck the desk with her stick and stood for a moment twisting her mouth to one side and staring at me before returning to her map. She pointed to three small dots in the sea to the south of Britain and turned to the class.

'These are the Channel Islands and here is Guernsey which is where our new girl Dorothy *Oggyer* comes from.' Everyone was staring at me as I put up my hand.

'Yes, what is it?' she asked,

'Please miss, my name is Ogier – you say it like O*shear* not O*ggyer* – it's French, miss.' I remembered the Green Lanes headmistress saying this to me and I felt quite proud.

'Well, it's spelled like *Oggyer,* O-G-I-E-R, *Oggyer,*' she threw open her palms and the whole class chimed in with *Oggyer* and began laughing. Clitheroe shouted *Oggy Oggy Oggy* and they laughed again.

'Quiet class!' Miss Peacock snapped and they stopped.

'So, Miss *Oshear,* stand up and tell us what you call a person from Guernsey.' She tilted her head back and stuck out her chin. I stood up.

'A donkey, miss,' I replied.

'A donkey!' she shrieked, and laughed. 'Whatever next?' The class all started laughing again but stopped when she held up her hand. 'Why a donkey?'

My cheeks burned, I felt stupid. 'I don't know why, miss, my Grandpa Ogier told me we were all Guernsey donkeys but I didn't ask him why.'

'Then you must find out for me. Now sit down. Class, open your geography books to page ten.' I dropped quickly onto my seat and lowered my head. Vera shifted closer and pushed her book across to share it with me: she hadn't laughed at me. She flattened down the open page and smiled a willing humble smile at me. I smiled a real smile back. The bell rang to end the lesson and everyone began lifting the desk lids, putting their books away, and banging them shut. We all stood beside our desks and were ushered out in single file to the playground.

Clitheroe caught up with me and ran around me making *hee-haw* donkey noises and shouting *Oggy, Oggy, Oggy.* I ignored him and he got fed up and ran off. Lollie was at the far end of the playground aiming a ball at the ring of the netball post. She shot and the ball swished down through the string net. I wandered towards her aware of the other kids who pointed their fingers and stared at me.

'I'm in the netball team and I'm the goal shooter. We just played a match against Christ Church School and we won and miss said I was the best player,' Lollie boasted as I reached her.

'I wondered why you weren't in class with me. Have you seen Nunoos?' I asked.

'Nope,' she replied.

'Why are they all staring and pointing at me like that?' I asked.

'They think you're posh in that uniform and that stupid hat.'

'I'm not wearing my hat, it's in the cloakroom,' I protested.

'Yeh, but I've seen you in it and it looks stupid. You should wear normal clothes like everyone else – we don't have a uniform at this school.'

'They're just jealous,' I huffed, and strode off to find Nunoos.

She was surrounded by a small group of girls who were clapping while she sang and danced for them. She looked up and grinned at me and I waved and left her to her friends. Lollie ran up to me as the bell rang for the end of playtime and followed me back to our classroom.

'Who you sitting next to' she asked.

'Vera Crowthorne,' I replied.

'Not V-V-Vera C-C-Crowthorne?' she mimicked a stammer and laughed.

'Don't be so mean, I feel a bit sorry for her really and she's been kind to me.' I soon learned that Lollie was the class clown. She would thumb her nose and waggle her fingers from behind Miss Peacock, making everyone laugh, and she often got whacked for what the teacher called disrupting her lesson.

As we piled out of the school gates at the end of lessons for the day, Nunoos came running up to me, slipped her hand into mine and skipped along at my side.

'I've got some new friends, Emily and Sally and Mary, they are really nice.'

'That's nice,' I said, feeling a bit jealous.

'Have you got some new friends?' she asked.

'Yes I've got a new friend called Vera,' I replied, feeling guilty because she wouldn't have been someone I'd have chosen for my friend.

'Is that boy still kicking you, Nunoos?'

'No – I told the teacher like you said and now he's stopped doing it.'

'How did you like Miss Peacock?' Pamela, who was trailing behind us, interrupted.

'She couldn't even say my name properly and made the other kids laugh at me,' I moaned.

'Don't worry, the kids here don't know how to say our French names and some of them call us niggers or gypsies, but most of them are okay when they get used to you.' She began to skip in time with Nunoos and we all linked arms and skipped down the road. We pushed the door open and tumbled breathless and laughing into our house. Mum lifted my hat from my head and tossed it onto the table.

'You can leave that off now. Take the boys outside with you and play until your tea is ready and take the pram for Leonard. Go on, all of you,' she waved us out of the house.

Outside it was grey. A cold clinging dampness swirled around us but it didn't rain. I'd let Nunoos wear my red coat so she could feel posh and I felt the chill in just my blazer. Our neighbours' kids poured out of the terraced houses into the street and huddled in groups never too far from their own doorsteps. A girl aged about eleven dragged a rope across the street and a younger girl took the other end and with outstretched arms they slowly turned the rope and it slapped against the cobbles with each turn. The other kids in the street started to drift down to the skipping rope and the girls began to chant: '*I like coffee, I like tea, I like sitting on a black man's knee... Crawford's biscuits are the best, north and south and east and west....*' Boys and girls alike ran into the centre of the rope and skipped in and out again. Nunoos and Pamela joined in – they knew the words. I leaned on the pram handle and tried to sing along. The kids pushed each other in the back to hurry them towards the rope so they could get their own turn faster. Soon their cheeks became rosy as they tried to be the one to stay in the longest without tripping on the rope. Nunoos, who was sweating in my red coat and puffing as she jumped to clear the swinging rope, easily beat everyone. Doors began to open as it grew darker and mums called the kids in. I looked up the street and saw our mum waving at us too. Nunoos waved to the girls with the rope and told them she'd play with them again tomorrow if they liked and they could be her new friends. They agreed.

18

The air raid

We had potato soup flavoured with Oxo for tea again with plenty of bread to fill us up. We scoffed the lot and could have eaten more if there had been any. Mum told us that Uncle Chalky would be calling later, so we had to go to bed early. We had got used to carrying our gas masks around all the time slung over our shoulders but sometimes when we were playing we took them off and when we went to bed we had to put them under the bed just in case. That night as we clung to each other for warmth under the heavy coats the wailing noise of a siren sounded and I jumped out of bed in a panic.

'What's happening, what should we do?' I shouted.

'Quickly, put your coat and shoes and socks on, get your gas mask and go downstairs,' Pamela ordered. I did as I was told, and so did Nunoos. All around us the air was filled with this loud wailing siren and I was terrified. Mum rushed into the bedroom carrying Leonard and holding Little Cliffy's hand.

'To the shelter, come on, make haste!' She pushed us ahead of her down the stairs and out into the street. 'Dorothy, you hold Little Cliffy's hand and Pamela, take hold of Nunoos: keep running and don't you stop.' She was puffing and waddled along holding her belly with Leonard straddling her hip. People were running all the same way in the dark with little torches shining downwards to see their way towards "The Caves" – an air raid shelter built into the sandstone rocks. The loud humming of engines sounded overhead and bright searchlight beams crisscrossed the sky. We ran so fast I couldn't take a deep breath. I was being bumped and shoved by bodies but I held on tight to Little Cliffy's hand as we reached the entrance to the shelter where sandbags were piled high and people were pushing to get inside. I nearly lost sight of Mum but heard her shout out to our Aunty Elise and followed her voice down along the dimly lit tunnel lined with benches full of frightened people until I saw them together.

'Where are Pamela and Nunoos?' Mum asked looking over my shoulder.

'I don't know, I thought they were behind me.' I turned and saw Pamela squeezing between two large ladies blocking her way.

'Here they are, Mum,' I said. But Nunoos didn't appear.

'Where's your sister!?' Mum screamed at Pamela.

'She ran back for her doll Missy and you told us not to stop running so I just ran after you.' Pamela started to cry.

'Oh Jesus, she'll be killed! I've got to go and get her.' She handed Leonard to Aunty Elise and ran back to the entrance.

'Where do you think you're going, missus – you can't go out there, it's much too dangerous,' said an air raid warden who stood with his hands held outstretched blocking her way.

'My little girl Nunoos is out there, now get out of my way or so help me I'll….' She raised her fist and he stood back a bit startled, before another man grabbed her arm. She spun around and seemed to recognize him.

'You can't go out there in your condition, Dolly. Tell me where she is and I'll go for her.' Mum lowered her arm and held it to her chest breathing heavily.

'The silly little... she went back home for her doll!' She was angry but also crying and he patted her shoulder.

'Go sit with your kids, Dolly, I'll fetch her here safely for you.'

'Lend me your hat,' he said to the warden, who hesitated but then handed him his tin hat, which the man put on. He pulled up his coat collar and held it tight to his neck as he turned, then he stooped, held onto the front of the helmet and dashed out into the street. The people in the shelter turned their attention from Mum to their own kids and busied themselves reading to them and clutching them close. Further down the deep tunnel someone started playing a squeezebox and people began singing to drown out the outside noise. I went to stand by Mum and we stared beyond the soft yellow glow of the tunnel lighting towards the darkness of the entrance. I overheard someone behind us whisper that it was a long raid and I wondered how long a raid usually lasted. Mum put her arms over my shoulders and around my neck. She pulled me backwards into her hard round belly and kissed the top of my head. I turned my head to look up at her frightened tearful face and I was afraid too.

We waited for ages and Mum was muttering over and over, 'I'll never forgive myself if anything's happened to her.' Just then there was a shuffling noise in the dark. There appeared from the darkness a small pair of legs hanging beside a stiffened face staring out from under the big "W" painted on the tin helmet. The man had thrown Nunoos over his shoulder where she was hanging on to her doll and his face was white with fear. As he lowered her to her feet in front of us Mum grabbed her arm and shook her.

'Don't you ever go back when we run to the shelter, d' you 'ear?' she shouted at Nunoos who started crying, and then she picked her up and held her so tight that Nunoos tried to push herself away from her. Everyone cheered the man as he handed the warden his hat and walked down into the tunnel

'Who's that man?' I asked Nunoos later.

'That's Mr Jones. He told me he's a friend of Granny and Mum from Guernsey.'

'Did you see the bomber planes?' I asked.

'No I shut my eyes really tight 'cos I was scared but I could hear the stuff he called shrapnel falling and we had to duck into the doorways of houses. I started to cry and that's when he told me to keep my eyes shut really tight, so I did.'

The all-clear siren wailed and everyone began to gather at the entrance and walk slowly out of the tunnel. We stepped over shrapnel that was strewn all over the street but there was no sign of bomb damage to the houses. The boys picked the shrapnel up to use for collections and swaps even though their mums shouted at them to put it down and leave it alone. Dawn was already breaking; we'd been in there for so long. In the distance stood the big Wellington Mill building with its tall smoking chimney and rows of tiny square windows, all exactly the same size and set one above the other. It loomed above the workers' houses. The sky was streaked with pink, red and purple lines. *Red sky in the morning, sailors take warning...* I whispered to myself, believing something bad must happen to a sailor today. Our home was still standing and we trudged wearily inside and went straight back to bed. Mum stayed up.

'How many times does that happen?' I asked Pamela.

'Last year around Christmas we had lots of raids with houses not far away bombed and all that, but we don't have hardly any nowadays,' she shrugged casually.

'Do we still have to go to school today though?' I asked.

'Course,' she said. I stared at the ceiling remembering the time I watched the planes with Mrs Thornton, then I fell asleep.

19

Shifting house again

Mum told us at the dinner table that we were going to move to be
next to our Aunty Elise in Newton Street and the rag 'n' bone man
was going to help us to move with his horse and cart.

'Can I drive the horse?' Little Cliffy asked, jumping up and
down.

'We'll see – now don't wander off, tomorrow everyone must help,'
she said. We were to live in a converted stables building, next door
to Aunty Elise, called Newton's Whim. There was a door inside that
connected her house with ours so she could come through without
going outside. On the day of the move she came out of her house
to help carry some boxes into our house. She kept one eye shut
because the smoke from her fag was drifting into it and she twisted
her mouth in the other direction to try to send the smoke that way.
I wondered if I should tell her that if the wind changed she'd stay
looking like that – the way Vincent had told me once when I was
pulling faces into the spoon – but decided not to in case she gave
me a clout. The cart pulled up and the patient old blinkered horse
stood still and quiet amid the hustle and noise of Mum's shouted
instructions and being poked and patted by us kids. We didn't have
much, just a few sticks of furniture, and the rag 'n' bone man carried
the heavy stuff for us in return for some bits that we had no room
for in our new house. This was set back from the main road down
a smaller street that reminded me of the High Street in Guernsey
but with fewer shops and there was a church at the end. It had two
bedrooms upstairs, on each side of the tiny landing – one for the
boys and the other for the girls. The windows already had black out
curtains. Downstairs was one big room that the front door opened
into. It had worn-out grey linoleum around a square of threadbare
patterned carpet. Mum set the fireside chair and old heavy sofa close
to the cooking range and fireplace to make it look cosy. Outside in
the back yard was a lavatory, a coalbunker and in a lean-to building

at the back of the house was the scullery with a big square sink. Mum pushed the table and chairs close to the wall beside the scullery door. In the far corner of the room she put a single bed for her to sleep in. She draped two blankets from the ceiling beams to the floor as curtains for some privacy.

Over the next few days Mum got into decorating the living room to freshen up the brown stained wallpaper. She mixed up some whitewash and brushed it on the walls and when it had dried she dabbed all over the wall with a big scrunched up rag soaked in green paint. She was dabbing her last bit of wall when the baby started to come.

'It's coming but it's too early, bloody hell! Dorothy go and get Aunty Elise, make haste!'

'The baby's coming!' I shouted as I flung open the connecting door to Aunty Elise's house. She was standing at her sink. She wiped her wet hands on her pinafore and rushed in behind me. Mum was making short puffing noises and leaning back in the chair.

'Go to the end of the street to Mrs Hattersley's – it's the big house on the corner. She's got a telephone. Tell her I sent you to ask her to phone the doctor. Go on, run,' she pointed to the door. The kids were playing in the street and Pamela shouted after me as I ran past, 'Where are you going?'

'The baby is coming – go back. I'm going for the doctor,' I puffed. She ran back and when I got home again I joined my brothers and sisters who were standing around our groaning mum, eagerly waiting for the baby to come out. A puddle appeared on the carpet between our mum's legs and it got bigger as we stared at it.

'Look! Mummy's peeing on the floor,' Little Cliffy said, pointing at the puddle.

'Go outside and play until after the doctor's been.' Aunty Elise shooed us away.

'How will the doctor get the baby out of Mummy's belly, Dorothy?' Nunoos asked.

'Don't ask me, maybe he makes a hole and pulls them out,' I shrugged.

'Or maybe he'll pull it out of her belly-button, Nunoos,' Pamela chipped in.

I watched Nunoos as she dropped her chin and poked her finger into her belly-button through her jumper and after a little while she looked up at me and frowned.

'Does your belly button get bigger when you grow up then, Dorothy?'

I shrugged at her. The doctor came and then an ambulance and our mum was taken away. We all chased the ambulance until it turned out of our street and then we walked slowly back to Aunty Elise who was standing on the pavement with Leonard in her arms.

'You all come next door to me for your tea and Dorothy, you'll have to keep an eye on the kids for your mum until she comes home, d'you 'ear?' I nodded. The next day when she got back from visiting Mum in the maternity hospital she told us we had a baby sister but she was a bit small and had to be kept an eye on. Leonard stayed with Aunty Elise for the next few days and we had our meals in her house. We slept in our house and I was in charge but Aunty Elise left the connecting door open for us if we needed her. We had no school – it was summer holidays and we went to the park near our house to play on the swings or just played in the street. Nunoos showed Pamela and me how to do a crab. She did a handstand against the wall and gradually walked her legs down the wall until her feet were flat on the ground then she walked away on the palms of her hands and her feet, arched over backwards like a crab. Pamela copied her but my feet kept sliding sideways down the wall. Then Nunoos tucked her skirt up into the sides of her knickers and showed us how to do cartwheels. I failed at that too.

'Look I can suck my toe,' Pamela said as she sat down, pulled off her shoe and sock and pulled her foot up to her mouth with both hands to suck her big toe.

'Bet you can't do this then.' Nunoos sat on the ground and lifted her ankle with both hands and hooked it behind her neck. Pamela tried but couldn't get it quite high enough. I told them both they looked stupid and I didn't even try it.

We asked Aunty Elise at teatime when Mum and our baby sister were coming home. 'In a few more days, she needs the rest,' she said.

Mum stepped out of a taxi on the following Sunday. She was carrying a bundle wrapped in a shawl. The others ran out to meet her but I stood back and waited. She looked tired and thinner as she stood surrounded by her scruffy kids jumping up to try to look into the bundle.

'This is your new sister Sheila,' she said, lowering the baby to their eye level. They peered into her tiny face and she started to yell. Uncle Chalky came to see Mum and wanted to hold the baby but every time he picked her up she bawled and after a while he stopped coming around anymore. Sheila cried a lot over the next few months and Mum got tired and fed up with her and soon she was being dropped into the pram behind Leonard for me to take outside with the others so we weren't under her feet.

20

An accident in the park

Nunoos held on tightly as she stood up on the swing seat. It was swinging so high that it seemed to stop in mid air as the chain fixed to the seat slackened then got tight again on the downward swing – we called it "going up to the rattlers" because the chain gave a little rattle as it tightened. She was laughing and shouting, 'Look at me Dorothy,' just as Lollie appeared through the park gate.

'Hey, I just saw you and shouted out to you in the town market, Nunoos, why didn't you answer me?' Lollie called out to her.

'I wasn't in the market, I been here all the time,' she shouted back.

'You're a liar, I know it was you,' Lollie insisted.

'No I'm not – tell her, Dorothy!' She wasn't swinging so high now.

'She's been here all the time,' I told Lollie.

'Well you've got a double then,' shouted Lollie.

'What's a double? I haven't got a double – tell her, Dorothy'

'Well there's that girl I saw coming over, she's right behind you – look.' Lollie pointed and Nunoos turned her head quickly around to see. Suddenly the swing twisted, she lost her grip and she tried to jump off but fell backwards. We heard her head crack on the ground and she lay there quite still for a moment. Lollie ran to help her but Nunoos came to her senses and picked herself up and ran home crying.

By the time we reached our house Mum was standing on the doorstep with her hands on her hips. I pushed the pram up to the doorstep.

'What's happened to Nunoos? You were supposed to be looking after the kids!' She lifted her hand and I ducked and slipped by her to go inside. Nunoos was lying on Mum's bed in the living room behind the curtain and I pulled back the curtain to sit on the bed beside her.

'Why did you run away?' I asked.

'Because I was frightened of that "double" girl,' she replied.

'That was just Lollie teasing you, she wasn't really your double,' I said laughing at her. 'Did you cut your head? Is it bleeding?' I asked trying to look around at the back of her head.

'No, but Mum says I've got a big bump, and it hurts a lot.'

That night Nunoos had bad headaches and over the next couple of days she began to vomit and got a temperature, so Mum brought her downstairs from our bed to hers to keep an eye on her and sent for the doctor. While we waited for the doctor, Aunty Edna – our dad's sister who had also been evacuated to Stockport – came to visit and she went to sit with Nunoos to talk to her. Suddenly Nunoos began to scream and we rushed over and gathered around her bed.

'I can't hear you, Aunty Edna! What are you saying, why can't I hear you?' Aunty Edna gave our mum a worried look and patted Nunoos' hand to comfort her.

'The doctor is here,' Aunty Elise called as she came through to our house and Mum sent us kids outside so he could examine Nunoos. I stood in the open doorway to hear what he said and the others gathered around me.

'She's a very sick little girl, I think it could be meningitis,' he said, shaking his head as he came out from behind the curtain. 'She'll have to be isolated and taken into Cherry Tree Hospital immediately. I'll arrange it straightaway.'

'Is Nunoos going to die, Dorothy? I don't want her to die,' Pamela whispered. I quickly shook my head.

I started to miss a lot of school that autumn because I had to look after the babies when Mum went to the hospital to visit Nunoos. Sometimes the truancy man from the school would call but I had practised how to look really sick and tell him my Mum had gone out to buy medicine for me. It usually worked.

'Can Nunoos hear you speaking to her yet, Mum?' Little Cliffy asked after she had come back from a visit to the hospital.

'No not yet, but I gave her a little pad and pencil and we write each other little notes.' She patted his head.

'Can we go and see her?' Pamela asked.

'No. Children aren't allowed to visit and she's still in isolation and that means even I can't go in to see her.'

'How does she read your notes if you can't see her?' I asked.

'I write them and press them against the glass window of her room and she writes her answers and presses them against her side of the window. Go out and play now until your tea is ready.' We didn't have much to eat since Uncle Chalky had stopped coming around with stuff for us. And since we'd moved away from Great Edgerton Street we didn't even get free vegetables from our old neighbour Mr Unwin's allotment any more. Mum got extra eggs and milk for the baby and also because she was breastfeeding, so we had lots of milksop puddings – bread and margarine soaked in warm milk – but I was getting a bit fed up of that. We were all happy though because we'd just been on a visit to the Red Cross and Mum had kitted us all out in shoes and coats for the coming winter weather.

21

A welcome visitor

Outside it was grey and cold and it was raining hard. We were sitting on the floor huddled around the coal fire colouring in the few remaining pictures of my bumper colouring book from Glasgow. Little Cliffy had already scrawled over some of the pictures, which spoiled the end result after I'd spent time carefully trying to ignore the scrawl and keep colouring within the lines of the drawing. Mum was next door having a cup of tea and a chat with Aunty Elise so she didn't hear the tap on our front door or see it slowly open.

'Daddy!' Pamela shouted and ran to him. Our dad was standing there grinning broadly at us, raindrops dripping from his nose and chin. He didn't look like the picture in the silver frame in Glasgow at all, as his uniform wasn't nearly so smart. On his head a cap was tilted to one side and it looked too small for him; his jacket was thick brown army issue with a wide belt with a tin helmet and a long slim pouch hanging from it, and over his shoulder was slung a rifle with a long strap that he held with one hand. His other hand gripped a kit bag which he lowered to the floor to free the arm that swept up Pamela. He gave her a kiss on her forehead and was suddenly surrounded by all of us; the younger ones held up their arms to him and jumped up and down. He lowered Pamela and knelt down circling us all in his arms. I flung my arms around him and buried my face into his neck. It felt cold and wet and his jacket smelled of cigarette smoke. As I pulled back to look into his face he laughed and said, 'Here, I've got something for all of you.' He dug into his pocket and handed us each a small cone shaped paper bag with a twist at the top.

'Cor, Dolly Mixture sweets, thanks Dad!' Pamela yelled after untwisting the paper and looking inside the bag.

'Have you got some for Nunoos?' I asked. 'She's sick, Daddy, she's in hospital.'

'I know Dorothy, Mummy wrote to tell me and I've come to see her, love.'

Mum came through from Aunty Elise's and stood for a moment with a look of shock on her face, then she smiled and came over to our dad. As she reached him he stood up and she grabbed his rifle strap and reached for his hat and took them from him. 'You'll catch pneumonia standing around in those wet clothes. Get upstairs and change, there's some dry clothes in the wardrobe in the boys' room,' she fussed. He patted my head and followed the direction of her pointed finger. When he came down we bombarded him with questions about had he killed any Germans and Little Cliffy wanted to shoot his gun. Mum asked him if he'd be getting leave at Christmas but he shook his head and told her they were being sent overseas after this leave.

That night Pamela and I slept downstairs on the single day bed and Mum and Dad slept in our double bed. They got up late.

Aunty Elise looked after baby Sheila overnight. We were all hovering around the door at the bottom of the stairs waiting for our dad to come down but none of us were brave enough to go upstairs for him in case we got told off by Mum. When they got up he lit the fire and Mum cooked him eggs on toast and we were allowed to toast the bread for him over the fire. Little Cliffy dropped his piece of bread onto the coal and it was black, but Dad told him, after he'd scraped it off and eaten it, that it tasted great.

They went to the hospital after breakfast and we went next door into Aunty Elise's because our fire had gone out. Little Cliffy stood with his nose pressed against the front window staring down the street waiting for them to come home.

'Here they come,' he shouted, and Pamela and I rushed to look out of the window. We had to rub away the steamed-up patches from Little Cliffy's breath. They were walking slowly and Mum had linked her arm through Dad's arm. His hand was dug deep into his trouser pocket. He looked down at the pavement as he took a drag on the rollup fag cupped in his hand and held between his first finger and thumb. We ran outside and down the street and circled them, dancing, as though they were a May Pole.

'Did you see Nunoos, Daddy? Can she hear yet?' I asked, tugging his sleeve and tilting my head to look up into his face.

'I saw her but she couldn't hear what I was saying, no.' He pinched the top of his nose, screwed up his eyes and gave a small sniff.

'Get inside, all of you and I'll light the fire. Go on, make haste,' Mum shouted. Our dad disappeared upstairs for a while and when he came down we were soon climbing all over him again and asking questions about our sister. His eyes were red and puffy and he got a bit cross with us after a while, so we left him alone and went outside to play in the street. We had the best tea that night that we'd had for ages – a stew with neck of lamb and vegetables, the thick juice tasting of beef Oxo, and for pudding jelly made with gelatine mixed with raspberry drink and covered in custard. We kids licked our pudding plates clean – I'd forgotten all about table manners – and asked if there was any more. There wasn't. We were packed off early to bed and Mum and Dad went next door to spend an hour with Aunty Elise. The next morning they were up early as Dad had to get to Manchester to catch a train and Mum was going with him to the station. He gave us all a kiss and a hug and they were smiling at each other and our whole family was happy.

We waved and shouted 'Cheerie Dad' as they walked down the street and he turned to wave back to us. Mum leaned her head against his shoulder as they turned the corner and disappeared onto the main road.

Mum was a bit moody and angry for a while after he'd gone. Sheila still cried a lot and it got on her nerves. We were always hungry because Mum's food rations didn't seem to go far enough and sometimes she would just sit staring into the fire, ignoring Sheila's screaming. Aunty Elise told her she had the baby blues and it would soon pass.

The following week after we got in from school Mum was putting away her rations and she looked pleased with herself. 'I've spent most of the bloody day standing in queues for this lot. My feet are killing me and my back is aching but I've done us proud this week,' she grinned.

'I'll help you put it away, Mum,' I said trying to sneak a look into a bag as I lifted it from the table.

'And me I'll help,' Pamela shouted as she pushed another bag across the table towards our mum after having a quick root around inside it for treats. A brown paper bag next to Mum slid off the table. There was a soft-sounding splat and Mum looked slowly down at her feet. A yellowy slime was seeping out of the paper bag on the floor.

She screamed at Pamela 'You stupid…bloody…little… that's our week's supply of eggs gone…I'll bloody swing for you!' She raced around the table reaching for Pamela who jumped clear of her raised hand and ran to hide behind the sofa. Mum chased after her and grabbed the poker from the hearth before she pulled the sofa aside and held Pamela by her shoulder. The blows were swift and uncontrolled as she beat into Pamela's back as though she was beating a rug. Pamela screamed out in pain. I just stood there, unable to move or speak.

Little Cliffy screamed and pulled at our mum's skirt, 'Stop it Mummy, stop it, you're hurting Pamela!' I quickly came to my senses and ran for Aunty Elise who rushed back after me and grabbed the poker from our mum.

'Dolly, for Christ's sake!' she shouted. Mum just stared at her for a moment then fell to her knees in a crumpled heap and sobbed into her hands. Aunty Elise hurried Pamela and Little Cliffy next door to her house and I left Mum alone to cry while I cleaned up the smashed eggs. Pamela had to stay off school until the bruises had faded. They were told she had mumps and the man from the school board didn't want to get close enough to her to check. Mum was really sorry and tried to be extra nice to Pamela for a while afterwards but Pamela became wary of her and tried to keep a safe distance whenever she got angry.

22

Nunoos is sent away

Aunty Elise had been babysitting with us and she smiled at Mum who wearily stepped in through the front door. She had just come from the hospital and we ran to her, eager for news of our sister. 'How is she?' Aunty Elise asked as Mum dropped her shopping bag to the floor and unbuttoned her coat.

'They've cured the meningitis,' she answered.

We jumped up and down and cheered 'Hooray!' Mum gave us a quick smile and turned again to Aunty Elise. 'That was the good news. Anyway, when I got there the Matron told me she was out of bed and dressed and I could go into the ward today. Nunoos was all smiles and called out to me when she saw me at the door. She tried to run to me but she was a bit unsteady on her legs because her muscles are weak from being in bed all that time. They've been teaching her to walk again. They told her that her meningitis was cured and that she didn't need to be isolated any more, so she was expecting me to take her home with me. As soon as I sat down next to her bed she wrapped her arms around my neck and she squeezed so tight she nearly bloody choked me. So anyway, after we had a long hug I lifted her so she could sit on the bed. I'd just started to help her to pack up her things when the matron came over and said the doctor wanted a word with me.' Mum covered her mouth with her hand and swallowed hard. We moved closer to her and waited for her to continue but she didn't speak. Aunty Elise grabbed her arm.

'What is it Dolly, what did he say?'

'He told me that she'd remain deaf from the illness and that they were sending her to a special school for deaf and dumb children in Manchester.'

'Manchester, that's a long way to go to visit her, Dolly,' Aunty Elise said.

'Oh, I'll manage that, Elise, but it broke my heart to have to write her that note to tell her she wouldn't be coming home.'

We'd all gathered so close around Mum that we were almost touching her. She started talking again.

'When I went back and sat on the bed beside her she couldn't sit still, she was trying to put her doll Missy into my bag and telling me how she wanted to go home to play with her brothers and sisters.'

'Poor little love,' Aunty Elise whispered.

'Poor Nunoos,' Little Cliffy said, and Mum nodded.

'So I shook my head at her and scribbled down what the doctor had said on a piece of paper. I had to hold it in front of her face so she'd sit still and read it. She read it, looked up at me and slowly read it again. The happiness drained from her little face, her eyes filled and she gazed up at me all confused and hurt. Oh Elise, I'll never forget that look. "But it's nearly Christmas, Mummy," she said to me in a quiet voice with tears streaming down her cheeks. "You told me I could come home for Christmas if I was better and I'm better now – the nurse told me yesterday." "You promised, you promised," she kept saying over and over between big sobs.' Aunty Elise steered Mum to a chair to sit down. We followed and knelt down on the floor around her feet. 'Even though she couldn't hear me I kept telling her that I was sorry and that I didn't know about the deaf school,' Mum sniffed. 'But then the matron came over and told me I should leave so they could calm her down. Oh Elise, it broke my heart to leave her. She was straining to pull her hand out of the matron's grip and calling out to me, "Please Mummy, take me with you, please Mummy don't send me away!"'

'Over and over she called out to me.' Mum clenched the hanky in her fist. 'I turned back but the matron shook her head and waved me to go.' Mum wiped her eyes and blew her nose into her hanky and Aunty Elise patted her shoulder. I moved away from them all, went to the old sofa and slumped down into it with my hands clasped in my lap. Pamela flopped beside me and as we looked at each other I could see the sadness in her eyes. I put my arm around her and she leaned into me.

'Don't cry Mummy,' Little Cliffy said, tugging at her sleeve. She put her hand around his head and pulled him against her.

'I'll make us some tea,' was all she could say as she heaved herself out of the chair and went to hang up her coat.

'We'll talk later when the kids are in bed,' Aunty Elise whispered to her through the scullery door as she went back through to her house. There was a heavy sadness in our house and we ate our tea in silence except for baby Sheila's quiet sniffs for air as she suckled on our mum's breast.

23

A visit to Nunoos

Christmas went by and was just like the ones we'd had in Guernsey except that Dad and Nunoos weren't there. We got second-hand toys. There wasn't much food in the house and we didn't have a Christmas tree, but most of all we missed Nunoos. Still, we played with Aunty Elise's kids and we all visited our dad's sister, Aunty Edna. After that we called on our cousins at Granny's. By the end of the day we had eaten something at everyone's house and the grownups had drunk plenty so they were in good spirits. Everyone knew though that it was at these family gatherings that Nunoos would have been the star attraction, put in the centre of the room to sing and dance and entertain to cheers and clapping from us all.

By the summer of 1942 there were fewer air raids and people were beginning to get back to a life as near normal as possible. Some had even stopped carrying their gas masks around with them even though they would get told off by the warden. Every two weeks Mum travelled to Manchester to visit Nunoos and on her return we hurried down the street to meet her to find out about our sister.

'She's been asking all the time to see you all and they've told me that I can take you to see her on my next visit,' Mum replied to our usual questions.

'Can I come too, Aunty Dolly?' asked Winston, Aunty Elise's son, who'd been playing marbles in the road with Little Cliffy and ran to greet her with us.

'I s'pose so since your mum will be minding Leonard and Sheila for me,' she replied.

He ran inside to tell his mum and we followed our mum into our house with questions about how far it was and how long did it take to get there until she got fed up and sent us outside again to play.

On the day of the visit we were up early and I squeezed into my sailor dress, which was getting too tight across the chest and arms. Pamela put on what used to be *my* pale blue frock and it fitted her perfectly. We brushed each other's hair and she tied a ribbon I'd saved from Glasgow into mine to make a ponytail. She was wearing my shiny black shoes because they didn't fit me any more and I had to wear my Red Cross lace-ups. Little Cliffy was dressed in his best jumper and shorts but he was complaining that his sandals were hurting his toes so Mum got him to take them off and she cut across the toes with a knife. When he put them on he wiggled the toes that were poking through the hole and ran to show Winston. Aunty Elise came through followed by Winston and Little Cliffy. Winston's hair had been smoothed down into a side parting and he was all dressed up in his Sunday-best. Mum handed her Sheila and she came to the door and shouted after us 'Mind you take care of my Winston. And you be a good boy for your Aunty Dolly, Winston.'

Through Stockport town I held Winston's hand and Pamela held Little Cliffy's as we ran to keep up with Mum who was hurrying to catch the train. When we arrived at the station Granny and Lollie were waiting for us and we clambered aboard just before the hissing steam and high-pitched whistle signalled it was time for the train to leave.

'You look posh,' Lollie said to Pamela and me as we sat squashed together on the seat.

She was getting big and tall for her age and had outgrown the dress handed out from my trunk last year. 'I just put this on: my mum said it was tidy enough.' She held open her cardigan to show us her school gymslip. We rocked from side to side as the train sped along making the fields and buildings outside the window flick by like an old movie.

'Yer we are, Manchester,' Granny shouted as the train slowed to a stop. A porter opened the door and we jumped down onto the platform behind Mum and Granny.

'This way, make haste,' Mum called back to us as she strode out into the sunshine of the street. People were hurrying in every direction yet nobody banged into each other. A tram rattled past with a row of faces looking out of the windows at us. There were soldiers standing beside a bookstall on the corner reading paperbacks. The bombing raids had left a tall building across from the station with a front wall and windows but nothing behind it and no roof. In other places were just piles of rubble next to buildings that seemed undamaged. We stayed close as we walked behind Mum and soon we came to a park with a pond. A statue of a man on a horse was high up on a stone base with seats underneath it. Set back from the road beside the park the school building was almost hidden amongst tall trees.

'That's the deaf and dumb school over there,' Mum pointed to the gate near the road. 'Now Granny and me have do some messages in town, so after you've visited your sister Dorothy, I want you to take the kids to play in the park until we come and fetch you. If you're all good, we'll take you to that British Restaurant across the street from the park for a treat.' I nodded to show that I'd understood. We followed her through the gates and up a long drive to the school's main entrance. Inside a teacher came up to us and smiled as she recognized our mum.

'Hello Mrs Ogier, are these Edna's brothers and sister come to see her?'

'Yes, but Grace and me have to go to do some messages in Manchester so could you take them in to see her for me? We're in a bit of a rush today.' She put her hands on my shoulders and pushed me forward.

'Yer's Dorothy, she's my eldest, she's in charge.'

The teacher nodded and smiled at us.

'Follow me, children,' she said, and we skipped alongside her, eager to see our sister. Along the corridors there were small kids making strange noises to each other and I felt a bit scared of them. Winston heard them too and gripped my hand. The teacher opened a door to a large room with wooden tables and chairs spread around them for visitors. I spotted Nunoos over in the far corner with a fair-haired girl about the same age who nudged her and pointed at us. Nunoos' face lit up and she came running over to us with her friend close behind. We laughed and hugged each other and she didn't want to let go of me.

'Oh, I'm so happy that you've come to see me. I've missed you all so much,' she said, beaming at us.

Winston pushed himself closer to me and looked around the

room staring at the kids waving their arms about, tapping their hands with their fingers and making strange noises.

'These kids are making grunting noises and they're scaring him, Nunoos,' I said. Her friend turned to face her and began tapping into Nunoos' palm. She waved a pointed finger around the room, all the time making the same sounds as the others. Nunoos nodded to her that she understood and gave me a disappointed look.

'It's not their fault, they can't hear themselves making those noises, Dorothy. I can't hear them but my friend can with her partial hearing. Her name is Sybil Wilson. When you talk she will sign for me, but she can't speak – she's dumb.'

Sybil smiled at us. She was quite a pretty kid, with hundreds of pale freckles. Nunoos told us all about how she'd got in trouble when she first arrived at the school because she told them she wasn't a bed wetter but she wet the bed the first night and was moved to a different class and dormitory. She told us all about how they spent their days with afternoon naps and visits to the park and sign language lessons in the classroom.

'When she first met me, Sybil thought it must be really hot where I came from 'cos I'm so brown. She asked me if we have coconut trees. Do we Dorothy?' I just shrugged. We mostly just let Nunoos do the talking as she had lots to ask us about, like what we were doing at home, but then she started to cry and said she wanted to come home with us. The teacher saw her crying and came and told us it was time we were going. We had long hugs and told her we'd visit again next time but she kept crying and as we walked away I saw Sybil put her arm around her and they both waved to us.

'Cheerie!' we all shouted and waved to her as the teacher closed the door to the room and ushered us out of the main entrance.

'I don't like those kids, they're scary,' said Winston as we trudged down the long drive.

'That means you don't like our Nunoos and you're just a silly scaredy cat,' Lollie snapped at him and clipped him around the back of his head.

'Ow! I'll tell Mum of you,' he shouted and rubbed his head.

We came out of the gates and turned into the park and went to find some swings to play on. Winston ran on ahead of us and called out when he'd found them way back behind some trees. Lollie caught him up and snatched the swing out of his hands. He tugged at it but she jumped on the seat and started swinging so he let it go.

'Dorothy, she took my swing and I had it first!' He started to cry, but I could tell he was putting it on.

A small girl on the swing next to Lollie's stepped off and gave it to him and ran over to her mum who was sitting on a seat under the statue. They took turns, on the swing, Winston and Little Cliffy, one pushing and one swinging, until they were bored with that and Pamela, who was on the other swing, said she was getting hungry. I'd been keeping an eye out for Mum and Granny but they hadn't shown up yet. Winston was hugging his swing and wouldn't let Lollie have another turn so she started turning him around and around making the ropes twist above his head until he had to duck and the swing lifted up from the ground.

'Oh tell her to stop, Dorothy, I want to get off,' he whined.

'Wheee!' Lollie laughed and let go of the ropes sending Winston spinning really fast until he jerked to a stop. He jumped off but this time he really was crying and he ran up to her, fists flying and boots kicking.

'Ooh I'm scared,' she laughed, then pushed him away and ran off.

'You're such a sissy, Winston,' Pamela sneered.

She turned towards me. 'Hey Dorothy, maybe we should go across the road to the restaurant and see if they're already there?' I waved to Lollie to come back and asked her if she thought we should go to find them and she agreed.

'I'm not coming if she's coming,' Winston pointed at Lollie.

'Please yourself,' she said and walked on ahead towards the road. Pamela, Little Cliffy and I followed but Winston just sat on the grass with his arms folded. I kept looking back as we got nearer the road and he was getting smaller in the distance but he hadn't moved.

'He'll follow us in a minute – you'll see,' Lollie said.

We crossed over and walked down the road until we came to the restaurant. We cupped our faces in our hands and pressed them against the steamed-up windowpanes. We could see people seated at tables tucking into plates piled high with food. Close to the window, a big table had a three-tier cake stand – just like Mrs Thornton's – in the middle of it, each tier with a layer of different cakes. I peered around the room but I couldn't see Mum and Granny anywhere. Lollie volunteered to go inside and look for them but I thought we'd better go and get Winston and wait in the park. We ran back to the park and over to where we had left Winston but he wasn't there.

'Everyone split up and go look for him and shout out if you find him, then we'll meet up at the statue,' I told the others. We began calling out his name as we looked behind bushes and around tree trunks in case he was hiding from us.

'Winston!' we shouted from our different search areas until we all ended up back at the statue without him.

'Aunty Elise will go mad if he's lost and Mum will give us a hiding. This is your fault, Lollie,' Pamela said. There wasn't anyone around to ask if they'd seen him so I suggested that we go to the restaurant so Mum and Granny could help us to find him. Outside the restaurant Lollie pushed open the door and tipped her head to one side to tell us to follow her in. We stood in the open doorway and searched the room for Mum and Granny but they weren't there. A man came over and looked down at us with a frown on his face.

'Do you have any adults accompanying you?' he asked.

'Yeh, but we can't find them, mister, *and* we've lost our little cousin in the park,' Lollie explained.

'Yeh, mister, and he's only four and he might have drowned in the pond for all we know, eh?' Pamela added.

'And he's my best friend,' Little Cliffy added.

The man stopped frowning and looked concerned as he turned to Lollie. 'Have you searched for him?' he asked.

'Yeh, but the little sissy's just disappeared,' she replied with a cocky grin.

'What's his name?' he asked.

'Winston, Winston Churchill,' Lollie answered, grinning again.

'Clear off you silly girl!' he shouted pushing her and us out of the open door.

'But wait mister, he really is called Winston Churchill.'

She tried to turn to face him but he closed the door behind her. Then he quickly opened it again.

'If it's true then go and tell a policeman.' He slammed the door and we stood in silence for a few seconds.

'Let's go find a policeman then,' Lollie said and we followed her along the road looking for a policeman. We didn't have long to wait before a policeman came out of a side road pushing a bicycle. He was wearing a helmet with the strap resting on his chin as though it didn't fit properly.

'Hey, mister policeman!' Lollie called out and ran across the road to him.

'Hello there lass, what's the problem?' he asked, leaning down towards her. We quickly crossed the road to join them and we all tried to talk at once.

'One at a time,' he protested holding up his hands. So Lollie took charge again.

'We've lost our little cousin in the park.' He took a black notebook and pencil out of his top pocket, licked the tip of the pencil with his tongue, and gave Lollie a very serious look.

'What time was it when you lost him?' he asked getting his pencil ready to write.

'I dunno,' Lollie replied.

'Hmm, all right, who saw him last?'

'Er I dunno,' Lollie replied.

'Hmm, well perhaps you *do* know his name, lass?'

'Winston Churchill, his name's Winston Churchill, isn't it?' She grinned and turned to us so we all nodded. He closed his notebook and started to put it back in his pocket.

'Run along home now and stop wasting my time. Don't you realise there's a war on... now get off, all of you!' He was really angry.

'Please mister, that really is his name, his mum is our Aunty Elise and she lives in the house next door to us in Stockport. Please can you help us to find him?' I pleaded. 'Pamela thinks he might have drowned in the pond.'

He looked at me, narrowing his eyes and I could see he believed me. 'Come on then, hurry up, let's see if we can find the lad,' he smiled, and we ran alongside him as he pedalled his bike along the road towards the park. As we got near to the statue we spotted him.

'There he is!' Pamela shouted and pointed to Winston sitting alone on the seat under the statue. She ran over to him and I turned to the policeman.

'Thanks mister, we've found him now,' I said.

'That's good lass, now don't you let him out of your sight again.' He shook his head and chuckled. 'Winston Churchill, well I never, the lads at the station won't believe this one.' Just down the road I could see Mum and Granny struggling with bags as they approached the park. I had to get the policeman to go before they saw us with him.

'Our mum's coming, we'll be all right now,' I smiled and he rode off still shaking his head and chuckling. We all swore not to tell anyone about losing Winston. Even Winston agreed after Lollie told him that if he didn't she'd give him a good whack. Mum told us we'd have to hurry to catch the train and we didn't have time to go into the restaurant. So, hungry and disappointed, we held hands and trudged along behind her and Granny.

24

Robert the rabbit

The following year Little Cliffy had started school in the September intake and was getting bullied. Mum told him he'd have to learn to fight his own battles but he had a gentle nature and he'd decided he would just have to learn to run fast to escape the bullies. It seemed that we were getting poorer than ever – we were often hungry and our clothes were the scruffiest in the street. The first time Little Cliffy got bullied was when he didn't have a shirt to wear under his jumper, so Mum pulled out one of my party frocks with a rounded collar and short puff sleeves that Pamela had outgrown and made him wear that, tucked into his shorts. She said that because the frock had a white collar it would look like a shirt above the neck of his jumper. He pleaded with her not to have to put it on but she raised her hand to him and he shut up. After school that day he was crying as he ran out to me at the school gates where we'd been waiting to take him home with us.

'What's up?' I asked.

'We had a games lesson in the playground and the teacher made me take off my jumper because she said I'd get too hot,' he sobbed, 'and the boys laughed and said it was a girl's blouse.' He dragged his sleeve under his nose and wiped the palm of his hand across his eyes. 'She made us run around, then the skirt of your frock dropped down out of the legs of my shorts and they all pointed at me and shouted at me calling me a sissy in a girl's frock.' Pamela started to laugh and I gave her a quick frown as I gave him a hug.

'I bet you looked funny though,' she said and laughed again. I tried not to look at her but couldn't help it: she was doubled over. I clamped my lips together to stifle any laughter but my cheeks filled up and I couldn't hold back, I just burst into laughter too.

'It's not funny, don't laugh!' Little Cliffy looked at us, surprised and hurt. We covered our mouths to try to stop. I looked at Pamela

– her eyes were merrily screwed up, her face was red and she was struggling to hold in her laughter.

'Don't laugh!' I finally managed to shout to her from behind my hand. Her eyes were watery and she turned away from us and bent over holding her belly. Then out it came, she gave a roar of uncontrolled laughter. I couldn't stop myself. I took my hand away and doubled over with laughter too. Poor Little Cliffy was really puzzled but then he caught our mood and started laughing too. As we walked home he pulled the skirt down his legs to show us what had happened and made us laugh even more.

Little Cliffy had made friends with a boy of around his age who lived nearby. He was called Edward, a cripple in a wheelchair and an only child. Little Cliffy used to go around to his house after school and during the holidays. On his way home from Edward's one day he met us coming back from the park. He was kicking the toe of his boot against the kerb edge and looking gloomy. His boots had come apart at the stitching around the front and had opened up. Whenever this happened we would say our shoes were "laughing".

'What's up?' I asked.

'Edward is going away with his mum to live with her sister because his dad's been killed in the war.'

'Maybe a new family will move into their house and you can make a new friend, eh?' I said.

'No,' he snapped, 'his mum said the house is being closed up until they come back one day.'

'There's no need to get shirty with us,' Pamela told him. I pushed the pram and he lagged behind as we headed home. Mr Jones was there when we went inside, having a cup of tea with Mum and Aunty Elise. After he left, Mum told us he'd called in to ask after Nunoos and to bring them the news he'd heard at the Stockport Channel Islands Society meeting. It was about the families still in German-occupied Guernsey, but there was no news of our grandparents, who were there. Most of the people who'd been evacuated to Stockport from the Channel Islands went to these meetings but Mum didn't go because she said she'd heard it was all poetry reading and churchy types – not her kind of people. Mr

Jones patted us all on the head and hurriedly left almost as soon as we'd stepped inside.

'I've got a secret, Dorothy,' Little Cliffy whispered to me as we played in the street a few days later.

'What is it?' I asked.

'You've got to promise you won't tell anyone else.'

'I promise. Now what's the secret?'

'Edward gave me his pet rabbit to look after. He's called Robert and he lives in a hutch in their backyard and every day I pick weeds and grass to feed him but I need someone to help me get more food for him because I think he's hungry.'

'Does anyone else know he's there?'

'Just me, I creep in the backyard gate so nobody sees me. I'll take you tomorrow but don't tell the others.'

I agreed not to tell. The following afternoon we slipped away pretending to the others that we'd been sent on an errand for Mum. We walked up through the narrow back alley between the backyards of the terraced houses until we came to Edward's house.

'Keep a look out for me,' Little Cliffy said as he lifted the latch and half-opened the gate to slip inside, then he grabbed my arm and pulled me in. There was a large wooden rabbit hutch with old lino draped over the top to keep out the rain. Robert was huddled in the corner until he saw Little Cliffy, then he hopped up to the wire mesh and pushed his quivering pink nose against it. Little Cliffy lifted his jumper and pulled out handfuls of grass and some carrot and potato peelings from our dustbin and handed them to me. He opened the hutch door and carefully lifted out the pure white rabbit.

'Hello Robert,' he said burying his face in its fur. He set it down on the ground and let it run around the yard but it came back when I dropped the peelings on the path.

'Will you help to find more food for him, Dorothy?'

'Of course I will. Can I hold him after he's finished eating?' In the end everyone in our house except our mum and the other grown-ups knew about Robert the rabbit because I always had to take them everywhere so they weren't under Mum's feet but we were all sworn to secrecy. For weeks we rooted through the dustbins up the backyard alleys to find any kind of vegetable waste for Robert and slipped in and out of the backyard to feed him every day. The house had been boarded up and nobody seemed to go there but us. We took turns cuddling Robert while Little Cliffy cleaned out his hutch, and he would even sit on Sheila's lap in the pram so she could stroke him and nuzzle into his fur. Back at our house I would stop at the door and put my finger to my lips and remind them it was a secret before we went inside.

I'm not sure how, but Lollie found out and wanted to come with us, and we let her come as long as she didn't tell. It was getting hard to find food because often we only had bread and Marmite ourselves and Robert didn't like that much. Leonard had decided he was a rabbit and kept hanging his hands like paws in front of his chest and screwing up his nose to show his front teeth and asking 'What's me?'

'A rabbit,' we all got fed up of answering and once Pamela said 'A dog!'

'Where have you lot been sneaking off to every day?' Mum asked as we sat around the tea table. I nearly choked on my bread.

'Nowhere special, to the park and that,' I lied.

'So why have you been seen looking in people's dustbins then?' She had her hands on her hips, her chin was dropped and she was looking straight at me.

'Oh, we were just playing a game lifting the lids and banging them down,' I lied again. She just tut-tutted and went back to the scullery. Our eyes darted guiltily from one to another around the table then quickly back down at our plates. Leonard was sitting in his high chair with his hands like paws screwing up his nose as she came back into the room and she looked at him quizzically.

'Eat your tea Leonard!' I snapped at him and he dropped his paws, a bit startled.

The next day Mr Jones passed us on his way to Mum's as we headed off on our secret mission and he waved. We'd decided to feed Robert in the mornings because later in the day people were at home and might catch us looking in their dustbins. We gathered what we could and Lollie had pinched some vegetable leaves out of someone's allotment so we had a feast for Robert. As we were leaving Robert, Lollie eased open the backyard gate to sneak back out into the alley but suddenly she slammed it shut.

'Bloody hell!' she gasped, and turned to face us. 'Mr Jones is in the alley and he nearly saw me.' I shushed her and we all kept quiet until his footsteps had faded into the distance, then we quickly crept out.

'Phew! That was close,' Pamela said, and we all nodded.

'Do you think he was following us?' Little Cliffy asked.

'Nah! He lives near here so this is most likely a short cut to his house,' Lollie replied. We headed off to the park and I thought about Nunoos as we stood on the swings and "went up to the rattlers."

The following Sunday we had played on the park all day and were tired and really hungry as we piled through the door and slammed it behind us.

'Mmmm I smell chicken, yummy,' Pamela said sniffing into the air of the living room.

'You can get the table laid, tea's nearly ready,' Mum called from out the back as she came through from Aunty Elise's.

We hadn't enjoyed a meal so much for ages and Little Cliffy asked for seconds but there was none left.

'That chicken was smashing, Mum' Pamela said licking her lips.

'That wasn't chicken… it was the rabbit you've all been feeding. Mr Jones fetched it and skinned it for me,' she scoffed. Little Cliffy dropped his spoon into his empty dish, stared at her in disbelief and his eyes grew as big as saucers… the colour drained from his face and he clasped his hands over his mouth.

'Oh no! Mummy, you killed Robert and made me eat him for my tea, I hate you! You're wicked! You're wicked!' He burst into tears and ran outside retching. Pamela held her stomach and her mouth tightened as a single tear rolled down her cheek. She pushed her plate away and turned to me with a look in her eyes that brought a lump into my throat and although she didn't speak, I understood the pleading question in her eyes: 'How could Mummy do that?' I slowly shook my head and she jumped up from the table and ran outside after Little Cliffy.

At the sound of "Robert" Leonard did his rabbit pose and asked 'Who's me?'

I stood up and shouted, 'Shut up Leonard, not now!'

'You needn't think you're going anywhere, lady, there's dishes to wash.'

I glared at her, 'He loved that rabbit, we all did, he was our pet and we were looking after him for Edward. I hate that Mr Jones.'

'Well I'm the one who sent him to find it. Look my girl, there's a war on and people are hungry, our food is rationed and I'm bloody struggling to feed you. As far as I'm concerned that rabbit is doing more good in you kids' bellies than sitting in some cage in a backyard!' She stormed outside and sent Little Cliffy, still sobbing, to bed and told Pamela and me to get up there too after we'd washed and dried the dishes.

25

Little Cliffy's shoes

Little Cliffy was sitting on the step outside our front door. He was wearing my old school hat because he'd been playing cowboys and Indians with some boys in our street. His grazed knee was bleeding and he was peeling back the leather upper from the toes of his "laughing" boots – it came right back to touch his laces.

'How did you do that?' I asked him, pointing at his knee as I squeezed out through the door behind him into the street.

'The sole of my boot peeled back under my foot when I was chasing the Indians and I tripped over,' he said, looking up at me.

'Come inside and I'll clean the blood up for you.' I held out my hand to help him up.

Mum was angry with him. 'Look at those boots: they're only fit for the dustbin and you've only had them a few months, I can't bloody keep up with you,' she clipped his ear and knocked off his cowboy hat. 'It's Monday tomorrow, you'll just have to stay home from school until I can find you something to wear, but Christ knows how I'm going to do that. Anyway you can take them off now and stay indoors.'

Pamela and I went to out to play after our tea and wandered up one of the back alleys behind our street; the dustbins were all out waiting for collection the following morning. Pamela lifted a lid and poked around inside the bin then she plopped it down and looked in the next one along.

'What are you looking for?' I asked.

'Some boots for Little Cliffy – maybe someone's kid has grown out of his and his mum has thrown them in the dustbin.'

'That's a good idea, I'll help you.' We took a side of the alley each and dug deep into ashes, wet potato peelings and other smelly rotten stuff, feeling around for a boot or shoe. We had no luck and had reached the end of the alley when Pamela pulled out a woman's shoe which had a heel but was a small size. She held it up while she rummaged for the other one and found it deep in the bottom covered in ash and dust.

'These might fit him 'cep' they're a lady's – oh well, they might fit us for when we play dressing up, eh Dorothy?' I took them so she could wipe her hands down her cardigan front and I saw they weren't even worn out, had laces tied over a tongue and the thick heel was quite high. It was getting late and there was that Sunday-evening quiet in the streets because all the kids were inside – it was bath night. We hurried home for ours.

'Where did you get those shoes?' Mum asked when she saw them in my hand. I had wiped them over with my sleeve – they were brown and quite shiny.

'We found them up the alley and kept them for playing dressing up,' Pamela answered.

'Give them yer and let me see if they'll fit me,' she said beckoning to me. I walked over to where she was sitting in the armchair with Sheila on her lap and she got up and put Sheila in the pram in the corner before sitting down again. She kicked off her old worn slipper and tried to slip her foot into one of the shoes.

'These are bloody small, she must have been a midget, shame 'cos they're like new.' She kicked it aside but then picked it up and examined it for a while.

'Come yer Little Cliffy, and try these on.' She turned her head to where he was sitting at the table watching us.

'Mummy those are girls' shoes. I'm not wearing those,' he protested.

'You get yer or you'll be sorry,' she shouted and he quickly came over and stood in front of her. She made him pull his socks up tight before lifting his leg and pushing his foot into the shoe. It slipped on easily and she tugged at the back of it to see if it was too loose – it wasn't. 'Put the other one on and turn around,' she ordered. He did as he was told and grew instantly taller as he wobbled about on the heels. 'Go and fetch me the bread knife, Dorothy.' I went to the scullery and returned with the knife. Mum was standing at the table holding down one of the shoes on its side. She took the knife and began to saw across the heel until it broke off, then she repeated this with the other shoe. 'Try them on now and turn around again,' she said looking pleased with herself as she handed them to Little

Cliffy. He sullenly did so. The heels weren't cut level and he was a bit lopsided but at least he wasn't so high off the floor now.

'There you are: that's you sorted out for school tomorrow. Now get ready for your bath. Dorothy, help get the tin bath indoors,' she ordered.

The next morning as Little Cliffy walked sulkily ahead of us on the way to school, Pamela began to imitate his lopsided wobbling but every time he turned around she stopped so that he wouldn't catch her doing it. She did this all the way to school and soon I started to join in her game and we giggled together as we wobbled along in an exaggerated way. 'Stop it, it's not funny,' he shouted at us as he whirled around trying to catch us but we froze just like when we played statues.

'We weren't doing anything,' I lied, and covered my mouth so he couldn't tell I was trying not to laugh.

'I know what you're doing 'cos I seen you in that shop window we just passed – you're copying me walking funny in these stupid ladies' shoes.'

'Do you mean like this?' Pamela said, and threw her knees out wide and tipped her shoulders from side to side. I couldn't hold it in any longer and screeched with laughter – she looked so funny. This just encouraged her and she jerked her bum from side to side as well.

'Shuddup, I bloody hate you!' he shouted and ran off ahead to school. After school ended that day we waited for him at the gates and he came running out to us.

'You're not wobbling any more,' I said.

'I know, that's because the old man who's the school caretaker saw me and he took the shoes into his shed and fixed the heels and made them straight for me.' As we walked home we played "Old Mother Riley" – the game where you have to say "Old Mother Riley says do this" – and put your hand on your head, or your knee, or skip or jump and everyone does it but if you just say "Do this" and do something without saying "Old Mother Riley" first and someone does it then they are out. Little Cliffy kept getting out and soon got fed up and ran off when he saw a boy he knew in our street.

26

The Yanks

Things were changing in our town since the "Yanks" had arrived and they were often seen driving around in their strange cars without doors called "Jeeps". They threw sticks of chewing gum down to us as we chased their huge lorries, shouting "Got any gum chum?" They were always smiling and waving to us and I liked their light-beige uniforms better than my dad's or even Vincent's. The Yanks wore tight shirts and trousers and a badge on the collar of their jacket had two letters – GI. Aunty Elise's friend Ruth had moved in to live with her and they spent a lot of time in our house talking about the Yanks and giggling like schoolgirls. Shortly after Aunty Ruth – as we were to call her – had moved in next door, Granny also moved into a house just a couple of streets away. The three of them and Mum would sit around at our house drinking tea and saying what they'd like to do with some of those *gorgeous Yanks*. They started to go out every Friday and Saturday night, although each week one of them would stay home to take a turn minding the kids. Aunty Ruth gave us her old wireless because she'd been given a better one for her and Aunty Elise. They would dance, twirling each other around in our house to Glenn Miller and his band on the Forces programme that played all the latest American bands and then they would go into the town.

'You ready yet, you?' Aunty Elise shouted as she tottered into our house on her peep-toed high heels one Friday night. She'd let down her long hair which she usually wore scooped into a crocheted hairnet called a "snood", which lots of ladies wore during daytime. Her flower-print cotton frock was belted at the waist to show off her slim figure. Our mum came downstairs wearing a dark blue frock with white polka dots that Aunty Elise had lent to her and her hair was as smooth as she could make it by wearing rollers all day. Her shoes had a lower heel and an ankle strap that was cutting into her flesh. She had reddened her lips with beetroot juice and paled her face with powder.

'Hurry up Dolly, I want you to do my legs before we go,' Aunty Elise said, kicking off her shoes and climbing up to stand on our table as Mum came into the room. She handed Mum an eyebrow pencil and pulled up her frock. I watched Mum start high up her leg and carefully draw a line from her knickers down to her ankle. She poked out her tongue as she concentrated on keeping it straight.

'How did you make your legs so brown, Aunty Elise?' I asked.

'I use a permanganate of potash mixture, my love,' she replied.

'Oh,' I said, without a clue of what those big words meant.

'There that's you done. Get down – now you can do me,' Mum said, straightening up and handing back the pencil. As they changed places and she climbed up on the table the door opened and Granny came in looking smarter than I'd ever seen her. Her hair was swept up into a "victory roll" and her lips and cheeks were bright red – a bit like a clown's. Her frock was black with big buttons down the front and her feet were squashed into wedge-heeled peep-toe shoes.

'You look pretty, Granny,' I said and she peered at me through her thick round glasses and smiled.

'You can do mine next Elise,' she said peeling off her shoes as she sat on the sofa. It was Aunty Ruth's turn to babysit and she came through with Sheila in her arms to see them off.

'If you can't be good, be careful and don't do anything I wouldn't do,' she laughed as they stepped out into the street. They giggled, waved and told her not to wait up for them. I watched my mum walking down the street with her hands out to her sides, palms facing down and fingers daintily stretched out and thought I'd never seen her walking so ladylike before.

It was late and everyone had gone to bed when I heard loud talking outside our house – then I heard our front door open and a man's slurred voice downstairs. I thought my dad had come home so I ran downstairs to greet him. I stood and stared at my mum who was holding up this soldier to stop him falling over and she was laughing and calling him darling and kissing him. She turned and saw me standing in my nightdress and said, 'Get back to bed, Mummy wants to talk to her friend.' I crept back upstairs and lay on the bed listening to the mumbling and squeaking sounds that floated up from below.

For some reason we started to get different food to eat. My favourite was frankfurter sausages that came in a tall tin you could heat up in a pan of water if you poked a hole in the top. Their thick skin was brown and the meat in them was pink and smooth. Mum would sometimes come home with tins of spam, which was pink too and salty and she fried it for us with mashed potatoes. It was good to not feel hungry as often as we used to. Mum still went to visit Nunoos every two weeks and once a month Lollie, Pamela and I went to visit her on our own.

'Does she eat frankfurter sausages in here?' I once asked Sybil, Nunoos' friend, who signed the question for her. Nunoos nodded and said she liked the smoky flavour of the sausages and licked her lips. Sometimes on our visits we would sit around at the table and she would try to show us how to do sign language. She was getting good at it and her fingers flicked across her palms and her hands flashed around in the air. The noises didn't bother us any more and we would end up laughing when we made mistakes with our fingers and she would tell us what we had just wrongly "said". Every time we left she began to cry because she wanted to come home with us, but she wasn't allowed and we all ended up feeling sad.

'Hello young lady, what's your name?' asked a handsome black man in a navy-blue uniform with silver braid on his shoulders and his peaked cap tucked under his arm. Mum had brought him home from Princes Street where she and our Granny and Aunty Ruth had been waiting for the men to come out of the cinema after the films had finished. I had been asleep on Mum's bed downstairs waiting for her to come home and they had awoken me.

'This is my daughter Dorothy,' Mum answered in her poshest voice before I had a chance to open my mouth. 'What are you doing down here – you should be upstairs, darling.' My eyebrows rose and I thought – *darling* – she's never called me that before, she usually only calls her men friends that. 'Sit down Abe, and I'll make us some tea.' She tiptoed daintily in her new way of walking to the scullery and left me in the room with him.

'You have lovely long hair, Dorothy, just like my little girl back home in the States,' he said in an American accent. 'I have a picture of her here in my wallet, I'll show you.' He took out his wallet and showed me a photo of a girl around my age with waist-length dark flowing curls like mine; she was sitting on his lap and they were smiling. Beside him sat a slim dark lady with a pretty face and long wavy hair, with a small boy of about two on her knee. Mum came back into the room to see what we were talking about and glared at me as she sat beside him. He talked about his family and how much he missed them and then he sighed, looked at his watch, stood up and said he had to go. Mum tried to snuggle up against him and threw me a glance casting her eyes towards the stairs so I'd leave the room but he held her away and slipped out of the door.

'Bloody hell Dorothy! Why do you always have wait downstairs? He was bloody lovely. Get to bed!' I ran upstairs and smiled to myself, glad that I'd spoiled it for her.

'My mum says your mum's a whore,' shouted a girl a few doors down the street whose mum worked at Kay's of Reddish. Kay's was a manufacturing firm that made cough mixture, firelighters and flypaper but since the war came it had started making sticky bombs for the soldiers to throw at tanks and they would stick on them and blow them up. I ran towards the girl pushing the pram up to her doorstep and she darted inside her house. 'She goes out whoring up Princes Street – everyone knows,' she shouted through the crack in the door that she was hiding behind.

'No she's not, your mum's a whore,' Pamela shouted and ran up to kick at the door that the girl had slammed shut.

'Come on, ignore her,' I called to Pamela and we walked on.

'What's a whore?' she asked, holding onto the pram handle.

'I don't know but it's something bad I reckon.' I decided I'd ask Aunty Elise when we got home.

'Where did you hear that and who were they talking about?' Aunty Elise asked, puffing on her fag, tilting her head and eyeing me suspiciously.

'Oh, I just heard one of the kids saying that word in the playground, I don't know who they were talking about,' I lied.

'Well it's a woman who goes about with a lot of men but it's not a nice word so don't you start saying it, d'you 'ear?' I nodded and ran outside to tell Pamela about the word but I didn't tell her about the men who came to our house at night.

The following Saturday night I was curled up in Mum's bed downstairs when I heard her shushing a noisy man's voice outside the front door.

'Not inside… let's go around the back,' she said in a loud excited voice. I ran through to the window overlooking the backyard, which was lit by the moonlight. I watched the gate swing open and she pulled a tall skinny soldier inside. He had to duck his head to get through and he closed it behind them. He staggered as she pulled him around and up against her as she leaned on the gate. Then she was hidden behind his towering frame.

'Whore, you're a whore, just like she said,' I whispered under my breath pulling the curtains across angrily before creeping back upstairs to bed.

'By Christ, I nearly broke my neck having a shag in our backyard last night. He was so tall I had to stand on the bloody dustbin,' Mum laughed to Aunty Elise the next day as I laid the table for tea. They were sitting on the sofa and as Aunty Elise's eyes darted across to me, Mum turned around to follow her eyes and lowered her voice. 'I didn't bring him inside because she's nosy and waits downstairs for me to come home.' Her voice dropped to a whisper, 'It's because of her doing that, that I'll never know if it's true what they say about black men.' She winked and nudged Aunty Elise, then laughed.

'Dolly! You shouldn't talk like that in front of her, she's just a kid.' Aunty Elise took a hairgrip out of her hair and squeezed it onto the end of a rolled up fag that was burned down almost to her fingertips. She held the hairgrip between her thumb and finger and tightened her lips so they wouldn't get hot as she took a couple more drags out of it before stubbing it out.

'You'll be sorry when Dad finds out you've been a whore,' I snapped at Mum.

'Well he won't if you don't tell him, will he?' She spoke to me differently these days – not like a child but like a grown-up. I suppose I'd taken the job of looking after the kids off her shoulders but that didn't make me a grown-up and I didn't like the way she made me part of her dirty secrets. Pamela came running in from outside carrying Leonard in her arms, he looked pale and limp. Mum jumped up straight away and took him out of her arms.

'What have you done to him?' she scowled.

'Nothing Mum, honest. He just started being sick in the street and then he fell down and didn't move.' Aunty Elise ran out to call for the doctor and while he examined Leonard on the downstairs bed we kids had to wait outside in the street.

'He's got to go to hospital 'cos the doctor thinks it's shingles but he's going to be all right, so stay outside and play, all of you,' Mum told us, after she'd seen the doctor out. Mum wrote to tell Dad about Leonard and after what seemed like ages she got a letter back from him. She sat down and read it then passed it to me to read. It had lots of blacked-out words. He wrote that he missed his kids, that he thought about us all the time and was longing to see us all again, and that he hoped Leonard would be better soon. We handed it around and everyone wanted to read it over and over until it became tatty and crumpled from our grubby hands.

27
Another brother or sister

'Oh Dolly, you're not!' Aunty Ruth said, holding her hand over her open mouth. 'What about Cliff – he'll kill you when he comes home. Are you sure?'

'I think I've had enough kids to know when I'm in the family way.' Mum sighed and patted her belly. I'd been kept home from school to mind Sheila while she went to the hospital to see Leonard and I was listening as I made them a cup of tea in the scullery.

'How far gone are you?'

'About six months judging by the way I'm feeling. At first I kept trying to tell myself I was just a bit late but as time went on I just had to get used to the idea.'

'Who's the father?' Aunty Ruth asked.

'I can't remember his name, I was too drunk.' She bit her bottom lip and glanced at me as I came into the room with their cups of tea and she nudged Aunty Ruth as I handed them the cups.

'She keeps giving me these looks, Ruth – as though she's mother bloody superior, and I'm some wicked sinner,' she rolled her eyes upwards.

'Well, now Dad will find out you've been a whore, that's for sure, and that just serves you right,' I spat out, quickly stepping back as she raised her hand.

'Get outside and play, school's nearly out and the truancy man from the school won't be around this late – go on, get out you cheeky little mare.' I stormed outside and sat on the front doorstep with my chin in my hands thinking about what would happen to us kids if my Dad killed her as Aunty Ruth said he would, and I remembered the fights in Cornet Street.

It was a week later when someone bumped me from behind and I stepped into the road nearly into the path of an oncoming lorry. Luckily it was travelling really slowly. People were standing three or four deep on the pavement waving and cheering at the cavalcade of old lorries towing trailers adorned with ribbons and flowers. A couple dressed up as the King and Queen and some other grown-ups were sitting on the back waving at the crowd. It was the annual Stockport Carnival and Lollie and I had sneaked off without the others to watch as it drove into Greek Street. She pulled me back to the kerb. There must have been hundreds of people lining the street and everyone was smiling and happy for a change. After it had passed by, everyone began to cross the street chattering away and some of them went into the Nelson Pub opposite to where we were standing. We decided to go home and I stepped into the road again to let a lady pushing a pram go by on the pavement. I peeped into the pram, to see the baby, which was sound asleep.

'Guess what? Mum's having another baby,' I said to Lollie who was walking with one foot in front of the other, arms outstretched, balancing on the kerb edge.

'That's funny, so's mine,' she said, 'I heard her telling Aunty Elise.'

'Yes but it's not my *Dad's* baby my mum's having. She made it with a soldier and Aunty Ruth told her that Dad's going to kill her when he comes home from the war and finds out she's been a whore.' I was standing still now staring hard at her to try to make her see how frightened I was.

'What's a whore?' she asked. I told her what Aunty Elise had told me. 'Well then my mum must be a whore too because my dad's in Guernsey, so she couldn't have made a baby with him, eh?' She had turned to face me and she shrugged. 'Anyway my dad wouldn't kill my mum – he's too scared of her, and he wouldn't hurt a fly him. I wonder if I'll get a brother or sister this time?' She thought for a moment, a pointed finger under her chin, then said, 'A brother, yeh, I like my brothers best.' She grinned at me. 'I'll race you to my house.' And she was off.

A month had passed and Leonard was cured of his shingles and back home from the hospital and Mum was looking after him. That meant I was allowed to take Pamela with me to visit Nunoos on our own. We were sitting around the table at the Deaf School with Nunoos and her friend Sybil. Pamela had gone to the lavatory when I said 'Mum's having another baby, Nunoos,' and Sybil smiled at me then signed it for her.

Nunoos looked puzzled and said, 'I know that already, I saw that Mummy's belly was big with her coat undone when she came last time. I asked her if she was having a baby brother or a baby sister for us this time, but she just told me she didn't know, and that the baby wasn't our daddy's. I didn't understand what she meant. What did she mean, Dorothy?' She raised her eyebrows and twisted her mouth to the side.

'She made the baby with a soldier on the dustbin in our back yard.' I whispered this to Nunoos and Sybil's eyes widened before she signed to repeat what I'd said.

Nunoos said 'Oh,' but I don't think she really understood. We talked about other things, like school and life in our street; then later as we signed to say goodbye and I gave her a hug, she started to cry again.

A few days later I was crossing the high street to the butchers shop with Mum and as we were heading towards the back of the queue a voice called out to us. 'Here love, you can go in front of me, I know what it's like standing around in your condition myself. When's it due?' A round-faced lady in a broad-rimmed hat and heavy coat smiled at Mum. She was holding a newspaper and a shopping bag, the same as our mum and all the other ladies in the queue. Ladies often let the ladies in *the family way* with a big bump go in front of them when they were waiting in long queues.

'Thanks missus – about three weeks or so,' Mum replied, stepping in front of her. I shuffled in alongside Mum.

We were quite near the front of the queue and someone further back called out to the lady, 'How do you know she's pregnant, it wouldn't surprise me if she had a cushion up there just so she can jump the queue.' It was the mother of the girl who'd said our mum was a whore. The kind lady and Mum turned to see who was calling out. Mum turned and pushed the bag and newspaper at me then strode up along the queue to face her. She pulled open her coat and lifted her smock to show her large bare round bump.

'Call this a cushion, you cheeky mare?' She glared at the lady.

'Well I'd say it's a lucky dip as to who's fathered that, seeing as your old man's away serving overseas,' she snapped back.

'Baise mon tchou!' Mum shouted and stomped back down to her place near the front, ignoring the whispers and mutterings of the other women and leaving her accuser looking puzzled. Mum winked at me and grinned and I covered my mouth with my hand to hide a smile. She had just spoken to her in Guernsey patois and said 'kiss my arse!' We shuffled inside the shop as two women came away from the counter and pushed past us through the open door.

'Yer, give me that newspaper,' Mum said and I handed her the sheets of paper as we approached the counter.

'Sorry Dolly, that was the last of it, no more tripe and the mince ran out ages ago.' The butcher smiled apologetically as he handed a wrapped packet to the lady in front of us. She stuffed the packet into her bag as she pushed past us to the door and Mum looked really fed up. I was glad because I hated tripe and onions and I gave the butcher a big smile. His counter was bare, and big empty steel hooks hung from the ceiling beams behind him. The butcher winked and smiled at me as he reached down under his counter where he had some meaty bones in a tray.

'Here Dolly, this is all I've got – you could make the kids some soup with these.'

'Oh you're a darling, Fred, yer wrap them up in this.' She handed him the paper but then she remembered the lady behind us and turned around to face her.

'You should have these really, missus, you let us in front of you.'

'You need them more than me ducks, we'll manage – I'll sort something out.' She smiled and waved us along as we left the shop. The disappointed ladies still waiting outside began drifting away from the queue grumbling to each other as they crossed the road. Mum grabbed my hand and we hurried home with our bones.

Mum gave us our new baby brother two weeks later. We'd all been asleep when she went to the new Maternity Hospital at Stepping Hill in the middle of the night. Aunty Elise looked after us until Mum arrived home on Friday morning a week later and showed us baby Terence. He was tiny and pale with fair downy hair and he was sleeping. She wrapped him up warm against the chill in our front room and put him in the corner, in an old wooden crib that Aunty Ruth had given her.

Terence was a good baby and he hardly ever cried except the time when he screamed solid and Mum told us he was constipated. We put our fingers in our ears to block out his yells as she came through from the scullery holding a piece of white soap shaved to a long narrow sliver as big as her little finger. She picked him up from his pram, sat down on the sofa, laid him on his back on her lap, and opened his nappy so it rested on her leg. We stood in front of her wondering what she was going to do. Pamela knelt down and stroked Terence's hair to try to calm him. His face was dark red with the strain of crying and the veins stood out on his head. Mum held his ankles in her left hand and lifted them up as she pushed the sliver of soap up into his bum. He straightened his legs and stiffened still screaming as mum pulled out the soap.

'There!' she shouted, as a thick yellowy spurt shot out of him. She scooped it up with his nappy and his crying changed to a sniffle.

'There Terence!' we all repeated and clapped our hands.

'Who's that screaming?' Aunty Elise asked as she came hurrying into the room.

'Terry was constipated and Mum made him better,' Pamela replied.

Aunty Elise touched Mum on the shoulder and leaned forward to whisper loudly in her ear so she could hear her over Terence's sniffles. 'Grace has had a baby girl – Ruth just told me. She was round at Grace's house when she started her labour and she went with her to the Maternity Hospital.' Then she spoke in a normal voice to us kids: 'Your granny's had a baby girl.' Once again she leaned over to whisper closer to Mum's ear, 'She's quite dark, and Ruth reckons the father is that black GI who was stationed at Heaton Moor last year.' Mum just nodded as she had the nappy safety pin clenched between her lips. Aunty Elise straightened up and said out loud, 'And both Granny and the baby are fine.' Our mum had changed since she'd brought Terry home – there were no more nights out with Aunty Ruth and no soldiers coming to our house. Our mum wasn't a whore any more and she was much nicer to us. She told us that our dad was in Burma fighting the "Japs" and when we asked what a Jap was she told us they were men with slitty eyes and yellow skin who were fighting against our dad in the jungle. But when Pamela asked her if she'd told Daddy about our new brother she didn't answer her.

Hardly any air raid sirens sounded over Stockport after the D-Day landings in Europe in June 1944. Aunty Ruth was in mourning for Glenn Miller – she was a big fan of his band's music. She told Mum that his plane had gone missing on its way across to France to entertain the troops. Mum shook her head and agreed it was a terrible shame and made her a cup of tea to calm her down. As winter approached the grown-ups would sit around the wireless in the evenings listening to the man from the BBC, who spoke proper English like the King. He told them the latest news of the war, like losing the battle of Arnhem in September, but as Christmas came around again it seemed as though we were going to win the war. It got dark earlier but the street lights were much brighter than they used to be; this was called "dim-out" instead of blackout. Mum told us we were going to get extra sweet rations for Christmas and she was to get an extra eight pence allowance for meat rations but that it wouldn't amount to much. On Christmas Eve the bombing over Stockport started again and we had to rush to the shelter. These were different bombs called V1-bombs – later we called them "doodlebugs" – and one landed in Garner's Lane, where two houses got flattened and hundreds of houses had windows smashed from the blast. Mum told us she'd heard a man had been killed.

On Christmas morning we were all worried another bomb would drop so Mum made us wear our boots and warm woollens and told us to leave our coats by the door even though she had made up a fire and the room was warm. Pamela and I got crayons and colouring books, Sheila a rag doll and Terence a knitted teddy bear from Father Christmas. The older boys got marbles and were warned to keep them away from Terence so he wouldn't choke on them. We had a big tray of corned beef and potato hash, all crispy and brown on top, for dinner with carrots and Oxo gravy and we each had a small bag of sweets. Our dad's sister Edna, Aunties Ruth and Elise and Granny came around bringing food and also our cousins came to play with us. Mum gave Aunty Elise a packet of fags and Aunty Ruth gave Mum a pair of nylons she said she'd got from a generous Yank and laughed as she waved them in the air. They drank booze, sang songs and the house was a crush with people and everyone seemed happy. The women passed Terence around kissing him and saying they wished they could take him home with them.

The new V1-bomb raids meant we had to start running to the shelter again when the sirens went but mostly the doodlebugs were flying over us and heading towards Manchester. We started using Granny's Anderson shelter in her back garden instead of running to the "Caves" but it was always cold and damp in her shelter with water up to our ankles. In the end we sat huddled together in the cupboard under our stairs. We used to listen to the drone of the bomb's engine and were told that as long as it didn't stop and it droned off into the distance we were safe. So once we heard it fading away we'd come out of our hiding place even before the all-clear was sounded. One night I couldn't sleep and as I stared into the darkness I heard the familiar drone of a flying bomb – it was faint but getting louder. I ran to the window and pulled back the curtain straining my neck to try to see above the rooftops. The sirens began to wail and I could hear our mum rushing upstairs to get us. I hid behind the curtain and pressed against the window as she shouted through the door for us to get downstairs into the cupboard. I didn't move when Pamela hurried the others downstairs still half asleep: I just stared up into the sky. At first the noise was overhead and then it passed over our house. I could see the flames shooting out behind the bomb as it droned on into the night sky but then the droning suddenly stopped. It was silent and I knew the silence meant it would drop from the sky. I held my breath and waited for a big explosion. My body stiffened; I was frozen to the spot waiting… suddenly I let out a scream as a hand gripped my shoulder and dragged me away from the window. It was Mum.

'Come away from that window and get downstairs.' She was pulling me down the stairs behind her when we heard the explosion and we both froze on the stairs for a second before diving into the cupboard.

'Were they aiming for our house, Mum?' I asked when she was tucking the younger kids into bed after the all-clear.

'No, they are after the viaduct 'cos the freight trains that cross it have tanks and big guns on them. They're heading to the ports to load them onto the ships and the Germans want to stop them from reaching there. It might only hit us if it went off course a bit but that's what the siren is for, to warn us, so you stay away from that window in future, d'you 'ear?' She stood up and wagged her finger at me. The next day Aunty Elise told Mum that the bomb had hit a building owned by the railways but it was only used for storage and nobody was killed.

28

Terence is taken away

By the time our new brother Terence was nine months old he had a head of blonde curls and was always smiling at everyone. Leonard was growing now and he drove Little Cliffy mad because everything he saw Little Cliffy playing with he wanted to take from him. There was lots of snatching and pushing and Leonard would run crying to Mum and Little Cliffy would get a clout because he was older and should know better. As I walked down the passage past Aunty Elise's open adjoining door I overheard Mum telling Aunty Elise that she'd written to our dad to tell him about Terence and was waiting for him to write back. Aunty Elise told her it was probably for the best because he would find out in the end so she might as well get it over with and give him time to get used to it. That night in bed I told Pamela what I had overheard and she said our dad would love Terence like we all did once he came home and saw him. But I couldn't help remembering Aunty Ruth's words: 'He'll kill you!'

It was a few weeks before Mum heard back from our dad – it was a Saturday. She stood on the front doorstep shifting from one foot to the other, nervously waiting for the postman to reach our house. He stopped in front of her and shuffled through some envelopes until he came to the aerogramme addressed to her. We dropped out of the skipping game. Pamela stood close to me and we watched our mum as she took it and went indoors, closing the door.

'Shall we go and see if it's from Daddy?' Pamela asked.

'No let's wait and see if she calls us. C'mon, let's carry on playing out here for a bit longer,' I said and we walked back to the other kids. She didn't call us in.

'Let's go in to see if Daddy is coming home,' Pamela said tugging at my sleeve and making me go all out of time with my rope-swinging. The girl jumping the rope in the middle of the street winced as the rope smacked against her ankle. She stamped her foot, put her hands on each hip and glared at me.

'Sorry, I've got to go in now,' I said, dropping the rope. I let Pamela pull me to our doorstep and we looked at each other – neither of us sure if we should go inside. I turned the knob and pushed her in front of me – Mum wasn't there but we could hear her and Aunty Elise's voices coming from the passage. Mum was shouting – she sounded upset and scared.

'He says here in his letter that he'll drown the little bastard and that's after I get what's coming to me. He's going to kill me, Elise! What am I going to do, he might come back from the war at any time without warning me?'

'Who is Daddy going to drown?' Pamela whispered as we stood as quiet as we could in the open doorway.

'Our baby brother Terence, like he drowned the kittens, and I think he's going to give our Mum a hiding and kill her too,' I whispered. We stared at each other. Pamela's face drained of colour and it was as though she had turned to stone, with her eyes fixed into an empty stare – I could tell she wasn't really looking at me any more. I shook her shoulder. 'Pamela don't do that, you're scaring me.' She blinked and gave me a puzzled look. 'You always do that when bad things happen – why don't you just cry like the rest of us?' I said.

'I don't know what you mean. Do what?' she asked.

'You know, you stare into space and go strange and scary.'

'No I don't!' she shouted.

'You do!' I shouted back. Mum came through from next door, she was clutching the crumpled aerogramme and her eyes were red and watery.

'What's all this shouting? You'll wake up Terence – get outside and play, both of you.' We turned and ran outside, back towards the girls skipping in the street, but we didn't join in with them – we walked on a little further and sat down on the pavement.

'Should we tell a policeman what our dad's going to do to our baby brother?' Pamela asked, staring at the cobbled street. Her chin was resting on her knees, her arms were wrapped around her shins and she rocked gently back and forth.

'If we did they might put him in jail forever and we wouldn't see him ever again as long as we live,' I said. In my mind I pictured my dad in his uniform standing with his hands gripping prison bars and looking really sad.

'Look Dorothy, here comes Little Cliffy and Leonard.' Pamela looked up and pointed down the street. Leonard was sitting in an empty wooden "Pears" soapbox holding a string between his fingers, his feet resting on a small plank of wood between two small pram wheels. and he was smiling. Little Cliffy was behind him pushing the box towards us. It had a bigger wheel on each side of the box and this made the *box cart*, as Little Cliffy called it, slope forwards.

'Don't you tell them about the drowning,' I warned Pamela. She shook her head. We all had turns in the box cart, pushing or riding in it until it was time to go in for tea. Our mum didn't say a word about the letter and we were too scared to tell her what we'd heard her say to Aunty Elise, so we acted as if everything was normal.

A few weeks later I was laughing at Pamela and Little Cliffy as they argued all the way home from school about who was the tallest. Little Cliffy pushed Pamela off the pavement into the street and walked alongside her nearly all the way home on his toes, which must have been painful because his boots were "laughing" again. Pamela ran ahead to our house and we chased her. She threw open the front door and we rushed inside after her. A lady we hadn't seen before was sitting on our sofa with Mum, Aunty Elise and Aunty Ruth and they gave us a startled look. The lady quickly stood up and smiled at us; she was slim and well-dressed in a smart coat, shiny silk stockings and lace-up shoes polished to a shine.

'Well I must go now, Dolly, but you can let Elise know when you've had time to think about what you want to do. She knows how to get hold of me.' She shook Mum's hand and Aunty Elise jumped up and followed her to the open door. She followed her outside, pulled the door closed behind her and said something we couldn't hear before coming back inside.

'Who was that lady?' I asked mum.

'Never you mind, go and lay the table for tea,' she said.

Nunoos was getting really good at lip-reading and on the last few visits we could talk to her without her friend signing for her. Mum had dropped us off at the Deaf School and gone into town. We had Little Cliffy with us and Pamela was playing cat's cradle with him as we sat around the table. Nunoos was unusually quiet. She kept lifting up her head as if she was going to say something but then she looked at Little Cliffy and changed her mind. I lifted her chin to make her look at my mouth and spoke slowly to her.

'What's up Nunoos?'

'I can't say.' She glanced at Little Cliffy, who had turned his head and was looking around the room, fascinated by the strange hand movements of the pupils and listening to the wordless sounds they made. She put her finger to her pursed lips and I nodded.

'Little Cliffy, go over to that lady teacher and ask her for some water for Nunoos,' I said, nudging him, and he slid down from his chair and walked nervously across the room to the lady by the door.

'I got a letter from Daddy yesterday,' she said as soon as he'd gone.

'Did he say he's coming home?' Pamela asked, forgetting to speak slowly.

Nunoos didn't respond but continued speaking. 'The teacher gave us our letters as usual so we could read them, then we're s'posed to give them back to the teacher so they can help us to write back, but after I read Daddy's letter I didn't want to give it back to her, so I hid it in my pocket.' She had dropped her chin again and I lifted it up.

'What did he write in the letter, Nunoos?' I asked, glancing at Pamela afterwards.

'He said Mummy is a bad Mummy and when he comes home he's going to take me, Pamela and you Dorothy and the others back to live with him in Guernsey but not our new brother or Mummy.' She started to cry and took her hanky out of her pocket to wipe her eyes before continuing. 'Later, when the teacher asked me where my letter was I told her I didn't want to show it to her because it wasn't a happy letter but she asked me to give it to her.'

'What did she say when she'd read it?' I asked.

'She told me not to worry and if I had family problems they would look after me. What's happening, Dorothy, why doesn't Daddy want our baby brother and Mummy to live with us?' Little

Terence is taken away

Cliffy had followed the teacher out of a door and hadn't come back yet so I told Nunoos what Pamela and I had overheard.

A few weeks later Mum sat us down on the sofa after school and told us that Terence was going to live with the lady who had come to our house.

'Can we go and play with him sometimes?' asked Little Cliffy.

'No she doesn't live around here – it'll be too far for you to go.' Little Cliffy's eyes filled up and he burst into tears.

'I don't want him to go away, Mummy, please don't send him away.' He ran over to Terence, who was sitting in the pram playing with a line of empty cotton reels fed onto string that was strung across it. He turned and stood in front of the pram facing us with his arms outstretched. Terence looked up, surprised at the noise, gave a wide gummy smile at Little Cliffy and clapped his hands.

'Your daddy doesn't want him, so he is going to live with this lady because she hasn't got any children of her own to look after.'

She walked over to Terence and tried to push Little Cliffy aside but he pushed into her belly with all of his strength and shouted, 'No Mummy, you can't give him away, I won't let you, let him stay with us please Mummy, please!' He looked up at her with tear-filled eyes and she grabbed his arms and pushed him away from her.

'Take him Dorothy,' she said still holding his arms and steering him towards me. I grabbed his wrists and he tried to wriggle free but I held on tight. She went back to the pram and picked Terence up. She stroked his loose blonde curls, then cupped his head in her hand and pulled it into her neck. 'It's for the best, he'll be very well looked after by that lady, son.' Little Cliffy reached out and as he stroked his brother's hand Terence took his finger into his tiny fist, held on really tight and Little Cliffy smiled at him. Pamela gave me that strange look of hers before running upstairs. I put my hands on Little Cliffy's shoulders and summoned up all the hate I could find inside myself and threw this look at our mother. She caught my look.

'I've got no choice, Dorothy, he can't stay here with us because of your dad.' I just glared at her and didn't answer. She sighed and handed him to me. 'Here take him for me while I get his things packed.' She turned away and went upstairs. Shortly after there was a knock at the door and I opened it to the lady who was going to take Terence away. She smiled at me – a quick short smile – then asked if Mum was at home and was Terence ready to leave. Later, as she gently lowered our brother into the shiny black pram she had left outside by the doorstep, we huddled around our mum who was standing on the step. She tried to give the lady a bundle of clothes but the lady waved them away and said she had plenty of new clothes at home for him.

'You mind you take good care of him or by Christ I'll come and get him,' Mum said in a lowered voice so the woman across the road, who had come out to see who the stranger was, wouldn't hear. The lady smiled and patted Mum's arm as she nodded. We watched her walk proudly away down the street and looked up at our mum who was crying. I quickly took hold of Little Cliffy who was about to run after the lady.

'No! Please bring my brother back,' Little Cliffy screamed, but I put my hand over his mouth and shushed him so the neighbour wouldn't hear. He turned to put his arms around my waist and buried his face into my chest, his body heaving as he sobbed, and I held him close.

'C'mon, let's get indoors,' Mum said, and as soon as we were inside she ran upstairs bawling her eyes out.

After a while we agreed not to talk about Terence because it made Mum either get sad and go quiet or snap at us. In bed at night though, I told them imaginary stories about him and of how he was living in a big house with lots of toys and plenty to eat. Little Cliffy liked these stories and as I told them I remembered my life in Glasgow, and I wondered if the Thorntons had a new little girl billeted with them now and if she was playing with my doll's pram. Aunty Ruth tried to cheer Mum up and she talked her into going out with her to the American servicemen's dances and to the cinema on Princes Road again. On Saturday nights they would get all dressed up and dance around the room to Glenn Miller music and pretend to be the Andrews sisters laughing and singing "Rum and Coca-Cola". Pamela and I imitated them and sang along with the chorus of the song. They pointed at us and laughed and we all danced like the Yanks. Then they would be out of the door and off down the street, Aunty Ruth with her wiggling bum and Mum with her dainty outstretched fingers.

Servicemen were thin on the ground now so Mum often came home alone except for the one night when she brought home a drunk soldier whom she'd known for years.

'Ben is from Guernsey, the same as us, Dorothy,' she said as she took his cap and told him to sit down on the sofa. She came over to me – I was on her bed – and flashed a silent message with her eyes to tell me to go up to my own bed. I got up and walked towards the passage door but he stood up and started to leave.

'I'd better be getting back to barracks, Dolly, or I'll be in trouble. Now where did I put my cap?' She turned to face him and held his cap behind her back.

'Oh don't go yet Ben, stop and have a cuppa.' She dropped the cap to the floor behind her and kicked it under the bed with her foot. She moved quickly towards him and pushed him gently back into his seat.

'Did I have my cap when we came in, love?' he asked me. Before I could answer she quickly shook her head and rushed towards me and stood very close with her back towards him.

'If you don't tell him where it is I'll give you a couple of bob,' she whispered. 'It's all right: he's just a friend – we went to the same school as kids and he's going back to the war in a couple of days.' She pushed my shoulder firmly and said, 'You get upstairs, it might be late when he leaves.' I crept upstairs so as not to awaken the others and drifted into sleep to the sound of hushed moans.

One afternoon a week or so later I overheard Mum talking to Aunty Elise through the open passageway door.

'It's no use Elise. I can't stand it any longer. I've got to get him back here with me where he belongs. It's breaking my heart not having him at home with us and the kids really miss him.' I crept closer to the door to listen.

'She won't part with him now, Dolly. I've heard she dresses him like a little prince and is telling everyone he's her late sister's orphaned child. Have you thought about what will happen when Cliff comes home?'

'Bollocks to Cliff, he'll just have to put up with it. I'm getting my Terence back and that's all there is to it.' I heard Mum approaching me and I quickly ran back to the scullery where I was peeling potatoes. She pushed past me and grabbed her coat from a nail on the back door. I didn't look up at her in case I looked guilty and she'd know I'd been listening.

'Mummy's going out. I won't be long, keep an eye on the kids until I get back d'you 'ear?' I nodded. Aunty Elise came rushing through clutching her coat and followed her to the door so I went to the door too.

'Wait, I'd better come with you Dolly – after all, it was me that put you onto her in the first place,' Aunty Elise called after her. They hurried down the street pushing their arms into the sleeves of their coats and pulling them on as they went. I went back inside and Pamela, who was playing in the street, came running in to find me.

'Where's Mummy gone to?' she asked.

'She's gone to bring Terence back home to live with us.'

'Hooray! I'll tell the others.' She raced to the door and I called her back.

'We're not supposed to know where she's gone. I was listening by the passageway, that's how I know, so don't say anything yet – pretend to be surprised, okay?' She gave a disappointed shrug then a big grin and went back out to play. It must have been a couple of hours before Mum got back. She was striding up our street with Terence in her arms, and Aunty Elise was walking a few yards behind her with her arms folded and her head down staring at the pavement. I was waiting on the doorstep for them to come back but Pamela saw them first and pointed them out to Little Cliffy who ran out shouting Terence's name. I hurried to meet them just as Aunty Elise caught up with Mum and I held my arms open to take Terence but Mum wouldn't let go of him.

'You didn't have to threaten her, Dolly: she was my friend and a good kind woman,' Aunty Elise scolded Mum.

'She wasn't going to let me have him back. I had to stand my ground – you would've done the same if it was your baby, don't say you wouldn't,' Mum snapped back.

'Well, I wouldn't have given a child of mine away in the first place….' Aunty Elise stopped short and covered her mouth. Mum looked hurt and shocked, she stopped walking and rounded on her.

'Well, you just go to bloody hell and stay out of my house – it was all your idea, you spiteful cow!' Aunty Elise tried to say sorry but Mum just stormed off into our house and we ran after her, happy that our little brother was back with us. Over the next week Little Cliffy stuck to Terence like a limpet – he wouldn't let him out of his sight and as soon as he got home from school he played with him until bedtime. Aunty Elise kept herself to herself next door but Mum was still friendly with Aunty Ruth.

29
The war in Europe is over!

It was nearly May in 1945 and the sun was shining. Mum still wasn't talking to Aunty Elise and she made us call her Mrs Churchill as she did when she spoke of her, and she had even locked our side of the door in the passageway. The teachers told us that we were winning the war and soon life would be back to normal. My schoolwork had suffered through staying at home to look after the kids and I'd lost interest because I never got any praise from the teacher. After school I waited outside the gates for Little Cliffy and Leonard to come out of their classes. Pamela had started walking home with her friends now so I was left to be the referee between the boys, who were always squabbling about something or other all the way home. Little Cliffy made straight for Terence when we got home and he took him outside and put him in his box cart to push him up and down the street. Leonard ran behind shouting that it was his turn now! Mum was on her knees scrubbing the doorstep with a dolly stone; the other women in our street often did this too. From time to time they would sit back on their heels and call out to each other with the latest gossip. I think Mum was really missing Aunty Elise's friendship since Aunty Ruth had gone off to live near where an American soldier she'd met was stationed.

'They're saying on the news that Mussolini has been killed by his own people,' Mrs Ashworth called out to Mum from her doorstep.

'I wish the bloody Germans would do the same to Hitler,' Mum replied. It's funny she said that because a few days later when we were in bed asleep she came running upstairs shouting 'Hitler's dead! Wake up, Hitler's killed himself!' I sat up, rubbed my eyes and squinted trying to see her face clearly in the dark as she came and sat on our bed. The others got up and huddled around her. 'The war will soon be over now and we can go back to live in Guernsey – won't that be great?' She was really happy and she hugged us all one after the other.

The war in Europe is over!

Aunty Elise's voice called up the stairs, 'Dolly, have you heard the news? That bastard Hitler is dead, he's dead, have you heard?' She came running upstairs into our room. Mum stood up and threw her arms around her and they danced around in circles.

I was glad we could stop calling Aunty Elise "Mrs Churchill" after that and that Mum had unlocked the adjoining door in the passageway so they could go in and out again. Little Cliffy was allowed to play with Winston and Aunty Elise shared her rations with us again, so everyone was happy. A few days later Mum called us in from playing outside to tell us that the Germans had surrendered to the Americans in France. She said there was going to be a big party the next day so we must all help. That night we stood at our bedroom window and watched the fireworks display. The skies glowed red from bonfires. It reminded me of the night that I watched the glowing sky from my bedroom window with Mrs Thornton, except that this was much closer and burned brighter. People were dancing and singing below in our street; they were doing a conga line and cheering. We watched until they had disappeared around the corner and the fireworks were over before climbing back into bed.

The next morning Aunty Elise was in our house at breakfast time and she and Mum were talking about what had happened last night in front of the Town Hall. 'Oh you should have seen us, Dorothy,' Aunty Elise said to me, 'we were cheering and singing, the Town Hall was all lit up and the street lights were glowing bright. The Corporation had decorated a tramcar with lights and a big "V" sign with a crown above it, and pictures of the King and Queen all done in little lights – oh, it was lovely! You couldn't move for people pressing against you, love, they were hugging and kissing and crying.' She took my hand in both of hers and pulled me close.

'Someone even burned a dummy that was dressed up like Hitler. That got us cheering, eh Dolly? Oh it's wonderful and this means we'll soon have our men back home with us again, eh Dolly?' Mum smiled at her and carried on cutting the bread for our breakfast, but she didn't answer.

Later that afternoon all the neighbours came pouring out of their homes carrying chairs and tables which they set up down the middle of the street. The big boys climbed ladders and tied bunting to lampposts so it criss-crossed the street above the tables. White cloths and a Union Jack were spread over the tables and women and children ran back and forth with armfuls of food. I asked Mum where the food had come from since we had all been rationed for so long. She replied that it was a case of pooling sugar rations to make cakes, and finding what they could in their cupboards, and that people from every household were chipping in with something. Even Mr Ogden, who people said was dealing in the black market, came out carrying a box of jam in jars and tinned fruit. His brawny wife was marching him out with it – pushing him forward when he tried to turn back to the house. There were flags everywhere, some real Union Jacks and others just scraps of red, white and blue material cut and stitched together. It was a great party – every single person from our street was there, all wearing party hats. Mine was made out of newspaper. We had Marmite sandwiches and jelly and cakes with pink icing and I ate and drank pop until I was so full up that my belly hurt. Leonard made himself sick from drinking too much fizzy drink and we all sang *Rule Britannia* with the grown-ups. Then we did the conga up and down our street. A man from the newspaper came to take our photo and we all cheered and gave him the "V" sign like Winston Churchill.

At home later we heard Winston Churchill's voice come over the wireless and he said 'Our dear Channel Islands are also to be freed today.' Mum and Aunty Elise hugged and cheered and we all cheered and danced around them.

'What does he mean, Mummy?' Little Cliffy shouted above their cheers.

'It means that the British troops will kick the Germans out of Guernsey, son, and we'll all be able to go back home to live on our island again.' Aunty Elise threw up her fists and shook them as she cheered again, and Mum swept Little Cliffy up and twirled him around and started singing *Sarnia Cherie* – the song that had become the Guernsey national anthem to the evacuees. Aunty Elise, Pamela and I sang along but the younger kids didn't know the words so they just clapped and cheered.

30

Vera's sick tortoise

Miss Peacock plumped up her seat cushion in her usual way before she sat down on her wooden chair in front of our class. She peered over the top of her glasses and announced that soon we would be saying goodbye to the evacuees who had joined our school in recent years, because they would be going back to their homes all over Britain and in the Channel Islands. She looked down at me as she said Channel Islands, but didn't smile. She had lost patience with me because of my frequent absences, and the fact that I'd fallen behind with my work because I was sick so often. I don't think she believed what my mum wrote in the sick notes that she'd sent me back to school with after my absences. I kept my head down and tried to catch up but I was always glad to hear the bell ring for home time.

'What's in that box, Vera?' Lollie asked our classmate who was leaning against the playground wall clutching a small wooden box at playtime break.

'It's my p-pet tortoise,' Vera stammered, 'I think he's sick because he didn't w-wake up after his h-hibernation time.'

'What's hibernation?' Lollie asked.

'It's when they go to sleep for the w-winter,' she replied.

'Let me see him then,' Lollie said, leaning over and poking at the crumpled paper that covered him in the box. Vera carefully reached into the box and lifted out the dome shaped shell with no arms or head or legs or even tail sticking out.

'Pooh it stinks!' Lollie said leaning back and holding her nose. It did smell bad and I stepped back too, but Vera couldn't seem to smell it. Lollie raised her fist and banged on the shell with her knuckles.

'Don't, you'll h-hurt him,' Vera said, pulling it closer to her.

'He can't feel anything, stupid, 'cos he's dead.'

'No he's not. I'm going to ask the teacher after p-playtime… she'll know what's wrong with him.' She put him back into the box. 'W-will you hold this for me while I go to the lavatory before the bell goes, Dorothy?' she asked, and handed me the box before hurrying away.

'Give it to me,' Lollie said, pulling the box away from me when Vera was out of sight. 'I've got an idea what we can do with it.' She was grinning and before I could ask what, she'd run off into the crowd of kids gathered in the playground. The teacher came out and rang the hand bell and we all stood in line and followed each other inside. I couldn't see Lollie anywhere but I turned and spotted Vera joining the end of the line. Lollie had managed to be first in line at our classroom door, which was open but we had to wait for Miss Peacock to come back from her break to let us in. She came striding up past us and stood facing us at the door.

'Go to your desks quickly and quietly now,' she ordered, and we filed into the room.

'W-where's Jack, my tortoise?' Vera stammered as she shuffled along the tipped-back desk seat to stand next to me and wait until we were told to sit.

'I don't know, Lollie snatched it away from me,' I replied.

'Is this something you would like to share with the rest of the class, Dorothy Ogier?' Miss Peacock shouted at me, and suddenly she was right in front of our desk.

'No miss, sorry miss,' I replied.

'Some of the children in this class who bother to attend school more often than the likes of you, Miss Ogier, come to listen to me, and to learn. I suggest that you be quiet and do the same. Sit down everybody.' She turned her back to return to her chair and I poked out my tongue at her. As she reached her desk she picked up the stick she used as a cane, tapped it on her desk and said, 'We know what happens to children who don't pay attention, don't we class?'

I bit into my bottom lip and clenched my fists ready to get called up to her as the whole class chanted slowly back to her, 'Yes, Miss Peacock,' but she put the cane down again and glanced down to check that her cushion was plumped before taking her seat. She had our full attention and we were all sitting upright, hands down by our sides, obediently waiting for her to teach us. She shuffled around on her seat, leaning to one side then to the other. She pulled a strange face and wiggled about some more – then someone sniggered at the back of the class.

Suddenly she leapt to her feet, lifted her cushion and jumped backwards. 'What on earth! Who did this?' she shouted. She picked up the tortoise that had been placed upside down under her cushion and a roar of laughter came from behind us – it was Lollie. Miss Peacock was holding the shell at arm's length and pinching her nose. She glared straight at Lollie, who was covering her mouth to hide the big grin on her face.

'Does this belong to you, Lollie Duncombe?'

'No Miss Peacock, it's not mine,' Lollie replied, trying to sound surprised.

'Well then, to whom does it belong? Own up now or the whole class will be punished.' Curious heads turned this way and that around the classroom – one or two looked straight at Vera but I turned back to look at Lollie, who was grinning widely.

'He's m-mine, Miss Peacock.' Vera was only half holding up her arm and her eyes were cast down at our desk.

'Come up here right now, girl,' Miss Peacock snapped. Vera slid out from the desk and walked slowly towards her then stood in front of her. 'Hold out your hands,' Miss Peacock demanded, and Vera held out both hands to take the tortoise from her – but instead of giving her the tortoise Miss Peacock took her cane in her free hand and swiped it across Vera's palms. Vera jumped back in surprise and began to cry.

I shot my hand up in the air to get Miss Peacock's attention. 'Miss! Please, miss!

'Put your hand down, Dorothy Ogier, unless you would like to come and have some of the same,' she snapped. I lowered my hand and turned to look at Lollie and she wasn't grinning anymore.

'P-please miss, my tortoise is s-sick, he didn't wake up,' Vera tried to explain through her sobs as she rubbed her stinging palms up and down her thighs.

'It didn't wake up because it's dead, you stupid girl, now take it home and give it a decent burial. Furthermore you can stay in after school for the rest of the week for playing that childish trick.' She thrust the tortoise at her and pointed her back to her desk.

'B-but…'

'Don't "b-but" me. Go to your seat unless you would like another stroke of the cane… well?' Vera hurried back to our desk and placed the dead tortoise on the seat between us.

I shifted away from it as far as I could without falling off the end of the seat. 'That was mean, you should have owned up and not let Vera take the punishment,' I told Lollie when we met at the school gates after school.

'Yeh you're right, but I didn't think she would give her the cane. I'll tell Miss Peacock tomorrow it was me that did it.'

'No, not tomorrow – you should go now so Vera doesn't have to stay behind just because of you. She's already had the cane....'

'Okay, bloody shuddup,' she interrupted. 'I'll go right now just to shut you up.' She smirked at me as she backed away and said, 'you have to admit it though, Dorothy, Miss Peacock's face wasn't half funny when she was wriggling around on that cushion.' Then she started laughing and turned towards the school. I remembered Miss Peacock's expression and I grinned as I watched Lollie skip back to the school's entrance door. She wasn't afraid of Miss Peacock, as we were. She was always playing up in class and getting the cane, and it didn't seem to bother her at all. I waited at the gates for a while after she'd gone back into the school and I was pleased when I saw Vera come out alone carrying her little box. I waved to her, she smiled and as we walked home together she asked me if I wanted to help her bury the tortoise. We walked to the edge of an allotment near her house and dug a hole with our fingers deep enough to take the tortoise box, which she gently lowered into the hole and covered with a pile of soil.

'We should say a prayer,' I said, I pushed my palms together, shut my eyes tightly and bowed my head and Vera copied me.

'Please God, take Vera's tortoise to live with you in heaven and be kind to him, amen.'

'A-amen,' she repeated.

31

Goodbye Mr Churchill

Everyone was talking about the election in our neighbourhood since they had all voted – but some of them weren't very happy about the result. I carried a bucket of water out to Mum, who was kneeling at our front door, and I heard someone call out to her, 'After all he's seen us through, it's a bloody shame to see him go.' It was Mrs Duckworth who lived a couple of doors along from us. They were both on their knees scrubbing their front doorsteps. Mum sat back on her heels and arched her back as she put down her scrubbing brush and spread her fingers across her lower back. She shouted back to her, 'Well, some says he was still thinking too much about the war instead of helping to get us people back on our feet. Look, I don't understands politics me – we don't have no party politics where I comes from, but it sounds to me like those Labour people are best because at least they wants to look after us and give us a children's allowance. Anyway I'm sick of this war me, I just want to go back to Guernsey with my kids and live in peace again.' She sighed and returned to her scrubbing. I jumped clear of the water as she sloshed it over the doorstep. It seemed to me that it didn't make much difference whoever was in charge of the country because we still had food rationing and wore patched ragged clothes and "laughing" shoes, so not much had changed.

We were still at war with Japan and Mum hadn't heard from our dad since he'd written to her about drowning our Terence. She told us a while after she'd fetched Terence back to live with us that she'd written to tell him he'd have to accept Terence because she would never part with him, but she said she'd not heard back from him since. Even Nunoos hadn't got a letter from him and he used to write to her regularly. I asked Mum if the Japs had killed our dad and that's why he hadn't written, but she shook her head and told me she would have got a telegram telling her if he'd been killed.

Aunty Ruth – who had been away for a little while but lived next door again with Aunty Elise, because her soldier boyfriend went back to America without her – was in our house sitting on the sofa next to Aunty Elise and Mum. Someone knocked on our door and Mum told Little Cliffy to answer it. It was Mr Jones, who had killed our rabbit. He'd started to call around again lately to see Mum and tell her the latest news of which families had gone back to Guernsey. Little Cliffy still hadn't forgiven him for killing Robert and didn't answer him when he said, 'Hello Sonny.' As he came inside he winked at me and patted my head but I pulled away from him. He sat in the armchair at Mum's invitation and perched himself on the edge turning the brim of his hat through his fingers. He leaned forward and spoke to them in a hushed serious voice.

'Brian Le Page has come back from Burma with a medical discharge. He got gangrene in a wound in his foot and they had to take it off.'

Aunty Ruth interrupted him, 'Do you mean the Brian Le Page from St Martins who married Julie Queripel?' He nodded.

'Poor bastard,' she said.

Mum turned to me and said 'Don't just stand there, put the kettle on, Dorothy, and make Mr Jones a cup of tea… fill the pot, we'll all have one.'

'His wife is looking after him,' he continued. 'They're living in Reddish with their three children: that's where I went to see him yesterday. He told me he'd spent some time with your Cliff in the jungle fighting the Japanese, and that's why I've come around.'

'What did he say about my Cliff?' Mum asked, jerking forward. I'd filled the kettle and put it on the range, then I hovered in the kitchen doorway so I could hear what he told her.

'He said Cliff was still in one piece when he last saw him but their lives had been hell in that jungle. Our men have been dropping like flies with dysentery and malaria. Brian's best mate got killed right next to him in the trench. He told me they heard a Jap call out to them, "You no fight Tommy, why you no fight, Tommy bastard?" His mate stood up and swore back at the voice, then a sniper's shot rang out and Brian watched as a bullet hit the middle of his mate's forehead, went through and splattered his brains against the trench wall behind them.'

'Ugh!' Aunty Ruth said, covering her mouth.

'Did he shoot my Daddy too?' Little Cliffy cried out.

'No he didn't, and you shouldn't be listening – now get outside and play with the others,' Mum shouted at him. He hung his head and left the room, slamming the door behind him.

Mr Jones hesitated, but then he went on. 'Brian told me he watched his mate slide silently down the side of the muddy trench into the ankle-deep water, then he threw up and couldn't stop shaking.'

'Those bastard Japs,' Mum said. Aunty Ruth, who had cupped her nose and mouth into her hands in horror, gave her a silent nod.

Mr Jones shook his head slowly and said, 'He told me the Japanese soldiers had dug a maze of tunnels and you never knew how close they were. It rained in sheets, he said, and they were often wading through mud and slime up to their waists. He even saw a mule, laden with supplies, sink underneath the water and just disappear because they couldn't reach it. He reckoned the nights were the worst. That was when the Japs would taunt them over and over to try to make them fire back at them and give away their position. They would shout out "Hey Tommy, who fuckee your missus tonight?"' I watched my mum as she turned to look at Aunty Ruth and they both cast their eyes to the floor.

'How long ago was he with my Cliff?' Mum asked, without making eye contact with Mr Jones, 'Only he hasn't written for months.'

'About six months ago,' he replied, 'because Brian spent time in an army hospital since then. He told me that our boys out there are all feeling as though they've been forgotten by the British Government and our people since the war in Europe is over.' He licked his dry lips and Mum told me to hurry up with the tea. I grabbed the kettle and made the tea in the scullery, then I carried it through to them on a wooden tray, hoping to hear more about my dad, but Mum sent me outside to keep an eye on Little Cliffy and the other kids. I went looking for Pamela to tell her what I'd overheard. She was sitting on the front step of her friend's house across the street and I ran over to her.

'Dad's still alive, Pamela! Mr. Jones told us a man from Guernsey has seen him in the jungle.'

'Is he coming home?' she asked.

I shrugged and shook my head. 'It was six months ago when he last saw him so I don't know.'

We watched Mr Jones leave our house. He waved to us as he hurried down the street, and we gave a half-hearted wave back.

32

Victory over Japan

The homes in our street were already buzzing with the news about the atom bomb that the Americans had dropped on Hiroshima in Japan when the news came of a second bomb being dropped on Nagasaki. The grown-ups were all saying that the Japs would surely surrender and a week later they did, so we were treated to another street party. There were not so many people at this party because some of the dads had come home from the war in Europe and their families were already reunited. Even so, the street was soon draped with bunting and full of happy dancing people and kids gorging themselves again on magically produced food and drink. Mum got caught up in the singing and dancing and got special attention from the others because her husband was still out there in Burma. She got really emotional and cried, then laughed, and in no time she was crying again but she wasn't sad. After the street party, Granny, Aunty Elise, Aunty Ruth and all of their kids came into our house. The women were drinking booze and the older kids were excited and noisy and ran around, while the younder ones played on the floor. Veronica, Granny's little girl from the black American soldier, was becoming a really sweet-looking toddler with caramel-coloured skin and a head of soft dark curls. She was nearly as big as our Terence and they played happily together with their toys in the corner. Our dad's sister Aunty Edna had already gone back to Guernsey with her children and Granny was telling Aunty Elise that she was still waiting to hear from our Grandpa about whether the Germans had commandeered Brazil House and left it unfit to live in, or if they could go home. We hadn't seen much of Granny in the last year and Mum had hardly mentioned her during all that time. They didn't talk much to each other, instead they chatted with Aunty Elise or Aunty Ruth.

Pamela was showing Barbara how she could climb up inside the frame of the kitchen door by spreading her arms and legs and pressing them against the sides. She had got over half way up when Granny told her to get out of the way and clipped her across the ear. She slid to the floor, rubbed her ear, and jumped out of her way as Granny barged past her to get a bottle opener from the drawer in the scullery. The grown-ups were drinking heavily and after a few hours, as it got dark outside, their laughter and talking got louder and then Granny and Mum started shouting at each other.

'Don't you accuse me of shagging Mr Jones: you're the one who's sex-mad around here!' Granny shouted. We all stopped playing and looked up at her.

'Lollie! Take the kids next door into my house, go now!' Aunty Elise ordered. Lollie picked up Veronica and Pamela scooped up Terence and the rest of the kids all scurried next door after them but I just stood there.

'Well we both know how I learned about sex, don't we, you old cow?' They were standing apart but Mum had stretched her neck forward, pushing her face into Granny's.

'Come on now you two, break it up.' Aunty Elise held up her arms and placed them on each of their shoulders. Mum tried to shrug her off.

'Yer Elise, you asked me once what things had happened to me as a kid in Jersey. Well, you should ask her!' Granny's face drained of colour and she tried to push past Mum to leave, but Mum grabbed her sleeve.

'You're not going anywhere until you tell them what happened. I've had to live with the secret all these years – what about you, how have you managed to live with yourself?'

Granny tried to pull her hand away but Mum gripped on tight, her face twisted with rage.

'What's she talking about, Grace, what happened?' Aunty Ruth demanded. She had tilted her head to one side and was staring at Granny as she waited for an answer.

Aunty Elise was looking curiously at Granny too and she tightened her grip on Granny's shoulder as she said, 'Speak up Grace, tell us what happened.' Granny stood there tight-lipped, taking short breaths through flared nostrils as her face turned a bright red colour and her piggy eyes disappeared behind her fogged-up lenses. Mum was still staring at her and challenging her to answer.

'Lost your tongue have you? Well then, I'll just have to tell them the dirty little secret that you threatened to send me back to the children's home if I told anyone about, won't I?'

Mum was screaming at her now and the veins in the side of her neck were bulging out. The Aunties glanced at each other and then quickly turned their attention back to Granny and Mum. Granny's eyes shot in my direction – I was staring at her, holding my breath waiting for her to speak. My feet were fixed to the spot and my hand covered my mouth.

She turned back to Mum. 'You're drunk, I don't know what you're talking about. Let go of me.'

Mum let go of her and staggered back a few steps, then noticed that I was still in the room.

'You get next door with the others – don't just stand there, get!' She pointed towards the passage and stepped towards me so I ran out of the room.

I stopped at the door to Aunty Elise's when I realised Mum hadn't chased me down the passage. I tried to hear what they were saying but I couldn't so I crept back towards the living room door.

'Oh Christ, Grace, that's disgusting, you're perverted!' Aunty Ruth shouted.

Granny suddenly appeared at the door to the passage. She pushed past me but then stopped and returned to the door where she stood for a moment looking back at Mum who was crying into Aunty Elise's shoulder.

'You have a wild imagination, my girl. I don't have any dirty secrets and you're just an attention-seeking liar!'

She then moved quickly down the passage and into Aunty Elise's house where she grabbed Veronica from Lollie and stormed out into the street chased by her bewildered kids.

Aunty Elise took me aside and said, 'Don't you tell anyone what just happened, Dorothy – it's private family business, do you understand?' I nodded and she sent my brothers and sisters upstairs to bed. I waited and watched as our Aunties tucked Mum into her bed then hurried next door together whispering to each other before I followed the others upstairs to bed. Pamela asked me why Granny and Mum had been arguing and I told her it was only because they had drunk too much booze and to go to sleep.

33
Another baby on the way

Even though the war was declared officially over we'd still heard nothing from our dad and I began to think he'd gone back to Guernsey on his own and left us all to carry on living here in Stockport because he didn't want Mum or us anymore. Mr Jones, who visited us quite often, assured me that he hadn't gone to Guernsey. It seems that only people who still owned a home there or had relatives that could offer them a place to live were being allowed to go back. He told us that the Germans had damaged so many of the houses they'd occupied that the island was short of habitable dwellings. We'd left our Grandpa Duncombe behind living in Brazil House and I wondered if the Germans had thrown him out so they could live there. Aunty Elise told Mum that Granny had heard nothing from him at all, so we were all left to wonder.

It was a Monday and Mum and Aunty Elise were hanging out washing in their backyards, even though it was a cloudy day and I thought it might rain. As I carried out another load of sheets that I had wrung out for Mum, I overheard her telling Aunty Elise over the fence that she was in the family way again. I stood quite still and waited for Aunty Elise to say something but she didn't speak.

'At least I knows who the father is this time: it's Ben from Guernsey.' Mum sighed as she rubbed her hand over her belly. It wasn't round or sticking out and I wondered if she was just pretending.

'Have you heard from Cliff yet?' Aunty Elise asked as she bent down to pick up a towel to peg out. She didn't look up at Mum as she spoke.

'Not a bloody word,' Mum said, before she pushed a clothes peg into her mouth and stretched a sheet across the clothesline to peg one end. As she took the peg out of her mouth to peg the other end she gestured to me to put the sheets down on top of her pile of laundry.

'I wouldn't want to be in your shoes when he does turn up, Dolly – first Terence and now another one on the way, he'll bloody murder you!' Aunty Elise warned her. I leaned forward and carefully put my sheets on top of Mum's. As I stood up I pulled at the patch where the wet sheets had soaked through my dress and made it cling to my skin – it felt cold against my chest and I was shivering.

Aunty Ruth stepped out of the door behind me into our yard. 'Did I hear right just then? Are you pregnant Dolly?' Mum nodded and turning down the sides of her mouth gave a nervous laugh. 'Well now you're really in the shit aren't you?'

Aunty Elise looked serious. She cupped her right elbow in her left hand. She had taken her fag out of her mouth and was holding it up between the long fingers of her right hand; she stabbed it towards Mum to make her point as she spoke. 'She's right Dolly, and it's no laughing matter.'

'Look Dolly,' Aunty Ruth said, 'when you've finished pegging out that washing, we'll have a cup of tea and see if we can sort this mess out.' She put her hand on my shoulder and I turned to face her. 'Dorothy, you go inside and put the kettle on, and get out of that wet dress before you catch your death, my girl.' I ran inside, put the kettle on then ran upstairs to change into dry clothes. I pulled back the curtain and looked out of the bedroom window. The street was quiet. All the kids were at school except me – I'd been kept home with a bad cold. The stairs creaked as I tried to creep down and get close enough to hear how they were going to "sort this out".

'An abortion!' Aunty Elise shouted. 'That's too dangerous, Ruth – women have bled to death after those back street abortionists have finished with them.'

'Well we know what happened with your idea of so-called adoption, don't we?' Aunty Ruth replied. Aunty Elise didn't answer. I wondered what an abortion was as I sat on the bottom stair. I was cold. My knees were drawn up with my face buried between them and I tucked my arms under my legs.

Mum spoke then. 'He's not coming back to the kids and me. He's gone off with some woman, that's what's happened. There's no need to get rid of this baby, I'll manage once we get back to Guernsey.' So my dad wasn't coming back. She'd said it. He'd found a new woman and maybe a new family. Tears stung my eyes and I angrily thumped the panelling alongside the stairs, forgetting that I was listening in secret, and I waited for them to call out to me but they hadn't heard. I missed my dad. I wanted him to come home and for us all to go back to Guernsey so we could go to Herm Island again and see the porpoises and go to the beach as a family. 'Please God, make my dad come back to us,' I whispered.

34

The telegram

It had been weeks since Mum told us she was having another baby. On our last visit to the deaf school, when Mum had gone to talk to the teacher and couldn't hear us, we told Nunoos that we were going to have another brother or sister. She looked pleased at the news at first but then Pamela slowly mouthed the words: 'Daddy's going to kill Mummy twice now when he comes home, once for Terence and then again for the baby in her belly.'

Nunoos' bottom lip began to quiver and she searched my face hoping I would say it wasn't true.

'Shuddup Pamela – anyway Mum reckons he's not coming back to us,' I said.

'Doesn't Daddy want us anymore, Dorothy? Is that why he's not coming back?' Nunoos asked.

I held her hand and squeezed it. 'I think he does want us but he's not happy with our mum so that's why he might not come back to live with us.' Mum had left the teacher and was coming toward us so we stopped talking about her. When we left Nunoos she was really upset and she cried big heaving sobs to come home with us, but when Mum asked us why she was more upset than usual at our leaving her, we just shrugged.

As Pamela and I were washing the dishes a voice on the wireless announced that it was midday. There was a loud knock at our front door. It was the postman and he was late for a Saturday. We rushed into the living room and watched Mum take a telegram from him and gently close the door. My heart sank when I noticed the telegram because I knew that wives got those when their husbands had been killed or were missing. Her hands were shaking as she read it and slowly she lowered herself into a chair before looking up at me.

'Your father is coming home next week,' she said, and bit into her bottom lip. I felt a surge of happiness rush through me but her face stopped me from breaking into a big happy smile.

'Hooray! Daddy's coming home,' Pamela shouted, and grinned at me as she ran outside to tell the others.

'You know what this means, don't you?' Mum said after she'd gone. She looked down and spread her hands over her belly. 'I've got to explain this and then there's our Terence. You remember that letter from him. What the hell am I going to do?'

Her face went pale and her eyes misted up. 'Go and fetch Aunty Elise for me and tell the kids to stay outside.'

I did what she'd asked. I put the kettle on for a cup of tea while Aunty Elise and Aunty Ruth sat around the table with Mum and took turns reading the telegram.

'It doesn't say what day he's coming – he could even turn up on Monday,' Aunty Ruth said. 'Come on Elise, we've got to come up with a plan of how to help poor Dolly.'

The front door was flung open and Pamela came in and started to say something but Mum cut her off and shouted, 'Play outside I said!' and she pointed out to the street.

'But Mum, Sheila's hurt herself,' Pamela protested.

'Go and see to her Dorothy,' Mum ordered, so I followed Pamela outside. Sheila was sniffing away the last of her tears as she looked up at me and I held out my arms to pick her up. She was rubbing her arm and Pamela said that she'd fallen out of the box cart when Leonard was pushing her too fast.

'When is our daddy coming home, Dorothy?' Little Cliffy asked as I hushed Sheila. My brothers and sisters surrounded me looking up into my face, hope in their eyes and smiles on their faces. They didn't know what Pamela and I knew about our dad's threats towards Mum – they just wanted to have him home with us again the way the other dads had come home.

'Next week – the telegram said next week,' I smiled and lowered Sheila back into the box cart.

'Hooray! Our daddy's coming home next week,' Little Cliffy shouted to the kids in the street, and a few of them ran inside to tell their mums the news. Pamela's friend Carol, who'd been playing with her earlier, overheard the news and came running towards us.

'Aren't you all scared though? I'd be really scared if my daddy had said he was going to kill my mummy when he comes home.' She looked at Pamela, then quickly at each face in our little group.

'Pamela you shouldn't have told her.' I glared at Pamela, then at Carol. The kids looked scared now and their eyes darted from me to Carol to Pamela and back to me.

'Are you happy now, big mouth?' I snapped at Carol. 'Clear off now, go on.'

'She's a liar, eh Dorothy. Daddy's not going to hurt Mummy, eh?' Leonard asked, and he shouted at her, 'Liar, liar, your tongue's on fire!'

Carol had started to run off but turned and shouted back at him 'No I'm not a liar. Anyway, everyone in our street knows that your dad is coming home to kill your mum and your brother Terence, so there.'

There was a look of horror on Little Cliffy's face as he took in what she'd said.

'Look, sit down on the pavement alongside me and I'll tell you all about it,' I said, pulling my skirt into the back of my knees as I lowered myself on to the pavement.

They sat or squatted around me and Little Cliffy began to shout at me, 'I won't let Daddy hurt Terence, I'll kill him if he kills Terence.' I held his hand tightly and shushed him.

'Listen, be quiet and listen to me,' I said and he calmed down. 'When Mummy told Daddy about Terence in her letter, he sent her a letter back telling her he wasn't very happy with her.'

'He said he was going to drown Terence like he did with Tibby's kittens,' Pamela interrupted.

'Pamela!' I hissed at her. She shut up when she saw the fear in their faces. 'He didn't really mean it: you know he was just letting Mum know that he wasn't very pleased. They'll probably have a big row like they used to have in Guernsey and then after a few days it will be okay, you'll see.' I had told myself this is what would happen and I found myself believing it even more strongly as I told them.

'Will they have a fight?' Pamela asked.

'Maybe, I don't know for sure,' I said looking down at my feet. The street had cleared of kids, it was a grey cloudy day and I felt sad. I sighed, stood up and took hold of Sheila's hand. 'Let's go in for tea' I said. Little Cliffy grabbed the string on his box cart and pulled it behind him as we crossed the street to our house.

Mum was inside peeling potatoes. 'Lay the table Dorothy, tea won't be long,' she said without looking up at me.

On Sunday night we all took turns in the tin bath washing our hair and scrubbing the tide mark from the back of the boys' necks. Aunty Elise lent Mum her kitchen scissors and the curls dropped one by one from my brothers' hair onto the floor as she hacked them off leaving them with bald patches above their ears and a crop of curls on the top of their heads. Pamela pulled a face at me and pointed at her hair, I shook my head and shrugged. Mum took a rest after she'd done Terence's hair and went to fill the kettle for a cup of tea. Pamela waited until she was out of sight in the scullery then grabbed the scissors from the table and pushed them underneath the cushion of the armchair. She put her finger to her lips and grinned at me. Later when Mum pulled Sheila up onto a chair for her haircut we couldn't find the scissors for her, even though we made a big show of looking everywhere in the room.

I couldn't get to sleep that night because my mind was full of re-runs of rows and fights between Mum and Dad. I was worried for our mum, yet I was excited about seeing my dad again. In the end sleep took over and I awoke the next morning to the shouts of the rag 'n' bone man. I ran to the window to see his horse waiting patiently as he loaded the cart. He didn't go into the house across the road any more since her husband had come back from the war.

'Up you get, you kids, make haste and put your best clothes on in case your dad comes home today,' Mum called upstairs. When we got downstairs she had made lumpy porridge which she made us eat all up before brushing the girls' hair and tying in ribbons. We looked as though we were going to church or a party – our white ankle socks were clean, our dresses had been ironed and starched and we gave each other admiring looks. The boys' pants were patched but their shirts were ironed and their shoes had been polished.

'You can do the dishes now, Dorothy. Pamela, you take the kids outside to play and mind they don't get dirty d'you 'ear?' Mum warned. They ran outside and she studied herself in the mirror. She was wearing the best of her cotton dresses that would still fit over her swollen belly – it was pale blue cotton with puff sleeves that cut into her arms. Her frizzy hair formed a full rounded shape that covered her ears and stood out from her neck.

'Do I look all right?' she asked, patting at the puffiness around her red eyes.

'You look nice Mum, that dress suits you, but… it shows a bit,' I replied.

'I can't hide it forever: he's going to find out sooner or later,' she snapped. I went through to do the dishes to keep out of her way and she sat at the table to read the crumpled telegram again. I looked out of the window into our backyard and pictured my mum on that moonlit night with the tall soldier and I remembered guiltily what I'd called her.

The sun was fighting to shine through the heavy smog from the factory chimneys. It would have dried the washing but today Mum didn't do any. She was staring at the telegram. I didn't know what to say to her so I went out to the yard and clicked the latch that opened the door to the outside lavatory. The wooden seat was warm against my legs and the metal hook that pierced through the newspaper squares was empty because Pamela hadn't been doing her job. Kay's brown sticky flypaper hung from the tin roof. It curled and twisted downwards and was encrusted with dried dead flies that looked like tiny raisins. Sunlight slipped under the gap beneath the door and reflected on the toes of my polished shoes. I sat quietly and waited, leaning on folded arms across my knees and swinging my feet back and forth. My stomach was in knots but nothing was happening and anyway there was no paper. I stood up and went back indoors where Mum was still at the table but she wasn't reading the telegram, she was looking at Terence who was having a nap on her bed. I let the door slam behind me and she jumped. Terence opened his eyes and turned his head and smiled at us. He didn't make a sound as he climbed down from her bed and walked towards her with his arms held up. Before he reached her Aunty Elise came into the room and swept him up into her arms. She gave him a big hug and as he giggled I watched Mum's strained face soften into a smile.

'Put the kettle on, Dorothy, and make your mum and me a cup

of tea, there's a good girl,' Aunty Elise said.

'I could do with something stronger than bloody tea, me,' Mum said to her. 'Something to give me some Dutch courage, that's what I need.' She pushed away the telegram. 'I've been living on my nerves for so long and now the time has come to face him, I feel sick, my guts is turning. I must be bloody mental because part of me really wants to see him again but that doesn't stop me being terrified of what's going to happen when he gets here.' She sighed and cupped her chin in her hands.

'Mummy, he's coming up the street Mummy, he's coming!' Pamela shouted, as she came running in through the open front door.

Mum jumped to her feet and threw a worried look at Aunty Elise, who tried to give her a reassuring smile as she patted her arm and said firmly, 'Dolly, remember what I said – you just shout if you need me.' As the two women's eyes met an unspoken message seemed to pass between them and Mum nodded at her. I knew they'd already agreed on a plan of escape. Aunty Elise was still holding Terence as she slipped quickly back down the passage and through the adjoining door that connected her house to ours. Mum had warned us, after she'd received the telegram, that things would be very bad for her when Dad came back from Burma. Pamela was standing in the living room surrounded by my other siblings who had followed her in. They were watching our mum and like me they were desperate to run down the street to greet our dad. Their young faces were set in slack-jawed uncertainty, their questioning eyes tinged with fear as they waited for her to tell them it was safe to go to him.

She swallowed hard and said, 'Go on and meet him then, but don't go telling him anything, leave that to me.' They rushed outside. I wanted to run after them but I hesitated and for a moment stood in an uncomfortable silence with her. She put her hands on my shoulders. 'And I don't want you putting your oar in either, d'you 'ear?' She looked scared for a moment but then she defiantly lifted her chin and said, 'Go on then, I'll wait here.' She waved me away. I ran outside and peered far down the cobbled street at a solitary soldier who was walking up the centre. He was still a long way away and the others hadn't yet reached him but they were running towards him as fast as their legs would carry them. The doors to the smoke-blackened terraced houses that lined both sides of our street began to open, and our neighbours stood on their doorsteps watching as he came slowly towards us.

Some of them waved and called out as he passed, 'Welcome home lad,' but none of them left their doorsteps – they didn't want to get involved. I glanced back and saw Mum standing half-hidden in the entrance doorway of our house. I started to run to catch up with the others and the soldier, still a good distance away, lifted his hat and waved it in the air. I slowed to a walk and felt a surge of disappointment as I decided he was not my dad – his hair was white and he looked older. I called the others back and they turned at the sound of my call. They stopped running but turned to look again at the soldier who was still waving to them.

'Come back, that's not our dad,' I called to them and they ran back towards me but Little Cliffy still kept looking over his shoulder at the soldier.

'Dorothy!' The soldier shouted and waved at us. I held my hand above my eyes to shade them from hazy sunlight. 'Hey Dorothy… Pamela…,' he called.

Pamela beamed at me and ran off down the street, waving and calling 'Daddy, Daddy.' We all ran after her and watched him drop his kit bag, lift her high in the air and swing her around before hugging her to his chest. I reached him next and he lowered Pamela and stood back to look at me. He held his chin thoughtfully with one hand and pretended he didn't know me at first, then he grinned and I ran into his open arms.

'You're all grown up, Dorothy eh,' he said, stroking my hair.

'I'm twelve-and-a-half now, Dad,' I said looking up into his heavily lined face that was burned a dark brown. His cheeks were sunken, his smooth white hair was shaven high above his ears and the top was longer and smoothed back.

'I'm nine-and-three-quarters me,' Pamela chirped in.

'I'm six-and-a-half, Daddy,' Little Cliffy announced, jumping up and down and holding on to Dad's sleeve. 'And Leonard is five and Sheila's three,' he said, pointing at Leonard who was standing back from us holding Sheila's hand – unsure of this Daddy that he couldn't remember.

Dad raised his hands in mock protest, then laughed and said

'That's a lot of birthdays, you're all growing up – I can see that.' He ruffled Little Cliffy's hair and moved me gently aside as he crouched down and held his arms open to Leonard and Sheila. Leonard glanced at me, then at Dad, then back at me. I nodded and smiled at him. He let go of Sheila's hand and went to stand beside Little Cliffy, and Dad put his arms around them both and pulled them into his chest.

'Come here my sons,' he said. Little Cliffy sank into his chest but Leonard was stiff and uncomfortable. Dad's cheeks were wet as he looked up at Sheila and held open his arm for her but she stood still and gave me a frightened look.

'It's okay, this is our Daddy,' I whispered to her as I took her hand and walked her forward into his arm. He picked her up and sat her on his forearm but she leaned away from him and turned to me with pleading eyes.

'She wants to get down, Dad, she's a bit shy of you,' I said. He lowered her to the street and she ran to me.

'Is your mum in the house, Dorothy?' he asked, picking up his kitbag and throwing it over his shoulder. His smile had disappeared and thin folds of empty skin hung at the sides of his mouth. I nodded.

'Let's go indoors then,' he said. The others ran ahead to the house but I walked alongside him in silence as he waved to the neighbours. I was glad he didn't have an arm missing, like Vera's dad, and he seemed to be the same as before the war except he looked different. But as I looked up into his face that was fixed in a frown with tightened lips, I began to feel afraid of him as we approached our empty front doorstep. Just before we reached our open front door I left him and ran inside – to find Mum standing in the middle of the room, facing the door, with the kids standing in front of her as though they were guarding her. I stood beside her and held her hand as we waited. My mouth dried up. I looked at Mum, then back at the door as the sound of his boots treading the pavement outside our home got louder and then stopped. His bony fingers gripped the doorframe and he blinked as he adjusted his eyes to the darkness inside the room. His eyes flicked across us one by one, then were fixed on our mum. She flinched.

35
Home truths

Once his eyes had got used to the darkened room, he stepped through the door and dropped his bag onto the floor. As he slipped his rifle down from his shoulder I heard Mum gasp and then give a sigh of relief as he rested it against the bag. He walked towards her and we all moved closer to her so that our bodies touched hers and I could feel her trembling as she grasped my hand tightly.

'Step aside now kids and let me get to your mother,' he said as he rested his hand on the handle of what looked like a sheathed knife attached to his belt.

'Please don't hurt our mummy, please don't Daddy,' Little Cliffy cried out.

'What's this, what's he talking about, Dolly?' he asked, taken aback.

'They know what you wrote in your letter, Cliff.' Her voice was calm but firm. 'They love their brother and I'm not giving him up, so if you can't accept him you'd better turn around and go back out of that door. We've managed without you during the war, haven't we kids?' We all nodded but kept our heads down so as not to look into his eyes.

'Look Dolly,' his voice was little more than a whisper, 'when I wrote those things I was angry and hurt. I didn't mean... I was stuck in that stinking jungle and you write and tell me that you've had another man's....' His voice tailed off into silence as he hung his head. Nobody dared to speak. Tears began streaming down into the deep lines that had aged his face and yet he looked like a sad and frightened little boy. I had never seen him cry and I wasn't sure that dad's were supposed to cry. Mum let go of my hand and gently pushed aside my brothers and sisters as she stepped towards him. She put her arms around his bent over shoulders and pulled him towards her. His whole body jerked and shuddered as he clung to her and sobbed uncontrollably.

'It's going to be all right now – you kids go outside and play for a while,' she said calmly. 'Dorothy you put on the kettle and make your dad a cup of tea.' The kids shuffled silently outside and Pamela pulled the door closed behind her. I went into the scullery to fill the kettle. When I came back into the room to put the kettle on the range they were sitting on the sofa. Dad was wiping his eyes with the butt of his palm and Mum was stroking his hair.

'It was just the thought of coming home to my family that kept me going in that bloody jungle. Christ, Dolly, you'll never understand what we went through in that disease-ridden godforsaken place, up to our waists in mud and blood.'

He leaned forward, rested his elbows on his knees and clasped together his thin, sunburned hands. 'When our little Nunoos wrote to me I just wept, I missed her and my kids so much. Then I got your letter about having another man's kid and I thought you'd go off with him and take my kids with you and I got angry and hurt. I'm sorry about what I wrote back to you. I wasn't the only soldier to get a letter like that from his missus down there me, but what made it even worse was that we already felt abandoned and forgotten by our country, so to think you'd lost your wife and kids as well....'

'It's this bloody war Cliff, it's changed people's lives,' she said. 'It wasn't of our making but we've had to live through it and survive as best we could.' She put her hand over his. 'Some of us have made mistakes that can't be ignored and forgotten like my little boy Terence, but he's part of our family now and we can't change that.' He shook his bowed head.

I poured the water into the teapot from the kettle, stirred it, then carried it over to the table and poured the tea into the cups adding milk and sugar, then I carefully handed them each a cup. Dad smiled up at me as he took his and Mum gave me a reassuring nod as she put hers down on the floor by her feet.

'I suppose I'd better meet this little boy Terence… where is he?' he asked her.

'Go next door and fetch your brother, Dorothy, and tell Aunty Elise everything is all right in here.' She smiled and tipped her head towards the passage door. I ran through to next door and found Aunty Elise standing close to her open door with Terence in her arms. She'd been listening, and she smiled as she handed my brother to me. I carried him back to our living room and stood in front of Dad on the sofa. I didn't speak.

'Hello little boy,' he said and gave a quick smile.

'Do you want to hold him, Dad?' I asked, moving closer to the sofa. Mum looked worried and leaned forward as if to take him from me but Dad held out his arms, took Terence from me and sat him on his knee. Terence gave him a big grin and put his finger on Dad's mouth. Dad opened his mouth and pretended to bite it and Terence gave a hearty laugh. Dad started to laugh too but his eyes filled with tears again as he handed him back to me.

'Take him outside to play for a while Dorothy, until I calls you all in later,' Mum said. I left them and went out into the street. The others weren't playing – they were huddled outside our door trying to hear what was happening inside.

'It's okay,' I told them. 'Daddy likes Terence, Terence made him laugh.'

'Hooray!' Little Cliffy cheered and the others joined in 'Hooray! Hooray!'

Mrs Duckworth was standing in her open doorway watching us. 'Is everything all right indoors, lass?' she shouted to me across the street.

'Yes thanks, Mrs Duckworth, our dad likes Terence, he made him laugh,' I called back and she smiled and went back indoors.

The next morning I felt happy as I opened my eyes and fixed them on the heavy curtain that Mum had nailed to the beams around her bed. Pamela was still asleep beside me and Mum and Dad were upstairs in our double bed. Our family were together again and there wasn't a row or a fight and everyone was going to be happy, I thought to myself. We were all to go to see Nunoos to surprise her and Dad had said he would arrange for us to go back to Guernsey as soon as he had returned to barracks and been discharged from the Royal Artillery.

'Why are you smiling?' Pamela asked, rubbing her eyes as she sat up.

'Because I'm happy that our dad has come home,' I laughed. 'Aren't you?'

She flopped back onto her pillow and said, 'I'm happy they didn't have a fight. When are we going to see Nunoos?'

I threw back the blanket and jumped out of bed pulling the pillow we were sharing out from under her head.

'C'mon, up you get, we can make breakfast for Mum and Dad.' She rolled over to face the wall.

'You're so lazy, Pamela!' I laughed, and went into the scullery to fill the kettle. I heard heavy footsteps down the stairs and ran to see if it was Dad, and it was. He was dressed in his uniform and as he came into the passage he patted my head.

'I'm going out for a walk, love,' he said and brushed past me.

'Is he going to come back, do you think Dorothy?' Pamela asked as he left.

'Of course he will, I'll go and ask Mum where he's gone to.' I ran upstairs and Mum was in bed staring out of the window, wearing a felt hat pulled down to her ears.

'Why are you wearing your hat?' She didn't answer. 'Where's Dad gone to, Mum?'

'He couldn't rest, he's just gone for some fresh air,' she replied.

The following day the train jolted out of the station on its way to Manchester and our family, all scrubbed and clean in our best clothes again, were squeezed into a compartment. There were arguments about who was going to sit next to our dad but Mum solved them by putting him next to the window and squeezing in next to him herself. Dad leaned his head against the window. He looked weary and closed his eyes as the train rocked from side to side. Sheila slept on our mum's lap, and we all stayed really quiet so we wouldn't wake Dad.

The teacher at the deaf school led us into the dayroom where Nunoos was sitting alone at a table – sent there to wait for her visitors. There was nobody else in the room. Her eyes grew wide as she saw our dad walk into the room ahead of us and she jumped down from her seat to run into his arms. He picked her up and buried his face into her hair; it seemed ages before he lifted his head, tears rolling down his cheeks, and kissed her forehead.

'Daddy you came back,' Nunoos said as she leaned back to look at him. She threw her arms around his neck and smiled over his shoulder at us. Once he'd put her down he sat at the table and we huddled around him while she asked him lots of questions and he answered her slowly.

'Was you scared in the jungle, Daddy?' she asked.

He laughed and said, 'Well now Nunoos, one day I was really scared. We were on the move and I'd only stopped for a minute to catch my breath but I got left behind. Suddenly I heard a noise behind me and I spun around thinking it was a Jap, but it wasn't… guess what it was, sweetheart?' Her big eyes were fixed on his mouth as she read his words.

'I don't know, what was it Daddy?' she asked and we all drew closer to him and waited for him to move his mouth slowly again. He smiled at us – he could see that he had us hooked.

'A big angry rhinoceros… it was stamping the ground and its head was lowered with the sharp horn on its nose pointed straight at me.'

'Did you shoot it with your rifle, Daddy?' Leonard asked.

'No son, Daddy turned and ran as fast as he could and climbed up a tree, but the rhinoceros chased me and stood under the tree snorting at me, so I had to stay there for ages and be really quiet until it got fed up and went away. Then only after it had walked away and I was sure it wouldn't come back did I dare to climb down.' Leonard looked a bit disappointed.

'Then did you chase it and shoot it with your rifle, Daddy?' he asked again.

'No son, I ran like the clappers to catch up with my mates.'

Mum laughed and he laughed and winked at her. Nunoos seemed unsure whether it was a scary or a funny story but she laughed along with the rest of us. When it was time to leave Dad told Nunoos that in a couple of days she'd be allowed to come home and we'd all be going back to live in Guernsey. She was so excited that for the first time she didn't cry when we all waved goodbye.

36

Our journey home

The day after Dad returned to barracks, Mum and Aunty Elise were having a cup of tea and laughing about the time an American GI had given Aunty Ruth an engagement ring that made her finger go green and they'd teased her and said he'd probably got it from Woolworth's. I had just come back from an errand and I was putting the food rations into the cupboard.

'Bloody men,' Aunty Elise laughed.

'Yeh bloody men,' Mum said. 'Do you know what, Elise, Cliff made me wear my hat before he would have anything to do with me in bed? He said he didn't like my bushy hair, but it's the same hair I've always had... I can't understand him, me.'

'But how did he handle you being pregnant?' Aunty Elise asked.

'He just stared at me and shook his head but he's just happy to be home with his family at the moment, so he's said no more about it.'

'Well I've got some news for you, Dolly' Aunty Elise said. 'My George is back in Guernsey and he's sorted out our house so me and the kids can go back home at last. So we'll all travel back to Guernsey together eh, and Ruth says that Grace and her lot are going to be coming as well. How are things between you and Grace these days? Are you still not talking to each other?'

'I haven't seen her for a few weeks but I bumped into her in town in Market Street the other week and we exchanged a few words,' Mum answered. 'You know Elise, I've never told anyone what she made me do before because I was too ashamed, and I don't know why it came out... I was drunk me, but I wouldn't make something like that up.'

'Of course you wouldn't,' Aunty Elise replied.

'She was really nice to me afterwards. I even started to feel as though she loved me and wanted me to stay with her and Dad so I went along with it.' She paused. 'I think at the time I knew it wasn't right but I didn't want to go back to the children's home so I kept quiet about it. When I was a little girl my real mum was always hugging me, right up until she got too sick and died. Then when I was in the children's home I never got any hugs – there was too many of us I suppose. I blame myself you know for letting it happen, that's why I've never told anyone, even my Cliff, I suppose I blocked it out from my memory and just got on with my life.'

'Well Dolly, it bloody shocked me and Ruth, I can tell you, and your poor Dorothy stood there and heard most of it.' I shut the cupboard doors quietly and slipped out into the yard.

The next day Mum and Aunty Elise went to collect Nunoos from the deaf school. She made friends with the kids in our street in no time and was outside skipping with them most of the day. Early in the morning on the day we were to leave Stockport, the neighbours came and carried off furniture and household things that they paid Mum very little for, and slowly the house emptied of everything except us and our clothes. Someone up the street had swapped three battered suitcases for our table and chairs, and I helped Mum to squash our family's clothes into them. Pamela sat on the lids so we could close them before Mum stacked them in the pram. Aunty Elise and Aunty Ruth were selling up too and by midday the neighbours were standing on their doorsteps waving goodbye to us all. One of them called out, 'Ta ra Guernsey donkeys… have a good trip home' and Mum and Aunty Elise laughed and waved back as we walked down the street for the last time on our way to the train station.

The train was to take us to the south coast of England so we could catch a boat across the Channel to Guernsey. Dad had made all the arrangements for our return home and was supposed to meet us at the station, but he wasn't there when we arrived. We saw Granny and her kids at the station. Ronald and Ernest, now in their teens, were struggling with Granny's cases. Lollie ran over to join us, she was really excited and I couldn't get a word in until we had all boarded the train. Dad still hadn't shown up and I asked Mum where he was.

'He'll probably meet us at the boat,' she said as she folded the pram to lift it into the carriage. The journey seemed to take forever. The scenery outside sped past and switched from countryside to the dirty backs of terraced brick houses, then to neat allotments with little wooden sheds, then the blackened skeletons of bombed houses, followed by more countryside. We changed trains twice and then rode on a bus to the Weymouth docks. As we walked along the docks Mum spotted three young sailors coming towards us. 'Yer, you look like strong lads!' she called out to them and they walked over to her. She asked them to carry the cases to the boat so she could put Terence into the pram to give her arms a rest. They nodded respectfully, lifted the cases out of Mum's pram and carried them towards the boat on their shoulders. The cases were heavy and one sailor mocked the others for struggling with the weight. Granny and Mum were back on strained talking terms, but they didn't talk as they wheeled Veronica and Terence along the quay towards the boat that was to take us home to Guernsey. A couple of smiling crewmen leaning on the rails having a smoke waved as we arrived at the boat. They flicked their fag ends overboard and skipped down the wooden gangplank to Mum and Granny. Lollie took Veronica and I held Terence while Mum and Granny folded up the prams so the crewmen could carry them aboard. We handed the toddlers back to our mums then snaked up the gangplank behind the crewmen and I gripped tightly onto the hand-ropes at the sides so that I didn't fall between the boat and the jetty. Following close behind us came the sailors who were stooped over and puffing with our cases. Aunty Ruth and Aunty Elise and her kids were a little way behind them on the jetty but they were soon clambering aboard too with their luggage.

'Where's Daddy? Isn't he coming back to Guernsey with us?' Little Cliffy asked Mum.

'He's s'posed to be yer, love. Mummy doesn't know where he could have got to – maybe the army wouldn't let him leave yet – but don't worry son, he'll come back to Guernsey soon.' A while later three excited girls – Lollie, Nunoos and me – stood on deck and peered over the rails. The buildings in the port of Weymouth grew smaller as we steamed out into the Channel. The sea was calm and the darkening sky made the sea turn black as a cold wind blew up. I thought about the last time the three of us were on a boat together and I shivered partly from the cold wind and partly from the memory. I found myself taking hold of Nunoos' hand and holding it tight and she looked at me and smiled.

'Get inside yer now Lollie, and you two, it's time to go to sleep,' Granny shouted.

Our families had been given a cabin and were squeezed in like sardines. The grown-ups and younger ones had the bunks and the rest of us curled up on blankets on the floor. It was an uncomfortable night and I didn't get much sleep. When I woke up Lollie had disappeared and Granny sent me to find her. I ran outside and found her standing on the deck leaning on the rail.

'Look, there's Guernsey just ahead on the right and there's Herm and Jethou islands – can you see?' she said, pointing them out as I stood alongside her. We were heading towards the Little Russell, the channel of sea between Herm and Guernsey. The sun was a bright yellow ball peeping over the top of Herm Island and its glowing light reflected in golden and copper coloured streaks across the rippling waves. On Guernsey I could see sparkling panes of greenhouse glass amongst the green fields and white cottages on the northern slopes below the Vale Mill, but the mill looked taller than I remembered it. The sky circling the rising sun glowed red, then spread into orange until it faded into a yellow hue high above. I looked up into the soft pale yellow of its cloudless expanse and saw that it was clean and clear of smog. I tasted salt as I licked my lips. A flock of seagulls swirled above us screeching as though they were welcoming us back. I felt a rush of excitement and joy as memories of happy times running from the waves on the first beach flooded my mind and I realised that we'd soon be back in Pedvin Street playing on Trinity Square with the friendly lion that spouted water for us. The rest of our travelling crowd and some other returning evacuees slowly appeared on deck looking crumpled and weary, but when they saw Guernsey the grown-ups started to cheer and laugh and hug each other. Mum began to shout at us telling us to make haste and gather up our belongings ready to go ashore, and as we steamed into St Peter Port harbour I overheard Aunty Elise asking Granny if she felt worried about what our Grandpa would say when he saw Veronica.

'I'm not worried about what he has to say, Elise,' she replied. 'He won't dare do anything to upset me if he knows what's good for him.'

'I can see who wears the pants in your house Grace.' Aunty Elise laughed and winked at her with the eye that wasn't already closed because of the fag smoke.

Displaced Donkeys

As the boat drew alongside the dock the crew threw heavy ropes to the dockers who slipped them over bollards and then secured the end of the gangplank lowered by the crew for us to walk ashore. There were lots of relations and friends on the dockside waiting to greet their returning families. Our dad's mum and dad and his brothers and sister and their kids were standing near the bottom of the gangplank waving and shouting our names. Standing just to one side of them was my Grandpa Duncombe and next to him a young woman with three small kids. Lollie ran to him and he swept her up into his arms and gave her a hug. Her brothers Ronald and Ernest and sisters Barbara and Delia were soon getting hugs and kisses from him too. Granny was carrying little Veronica as she walked down the gangplank followed by Aunty Ruth, then me, and Mum was behind me.

'Who's that with Charlie?' Aunty Ruth whispered back over her shoulder and above my head to Mum.

'I don't know me – I can't say I know her face,' Mum said, as she stretched to get a better look at the woman. Once we'd all stepped off the gangplank, we gathered around Grandpa Duncombe and the strangers with him and I noticed that the grown-ups all went quiet.

'Did you have a good trip, Grace?' Grandpa asked with a wide docile grin.

'Never mind that! Who's this woman and what's she doing here with these kids?' Granny snapped.

'This is Odette and these are hers and my kids.' He started to introduce them by name but Granny cut him short.

'I can see they're yours – they're not exactly bloody white, are they? And you, you cheating bastard… you've been living with this tart behind my back while me and your kids have been bombed and nearly killed!'

'Who do you think you're calling a tart eh?' the fiery Odette snapped. She was a small thin woman with flaming red hair and pointed features, and she narrowed her eyes and jutted her chin forward as she stepped towards Granny. The rest of our welcome-home party were all standing around them, silent spectators. Aunty Ruth gave Aunty Elise a nudge and smirked at her. Grandpa looked around at our faces all fixed on him and his eyes fell on Veronica in Granny's arms.

He pointed at her. 'Well *she's* not mine is she…who fathered her?'

Granny stiffened and spat out, 'He was a black American GI and he was twice the man you are!' She turned and stormed off towards the road with Barbara and Delia close on her heels. Ronald and Ernest gave their dad a disappointed look before picking up her cases and following after her. Lollie grabbed Veronica's pram, brought down the gangplank by a crewman, and glared at her dad before pushing the pram as fast as she could to catch up with the others.

'Well bugger me! This is a turn-up for the books, eh Dolly?' Aunty Elise said and took a drag on her fag as she eyed the woman and her bewildered kids up and down.

Mum glared at Grandpa and said, 'I hope they're not living with you at Brazil House, Dad, 'cos if they are you can bloody well get them out, 'cos that's where me and my kids are expecting to live.' At that moment Aunty Elise spotted Uncle George running towards us along the dockside and she waved to him. Her kids ran towards him shouting and waving and when they reached him he held onto them crying and laughing at the same time.

'I've got to go to George – will you be all right Dolly?' Aunty Elise asked.

'We'll be all right, you go,' Mum replied.

'La, you come yer to your Grandpa Ogier,' our Guernsey donkey Grandpa said, holding open his arms to us and we flocked towards him, smiling and eager for his warm hugs and for kisses from Grandma. Meanwhile our aunties and uncles gently ushered us along the dock to get well away from our Grandpa Duncombe and his new family.

Nothing much had changed in Pedvin Street – the houses and the square looked the same, and the friendly lion still spouted water. When we went back to school, we were told lots of stories about life in the island under the Germans. Many of our school friends who'd stayed behind in Guernsey were even skinnier than us and told us of how they were nearly starving by the time the Germans surrendered. It took time to get used to the sound of voices in our school playground shouting in the Guernsey accent but here and there a Scottish, Welsh or English accent could be heard among the returned evacuees. Local kids told us about the big concrete pillbox gun towers that the Germans had built all around the coast of the island and I realised that's why I thought the Vale Mill tower looked different from the boat that day.

Grandpa and Odette moved out of Brazil House with their kids. Mind you, before he left Mum screamed and swore at him and started crying because he'd sold all our furniture and beds during the occupation. Later on Grandpa left Odette and came back to be with our Granny and their kids, but only for a while. Mum had moved us into the top floor rooms in the house and was disgusted that we had to sleep in donated old German iron cots and under German blankets! The Red Cross gave her so many blankets that she folded them to make them thicker and nailed them down the stairs as stair carpet. We were still poor but at least we were back where we belonged – on our island, among our own people. A few weeks after we'd settled back into life in Guernsey, Mum went into labour and our brother Michael was born. The following day our dad came home from England.

Lightning Source UK Ltd.
Milton Keynes UK
07 April 2010

152440UK00001B/6/P